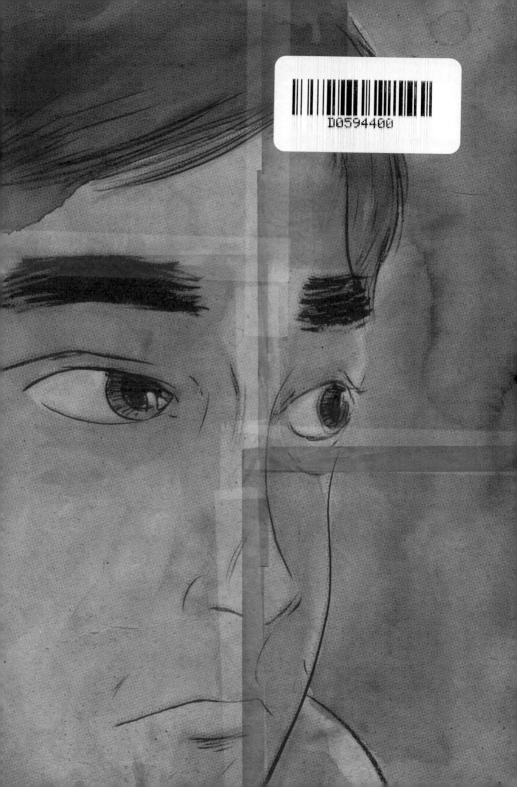

3
STORY

Editor
DIANA SCHUTZ

Assistant Editor
BRENDAN WRIGHT

Digital Production
CLAY JANES

Design
MATT KINDT

Publisher
MIKE RICHARDSON

Published by Dark Horse Books
A division of Dark Horse Comics, Inc.
10956 SE Main Street
Milwaukie, Oregon 97222
darkhorse.com

First edition: September 2009
ISBN 978-1-59582-356-4

3 5 7 9 10 8 6 4
Printed in China

THE
SECRET
HISTORY
OF THE
GIANT MAN

MATT KINDT

1ST
STORY

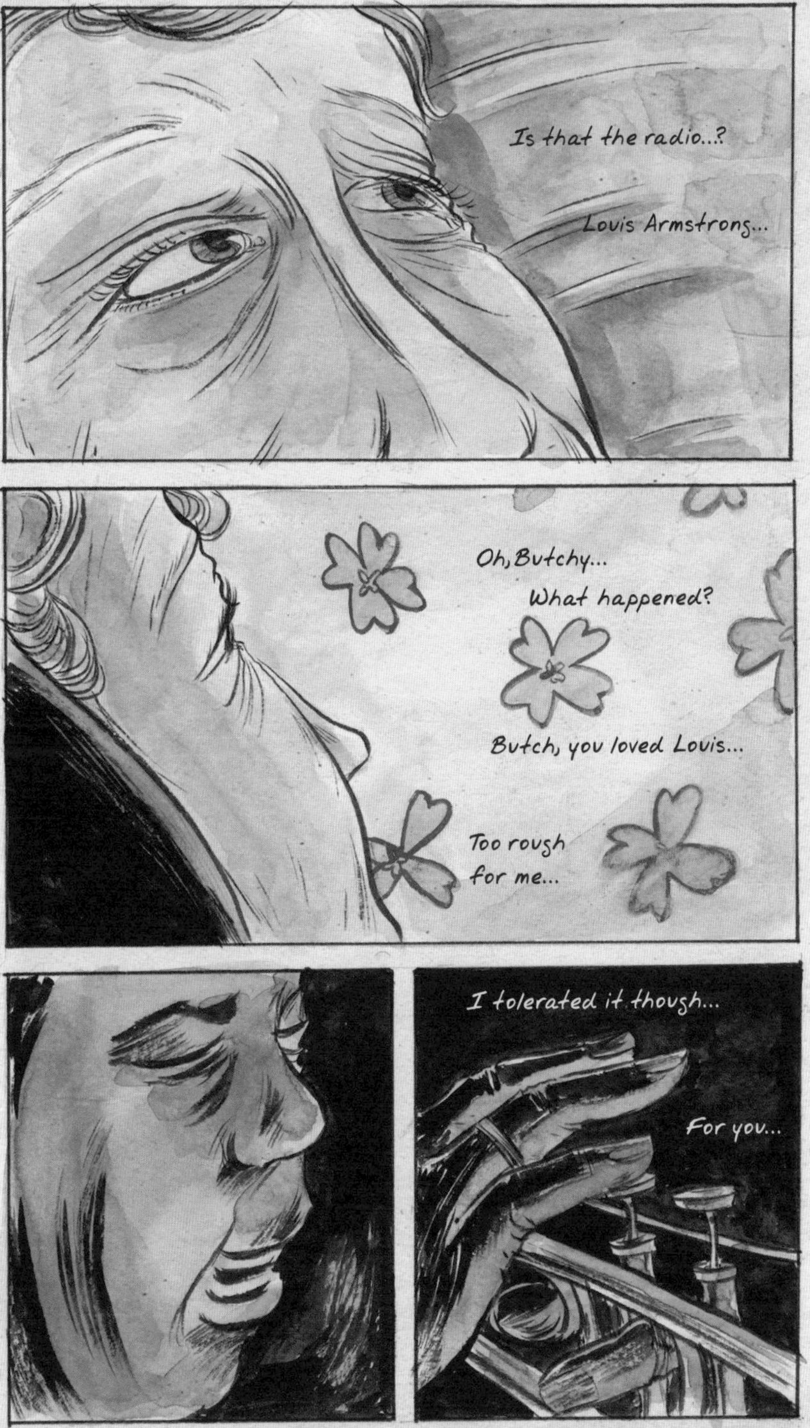
Is that the radio...?
Louis Armstrong...
Oh, Butchy...
What happened?
Butch, you loved Louis...
Too rough for me...
I tolerated it though...
For you...

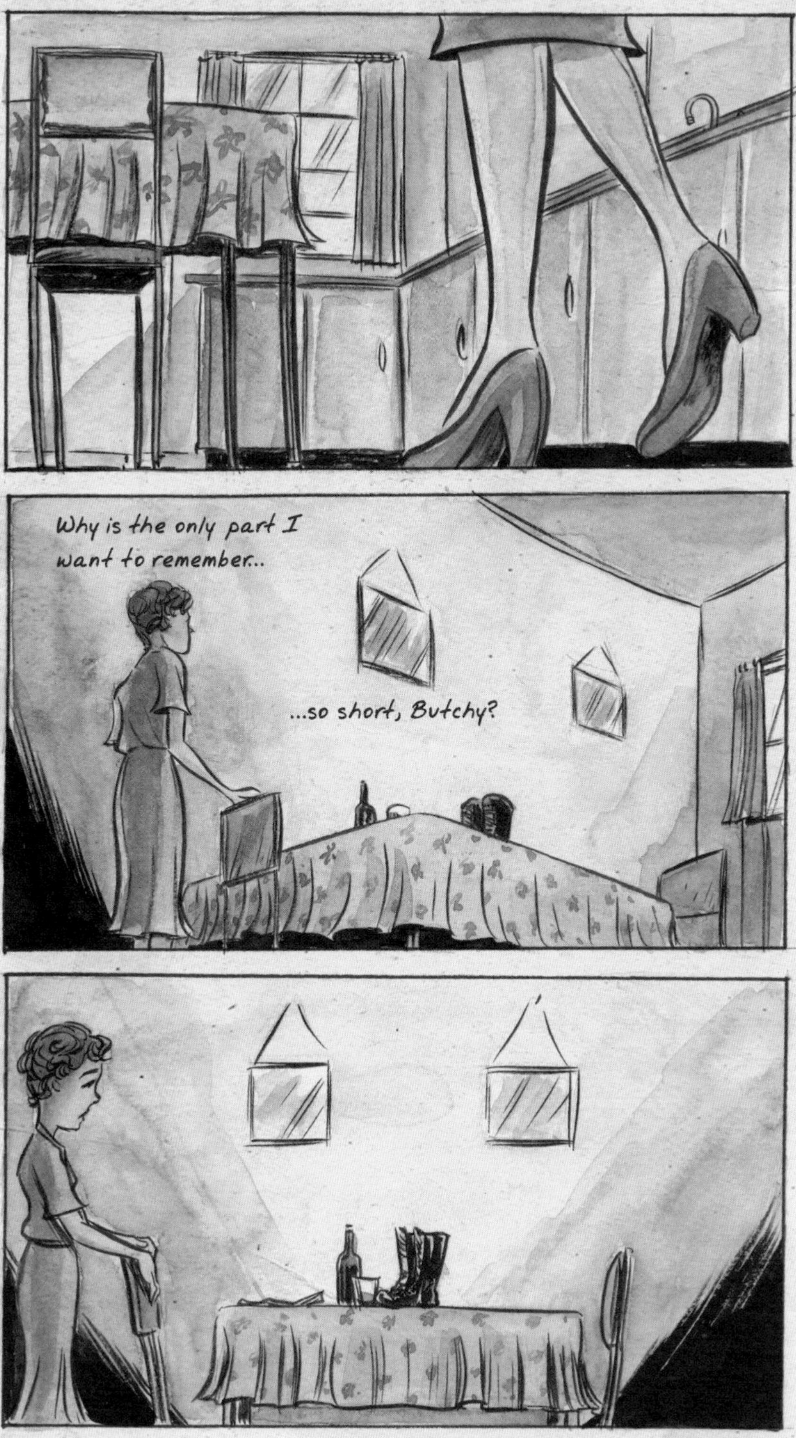
Why is the only part I want to remember...
...so short, Butchy?

And everything...

I want...

To forget...

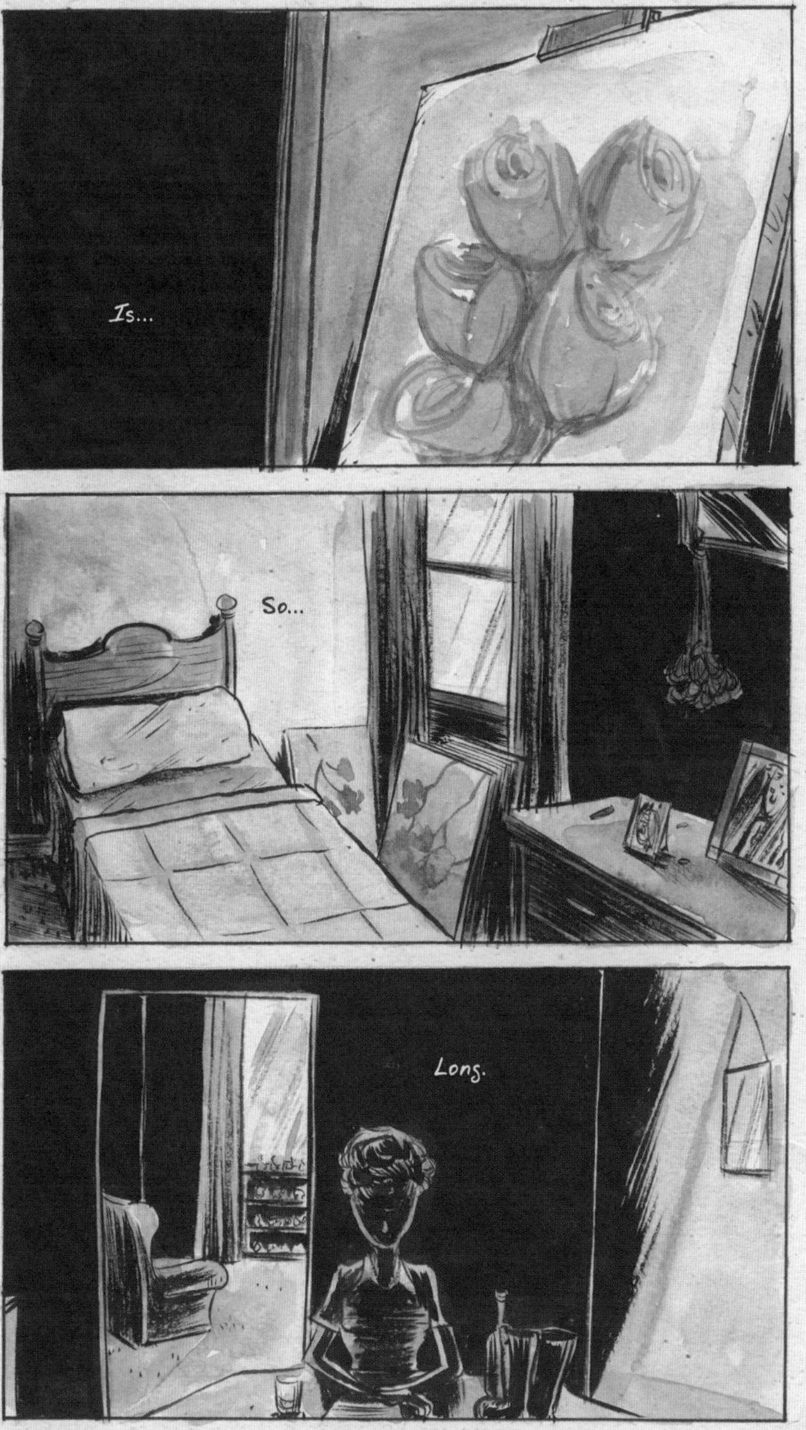
Is...
So...
Long.

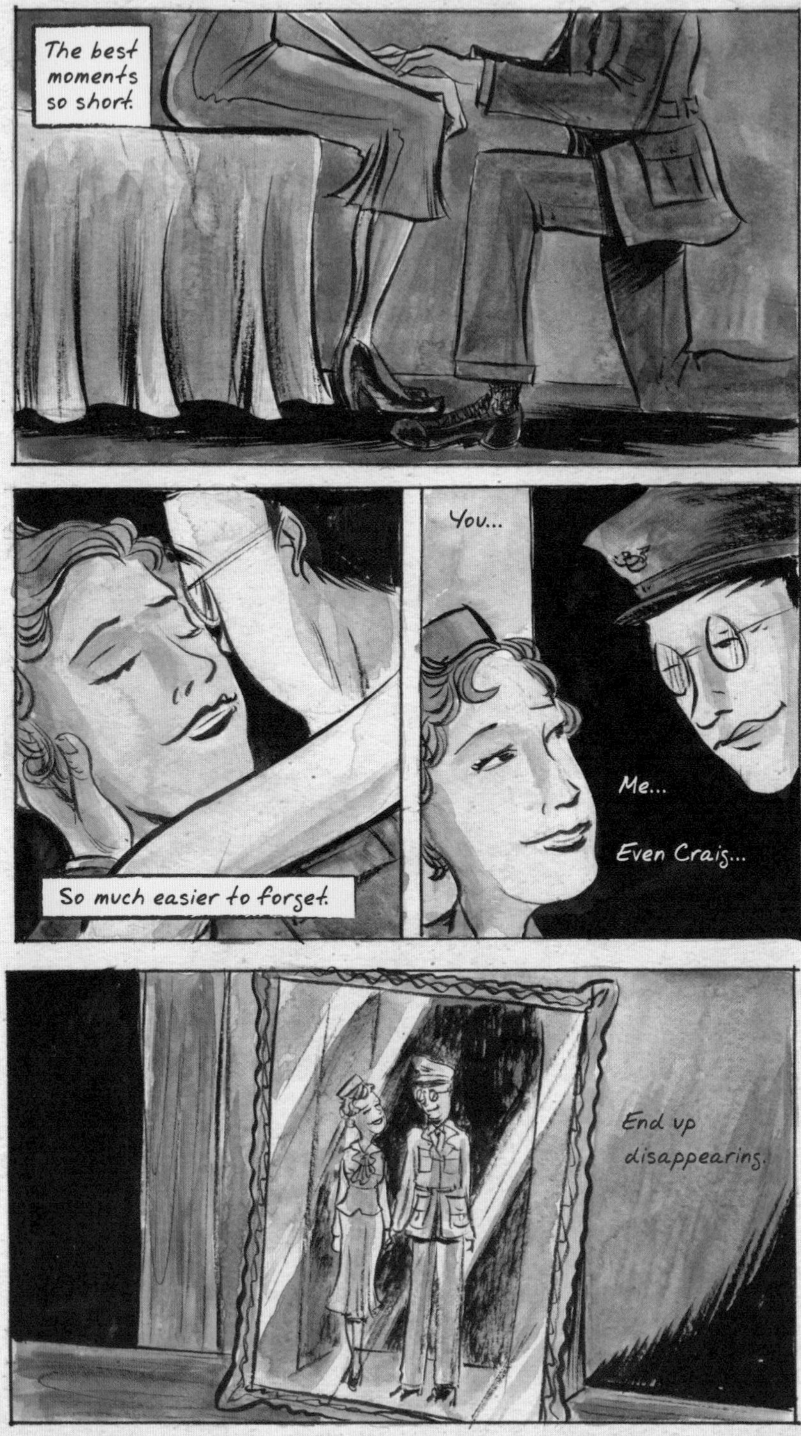
The best moments so short.
So much easier to forget.
You...
Me...
Even Craig...
End up disappearing.

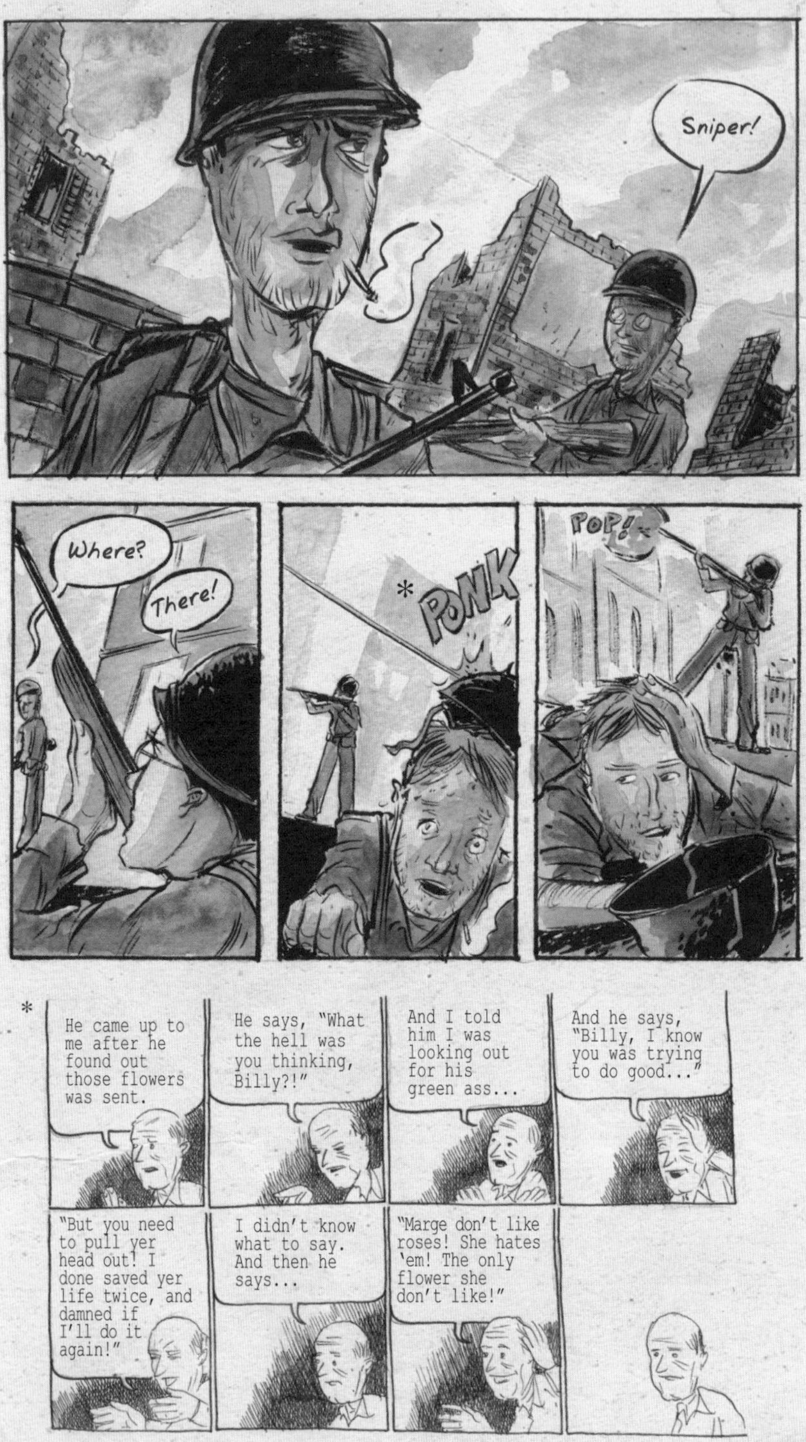
Sniper!
Where?
There!
*PONK
POP!
* He came up to me after he found out those flowers was sent.
He says, "What the hell was you thinking, Billy?!"
And I told him I was looking out for his green ass...
And he says, "Billy, I know you was trying to do good..."
"But you need to pull yer head out! I done saved yer life twice, and damned if I'll do it again!"
I didn't know what to say. And then he says...
"Marge don't like roses! She hates 'em! The only flower she don't like!"

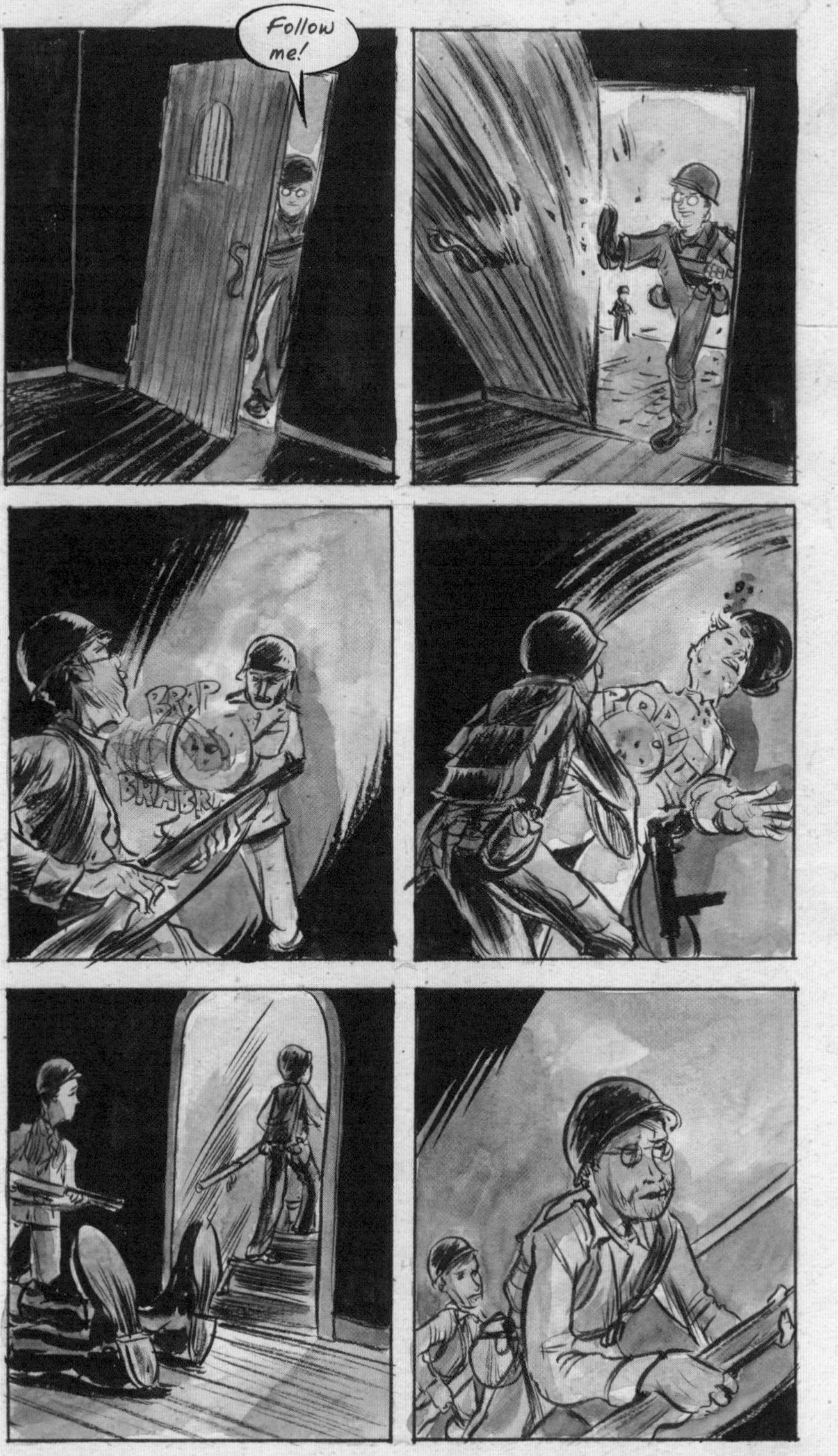
Follow me!

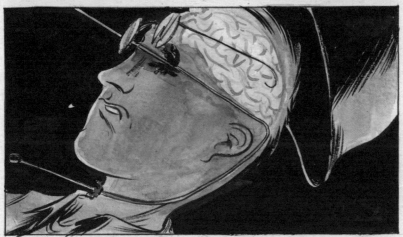

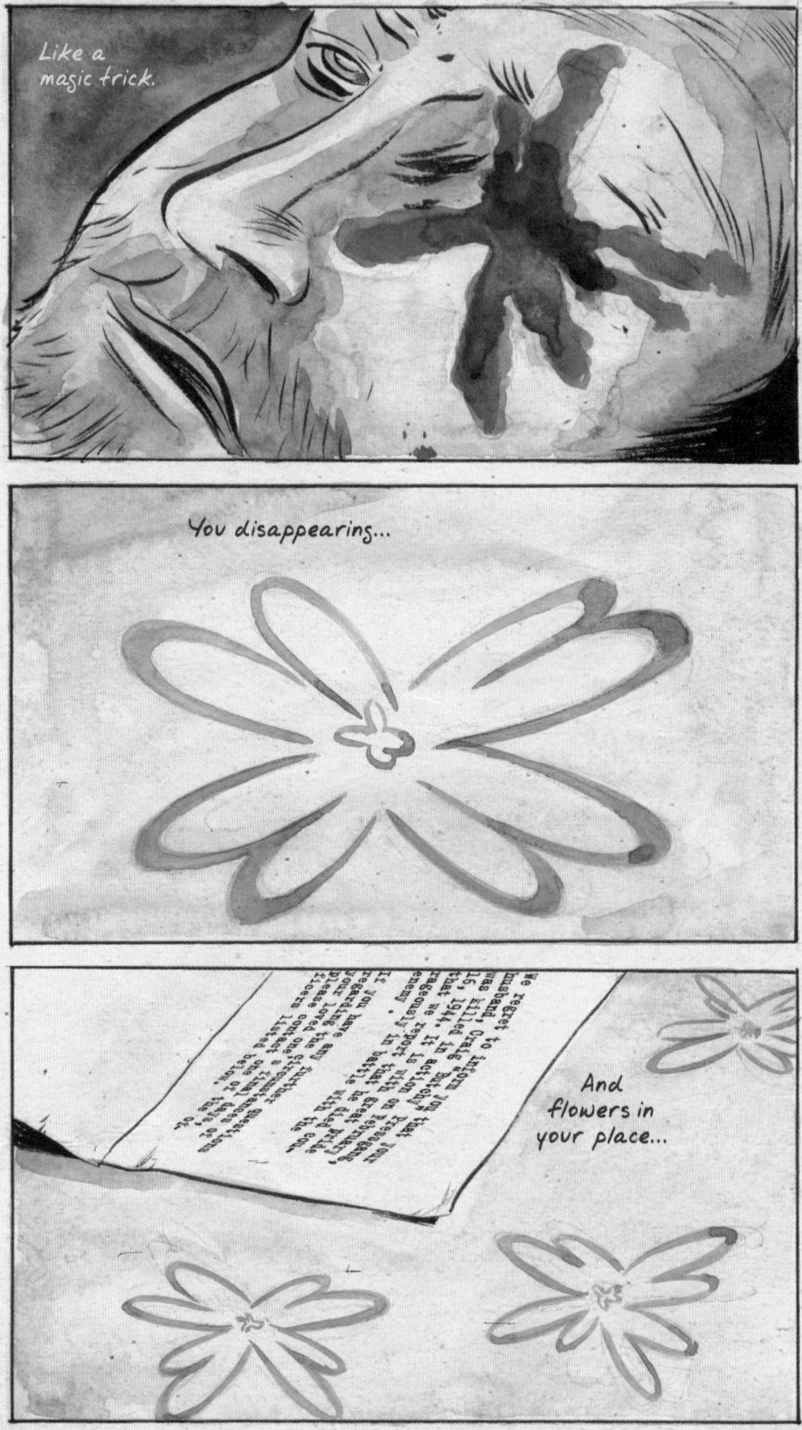
Like a magic trick.
You disappearing...
And flowers in your place...

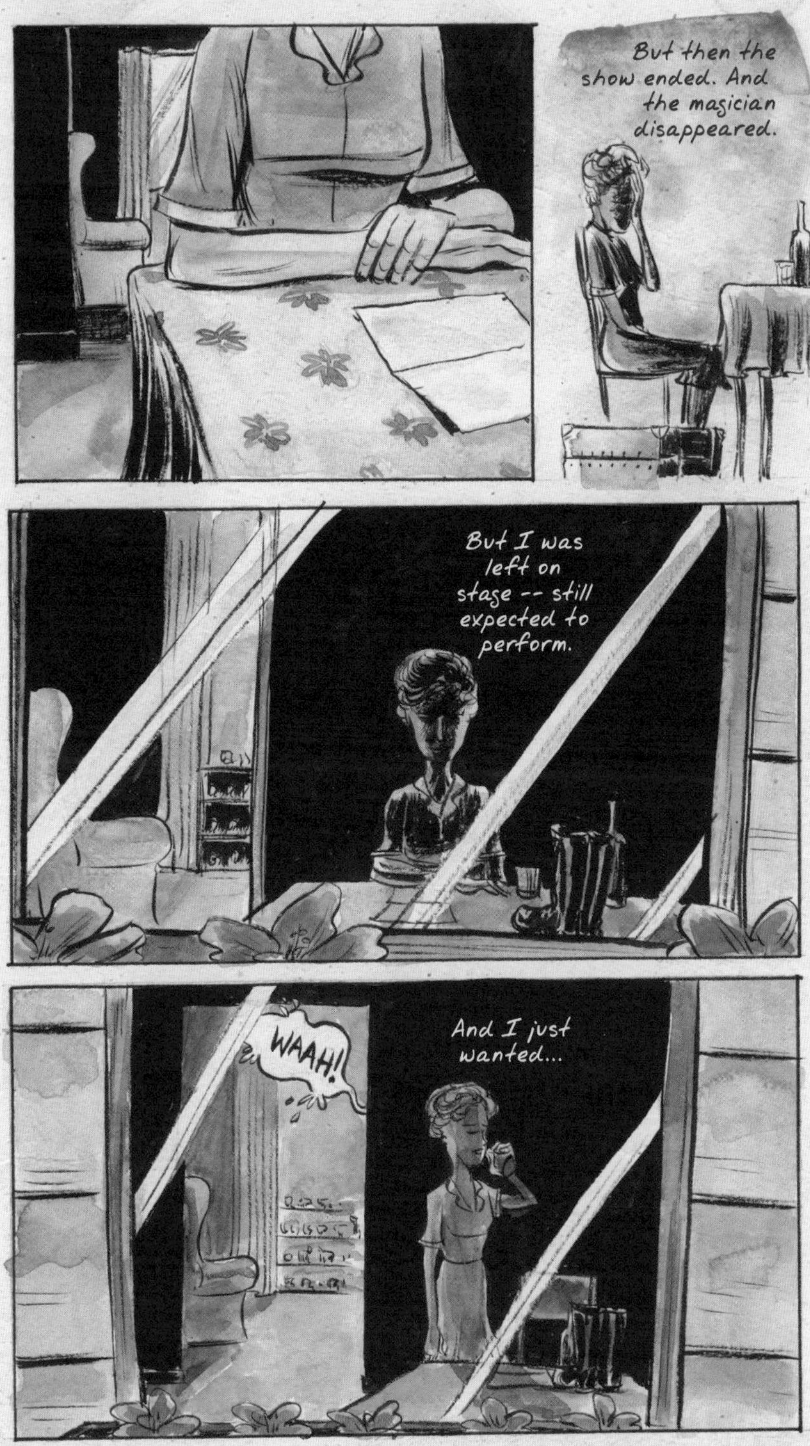
But then the show ended. And the magician disappeared.
But I was left on stage -- still expected to perform.
WAAH!
And I just wanted...

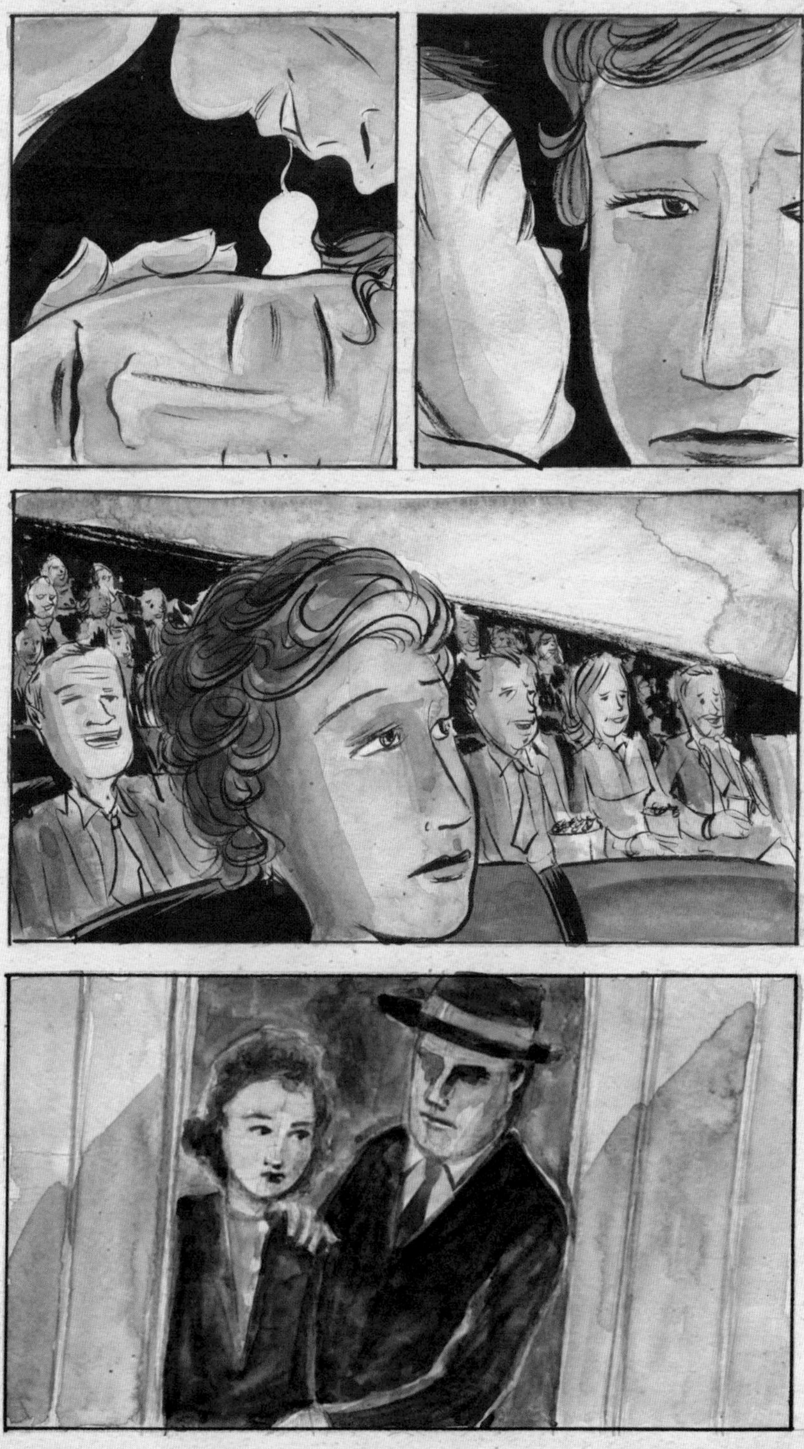

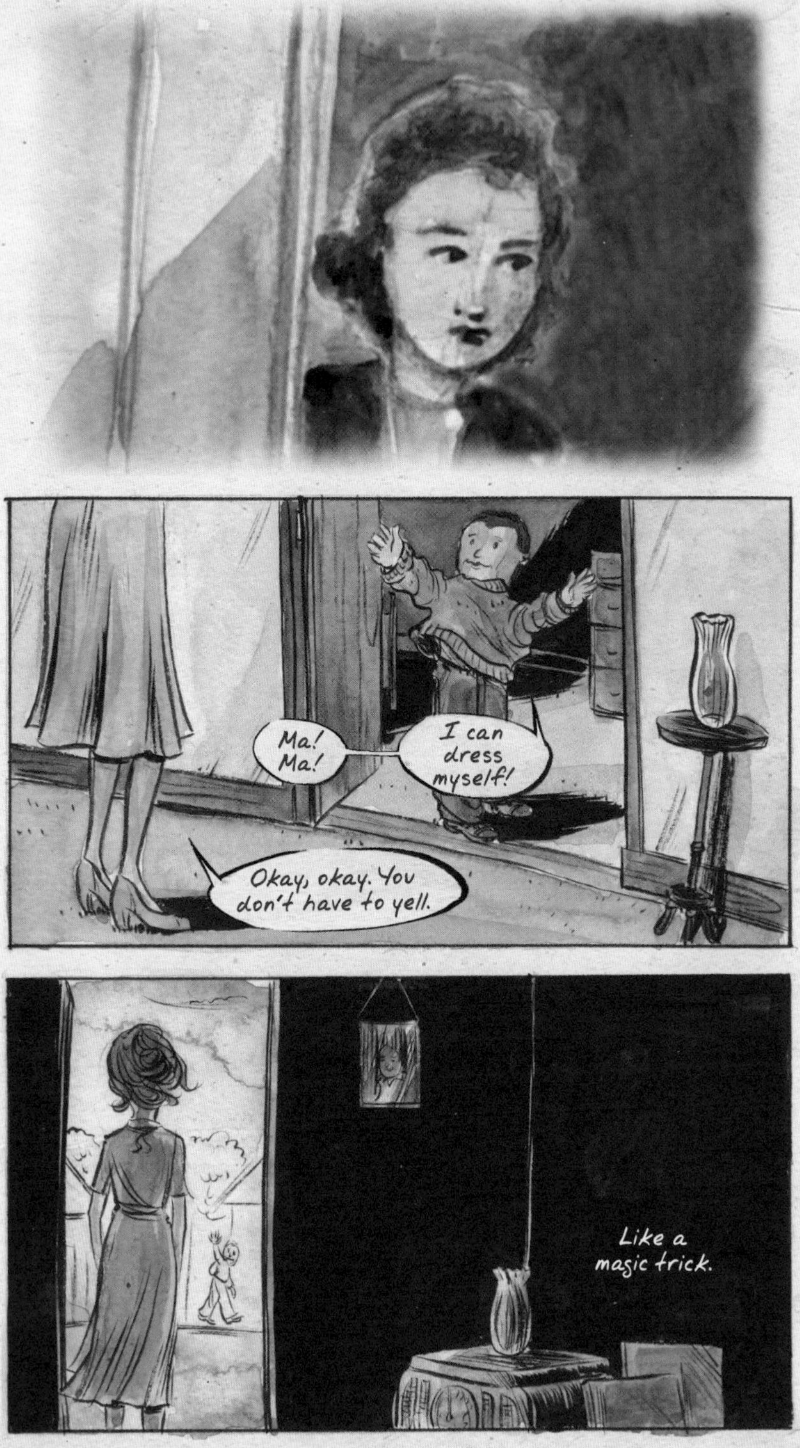
Ma! Ma!
I can dress myself!
Okay, okay. You don't have to yell.
Like a magic trick.

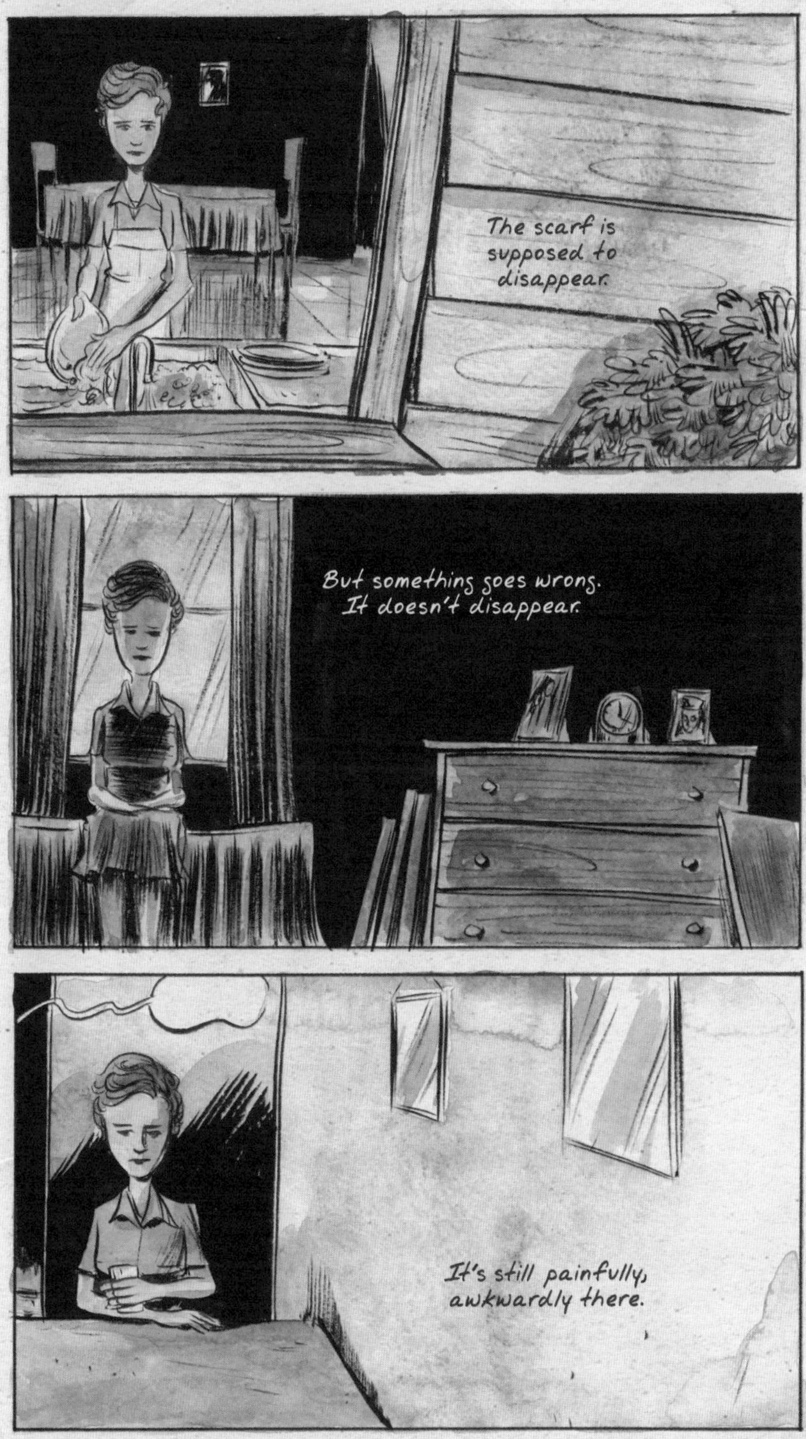

The scarf is supposed to disappear.
But something goes wrong. It doesn't disappear.
It's still painfully, awkwardly there.

Disappeared when he was eight.

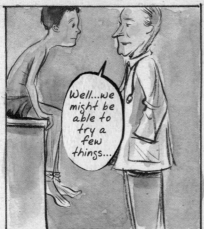

Well...we might be able to try a few things...

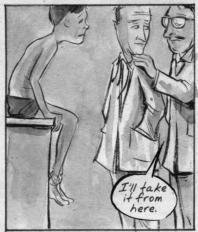

I'll take it from here.

And the bigger he got, the less I could hold on to him...or you.

More, please!

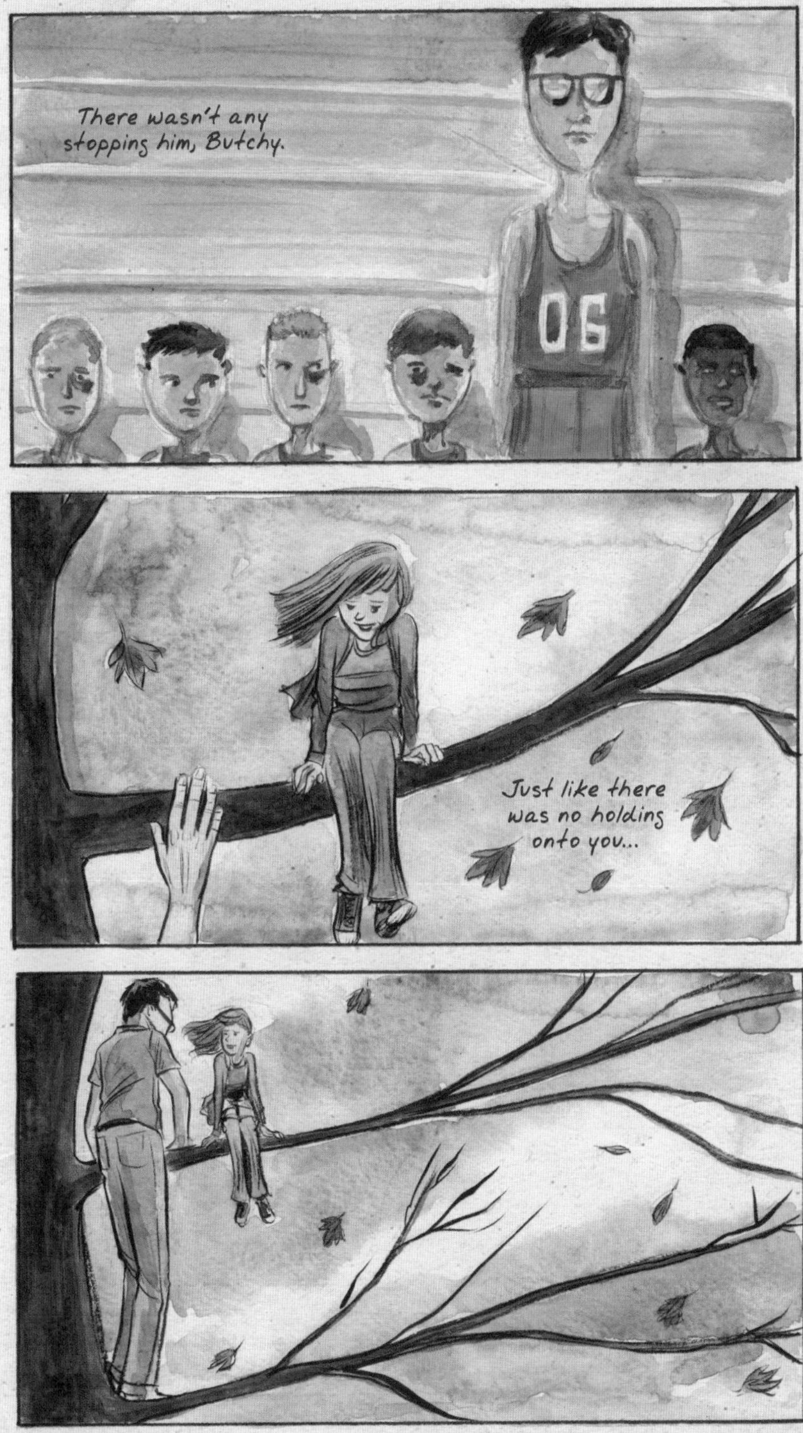
There wasn't any stopping him, Butchy.
06
Just like there was no holding onto you...

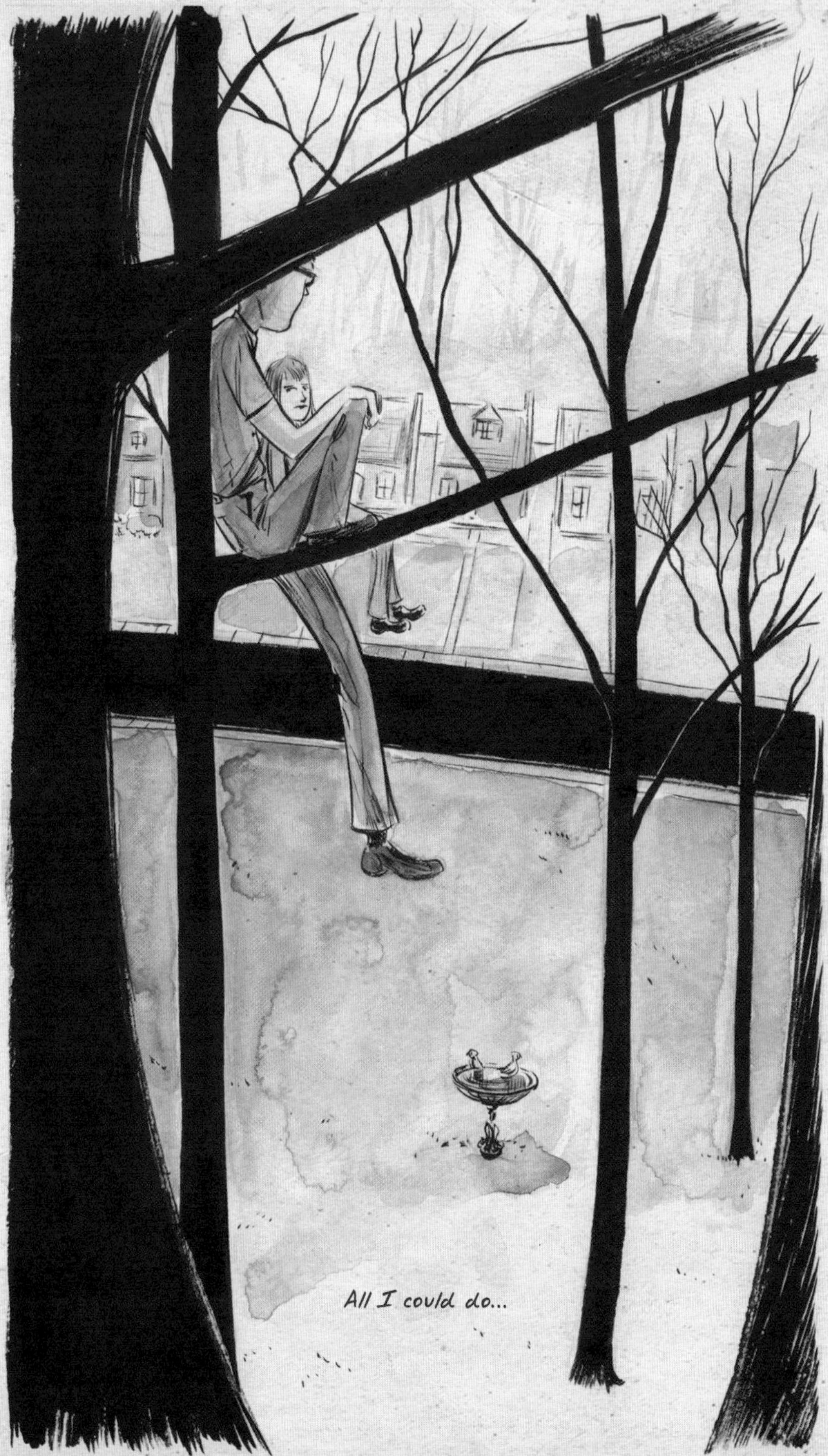
All I could do...

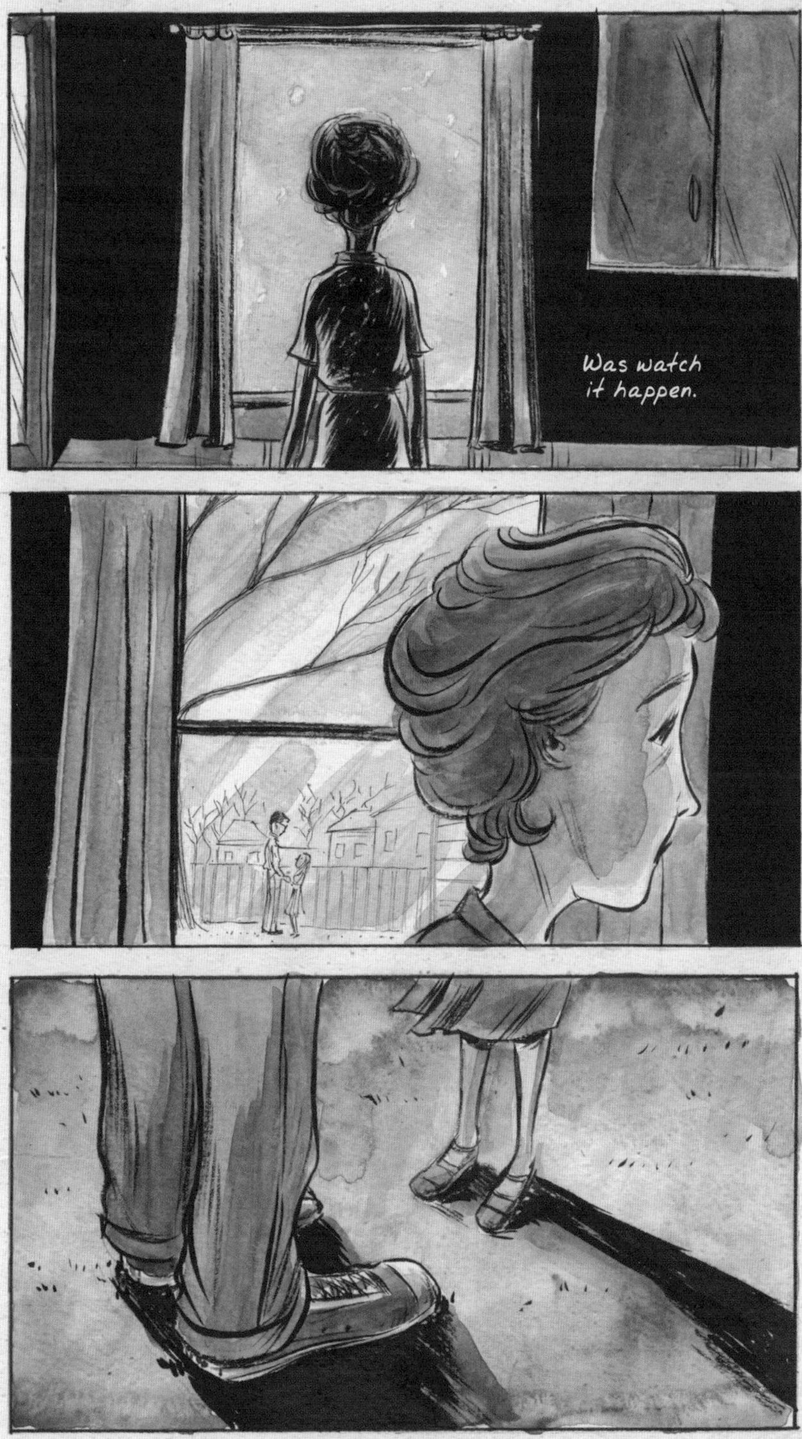
Was watch
it happen.

Giant Boy in Town!

Local boy Craig Pressgang has been making a sensation of late. He is currently the tallest 8-year-old in recorded history and is on pace to break Robert Wadlow's record-setting height of nearly 9 feet. When asked how he felt about being taller than all of his fellow classmates, young Craig replied, "No different really. I like cowboys and robots, just like the next fella."

Giant Boy Grows Up

Hometown celebrity Craig Pressgang is making headlines again. Since last we checked in with young Craig (age 10), he has grown a whopping twelve inches! We asked Craig's mother, Marge, how she's dealing with her son's incredible growth. "Well, I hope he doesn't outgrow the house. He's a good boy, though. Very mindful and loves to help around the house. He's a dream to have around when it's time to trim the trees."

Too Tall for Basketball

Craig "3 Story" Pressgang is making headlines again. But this time he's causing a little trouble. Neighboring towns are protesting the eligibility of Craig for the local basketball team, our own Buffalo Bills. Teams claim Craig's freakish growth spurts are giving him an unfair advantage against opponents, and they might have a point. The Bills have been trampling opponents in every game this season starting with their crosstown *(cont.)*

Giant Sighting

Craig Pressgang sightings have become akin to Bigfoot. Craig's mother informed the *Times* that he rarely leaves the house, but one eyewitness recently claimed she saw Craig's towering frame vacationing on the lake front in nearby Cheektowaga, New York. "He was lumbering around. It almost seemed like he was moving in slow motion. And I think I saw him with a girl. Maybe his mother?" Other sources are saying that *(cont.)*

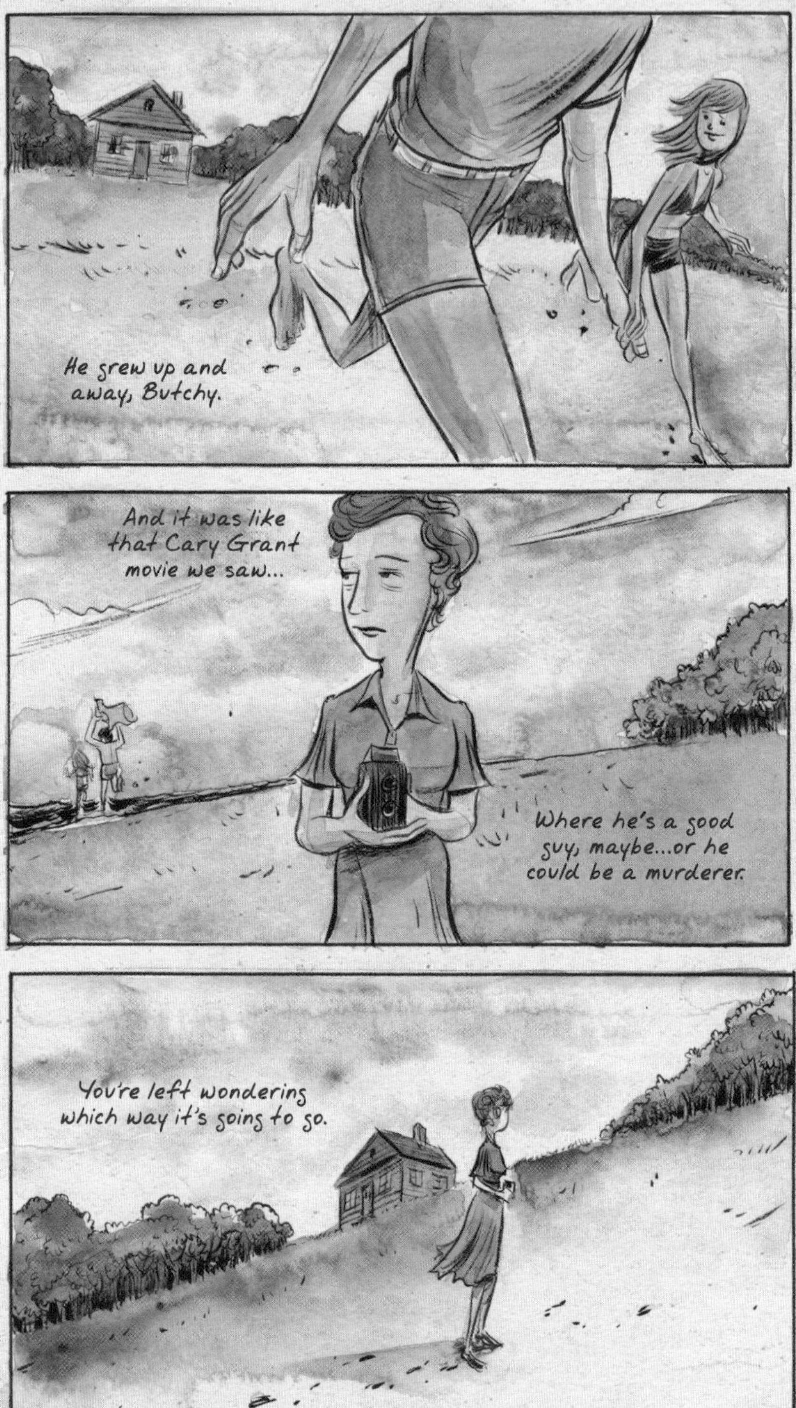
He grew up and away, Butchy.
And it was like that Cary Grant movie we saw...
Where he's a good guy, maybe...or he could be a murderer.
You're left wondering which way it's going to go.

And I liked to think it was going to go my way.

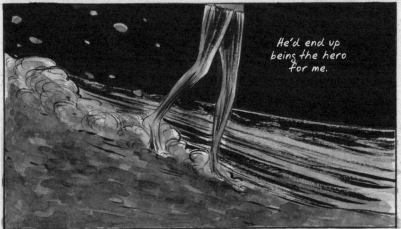

He'd end up being the hero for me.

But I realized that, either way...I wasn't Joan Fontaine to Cary Grant.

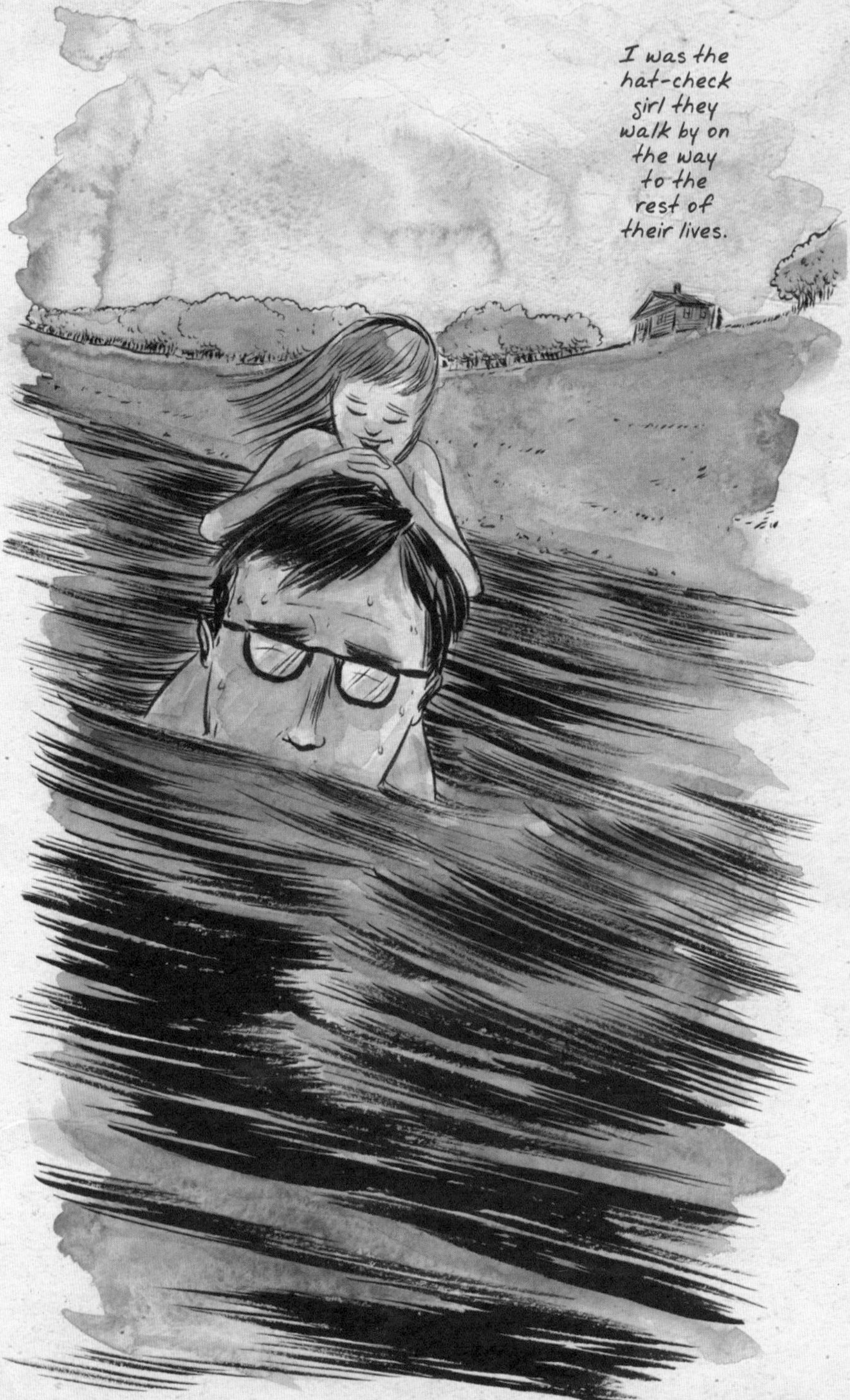
I was the hat-check girl they walk by on the way to the rest of their lives.

It didn't mean anything.

It ended up being like an early chapter in a long novel.

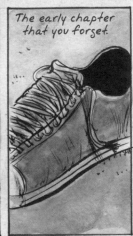

The early chapter that you forget.

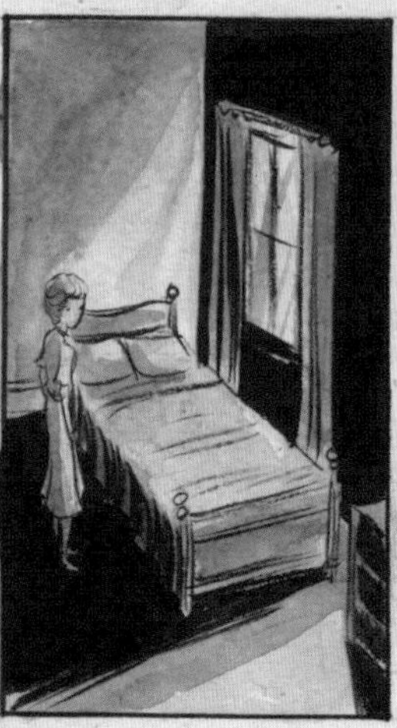

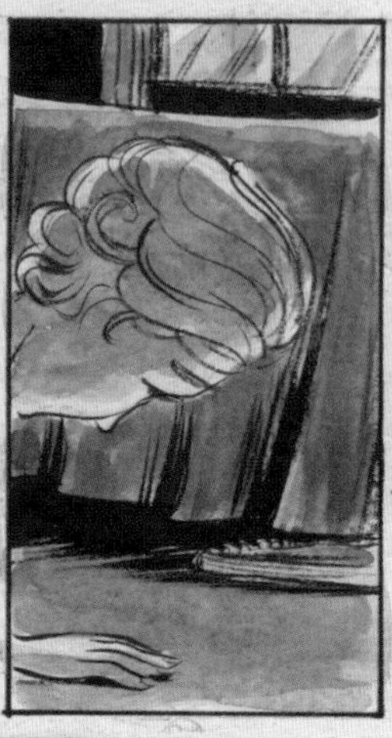

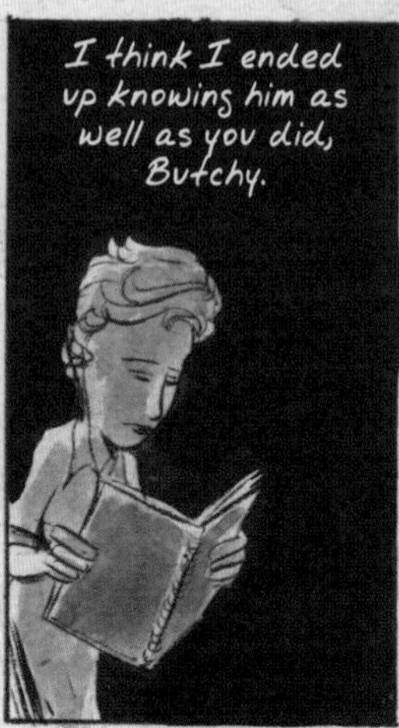
I think I ended up knowing him as well as you did, Butchy.

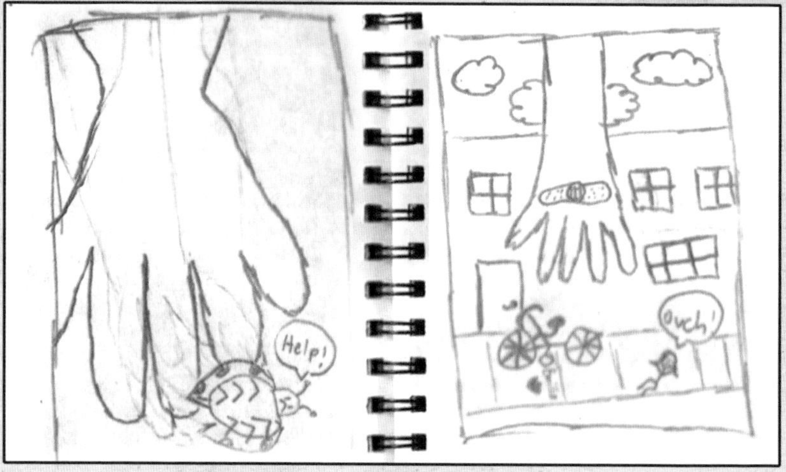
Help!
Ouch!

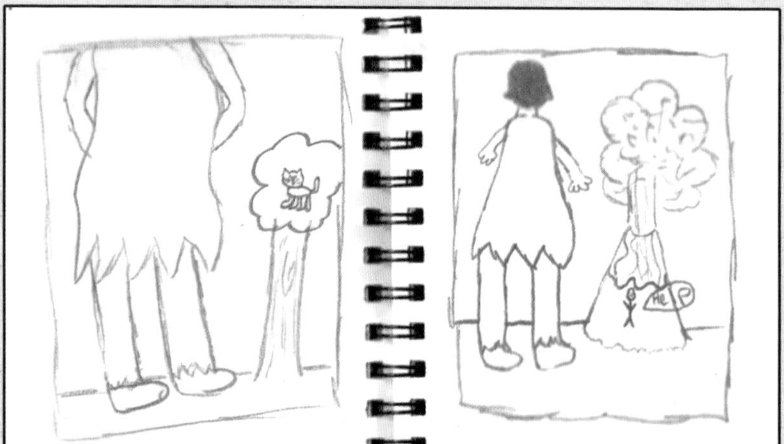
Help

sob

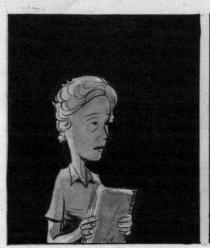

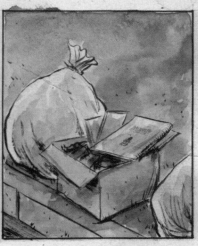

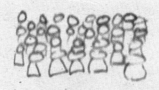

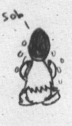

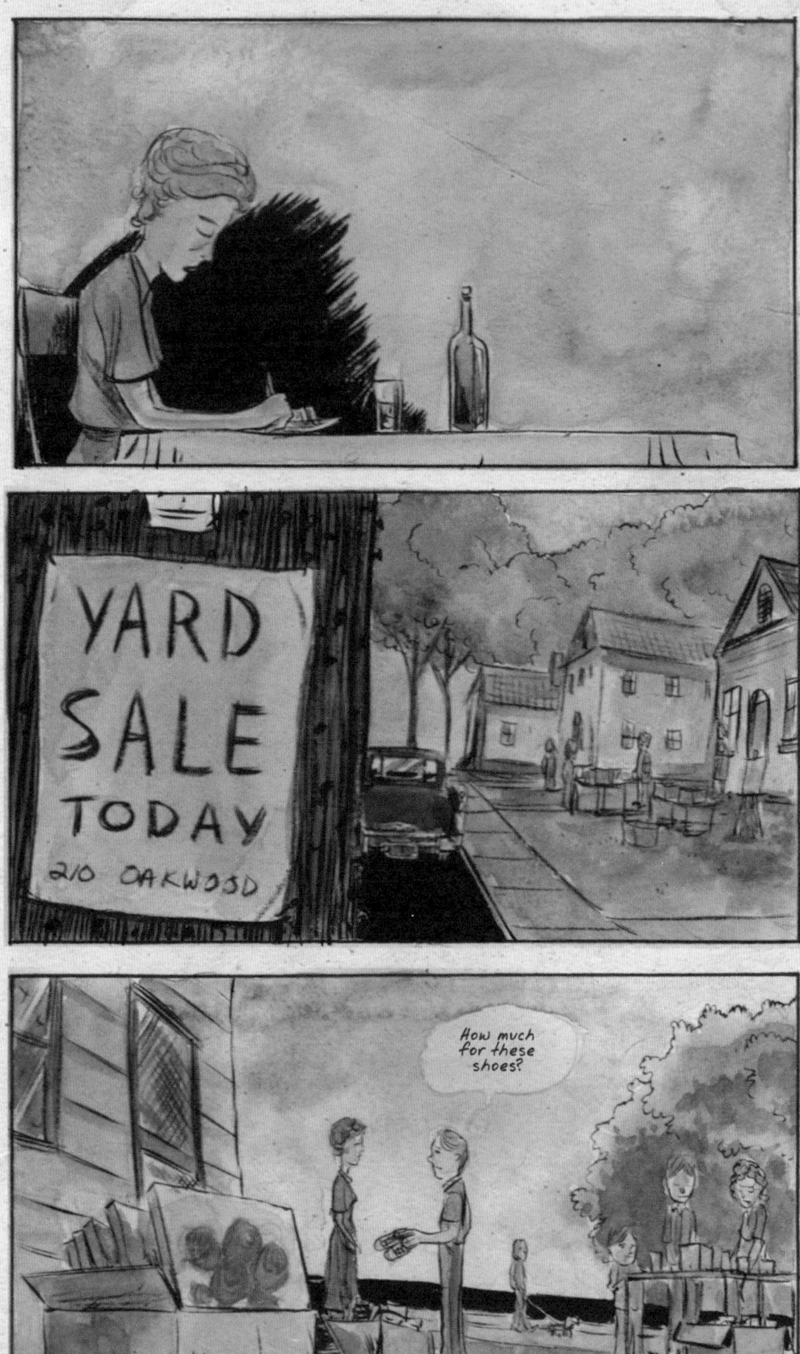
YARD
SALE
TODAY
210 OAKWOOD
How much for these shoes?

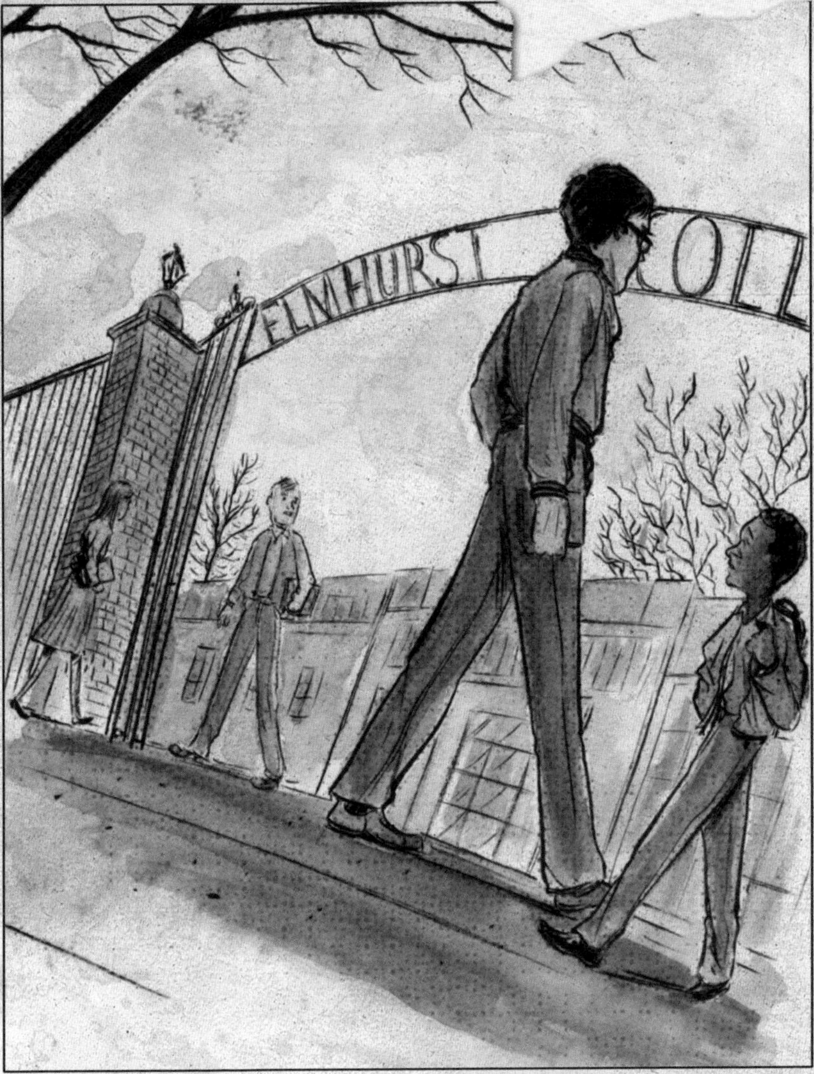
ELMHURST
COLL

Giant Education

Hometown icon and hero Craig Pressgang attended his first days of college at Elmhurst College in the suburbs of Chicago.

Craig's height of 9 feet caused distractions early on, but, from eyewitness reports, the student body quickly welcomed its newest and most famous student. Several colleges vied for Craig's enrollment, but Elmhurst finally won out.

Craig plans to study economics and business, but his major is still undecided. The campus has already taken steps to accommodate its largest student by modifying an existing dorm room to house Craig comfortably.

"I couldn't ask for a better roommate," Ray Cool said when questioned about rooming with the "Giant Man." "He's quiet and keeps to himself mostly. He's just a student like anyone else here on

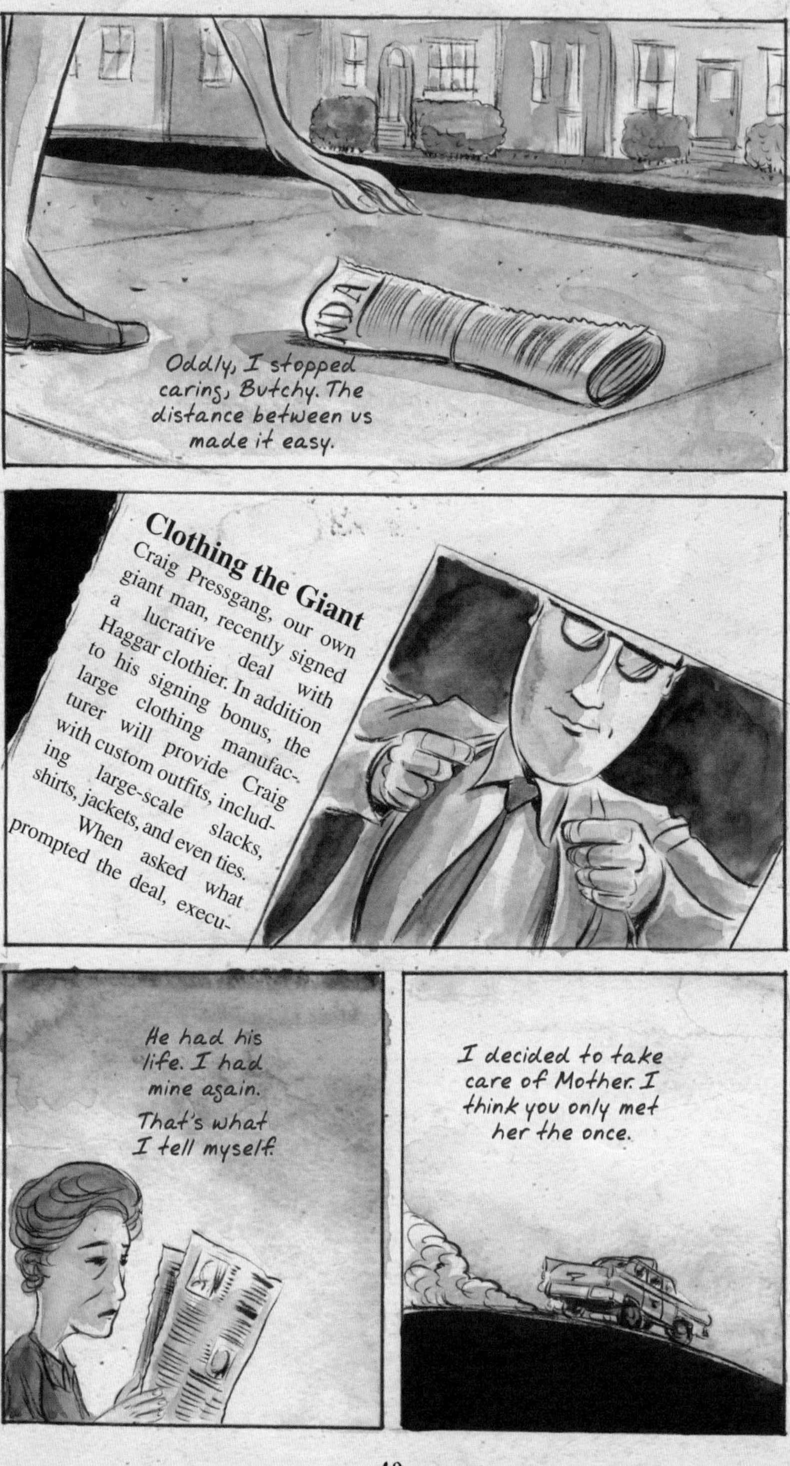
NDA
Oddly, I stopped caring, Butchy. The distance between us made it easy.
Clothing the Giant
Craig Pressgang, our own giant man, recently signed a lucrative deal with Haggar clothier. In addition to his signing bonus, the large clothing manufacturer will provide Craig with custom outfits, including large-scale slacks, shirts, jackets, and even ties.
When asked what prompted the deal, execu-
He had his life. I had mine again.
That's what I tell myself.
I decided to take care of Mother. I think you only met her the once.

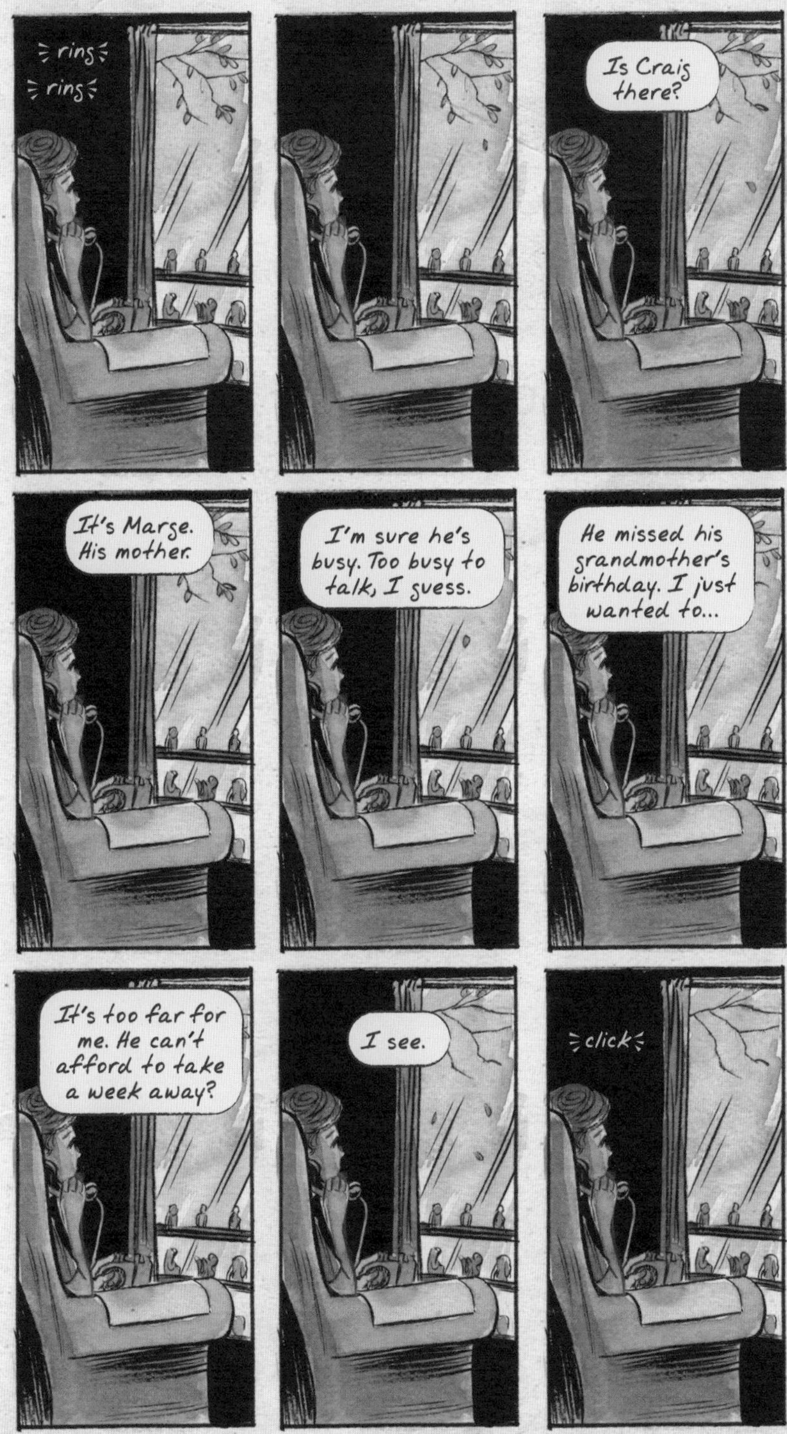
rings
rings
Is Craig there?
It's Marge. His mother.
I'm sure he's busy. Too busy to talk, I guess.
He missed his grandmother's birthday. I just wanted to...
It's too far for me. He can't afford to take a week away?
I see.
click

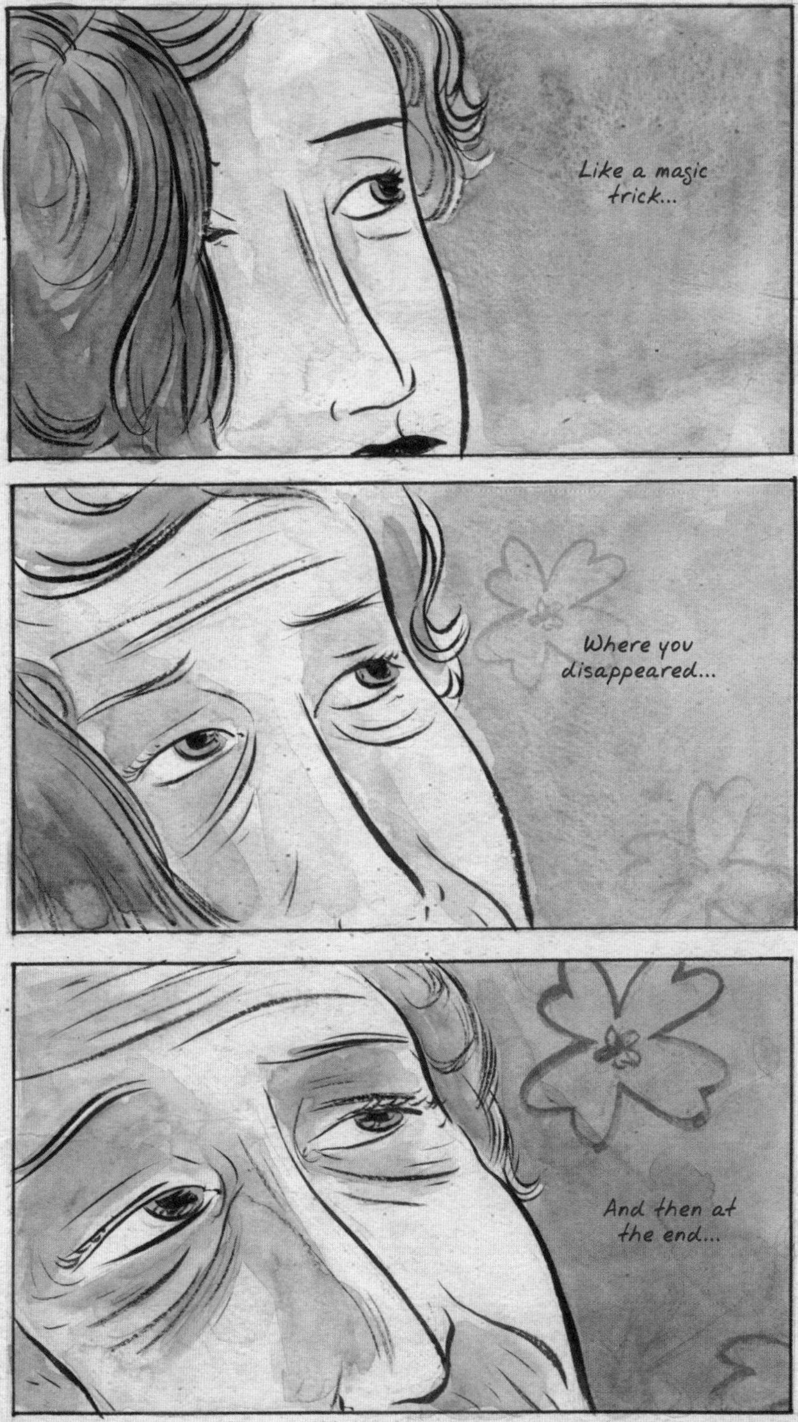
Like a magic trick...
Where you disappeared...
And then at the end...

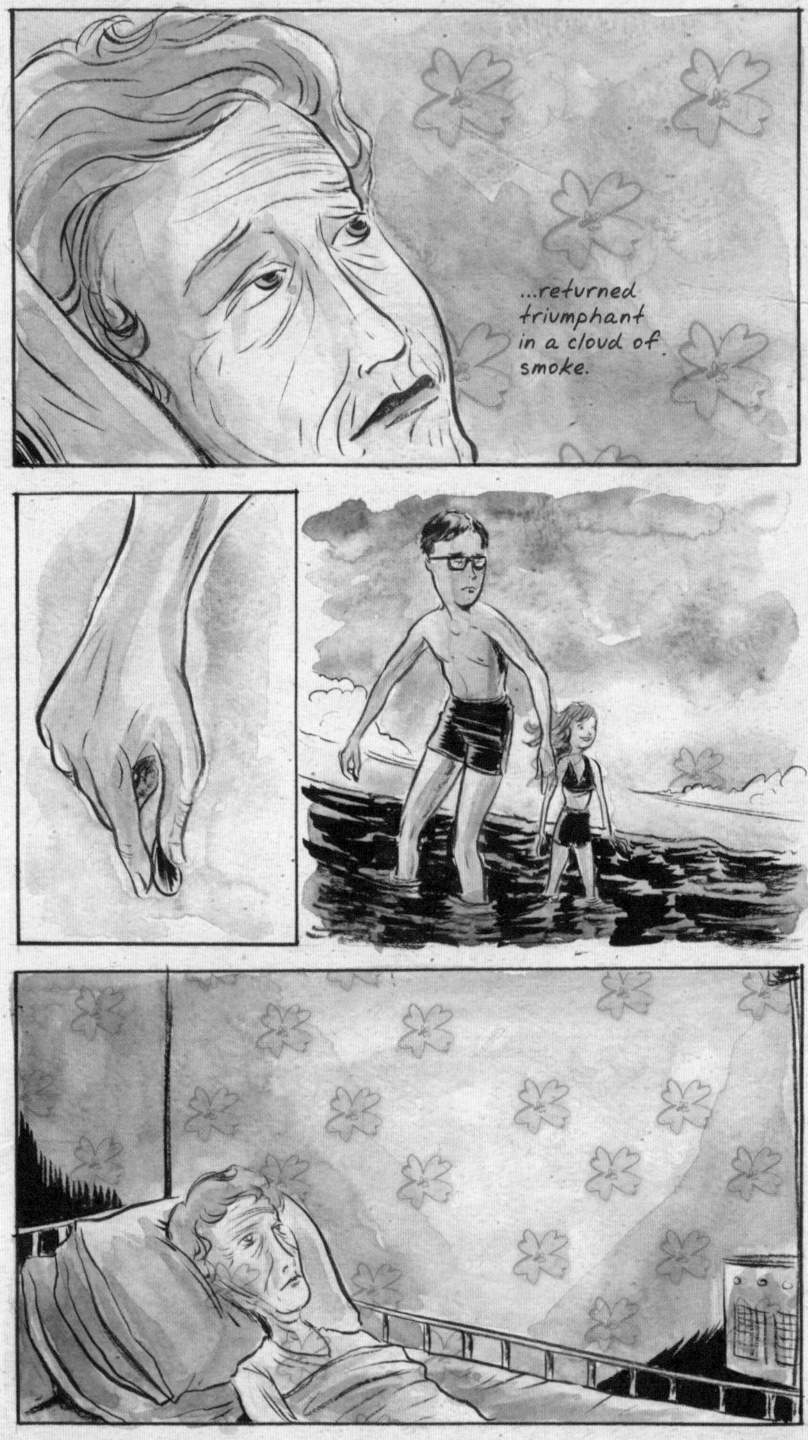
...returned triumphant in a cloud of smoke.

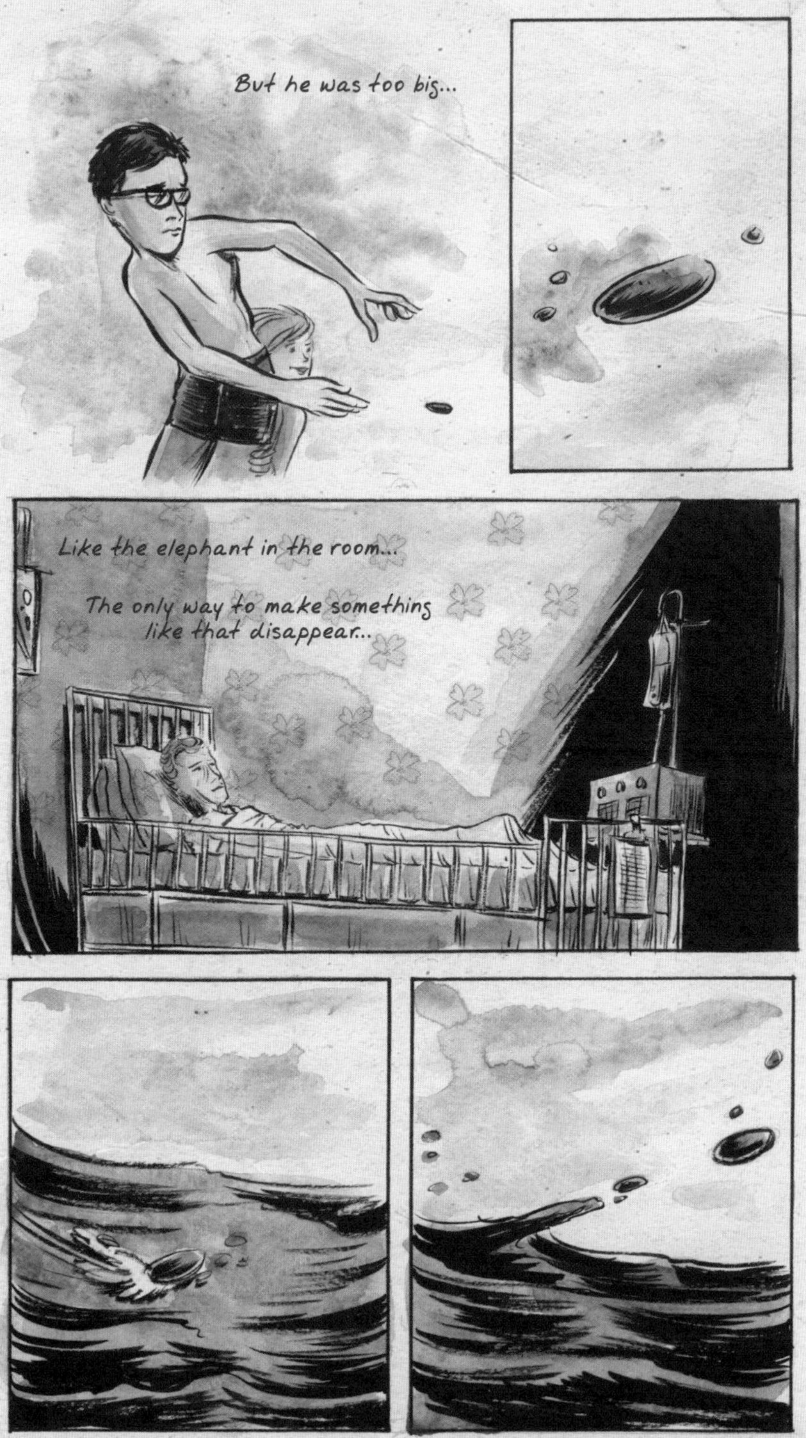
But he was too big...
Like the elephant in the room...
The only way to make something like that disappear...

Is to stop
talking
about it.

You knew
Cary Grant
would turn
out to be
innocent.

He was too big a star.

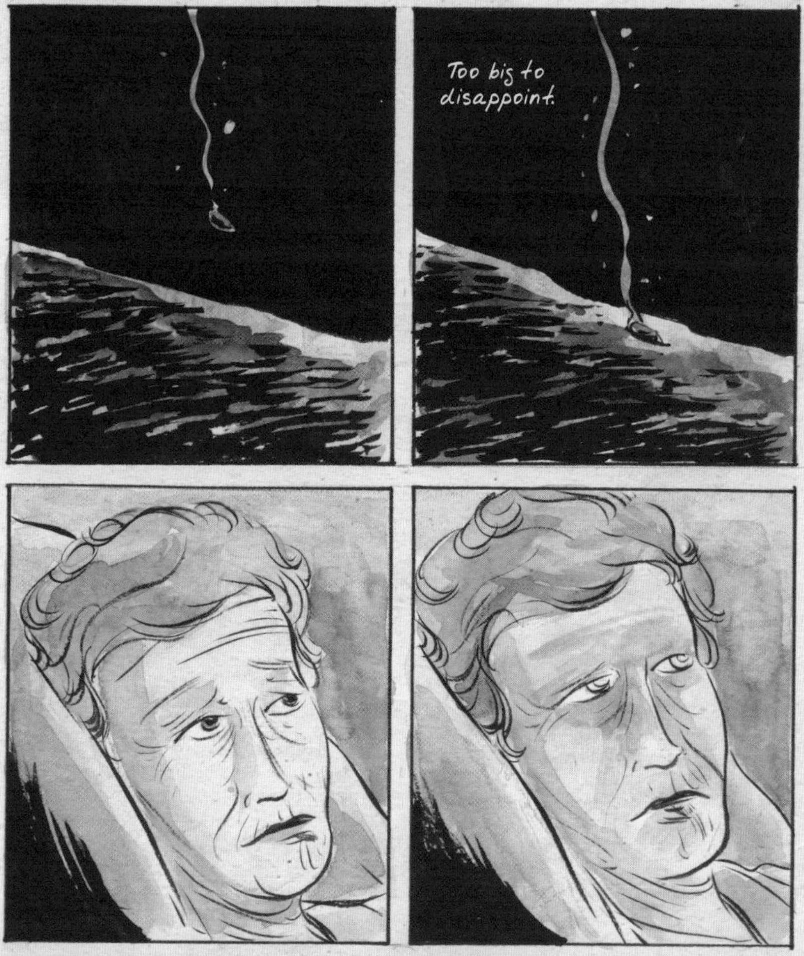
Too big to disappoint.

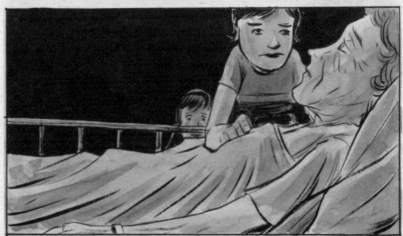

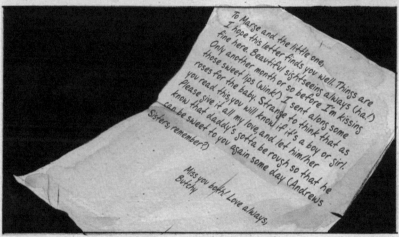

To Marge and the little one,
I hope this letter finds you well. Things are
fine here. Beautiful sightseeing always (ha!)
Only another month or so before I'm kissing
those sweet lips (wink!) I sent along some
roses for the baby. Strange to think that as
you read this, you will know if it's a boy or girl.
Please give it all my love, and let him/her
know that daddy's gotta be rough so that he
can be sweet to you again some day (Andrews
Sisters, remember?)
Miss you both! Love always,
Butchy

To Marge and the little one,
I hope this letter finds you well. Things are fine here. Beautiful sightseeing always (ha!) Only another month or so before I'm kissing those sweet lips (wink!) I sent along some roses for the baby. Strange to think that as you read this, you will know if it's a boy or girl. Please give it all my love, and let him/her know that daddy's gotta be rough so that he can be sweet to you again some day (Andrews Sisters, remember?)

Miss you both! Love always,
Butchy

2ND STORY

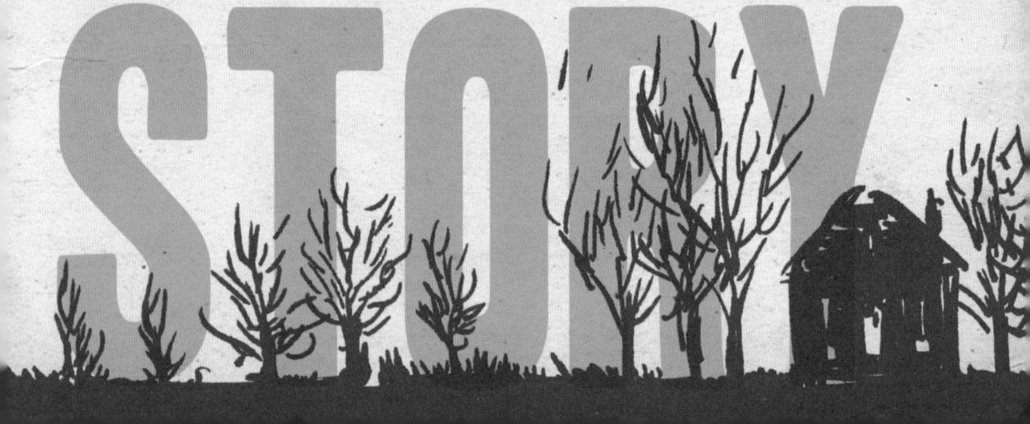

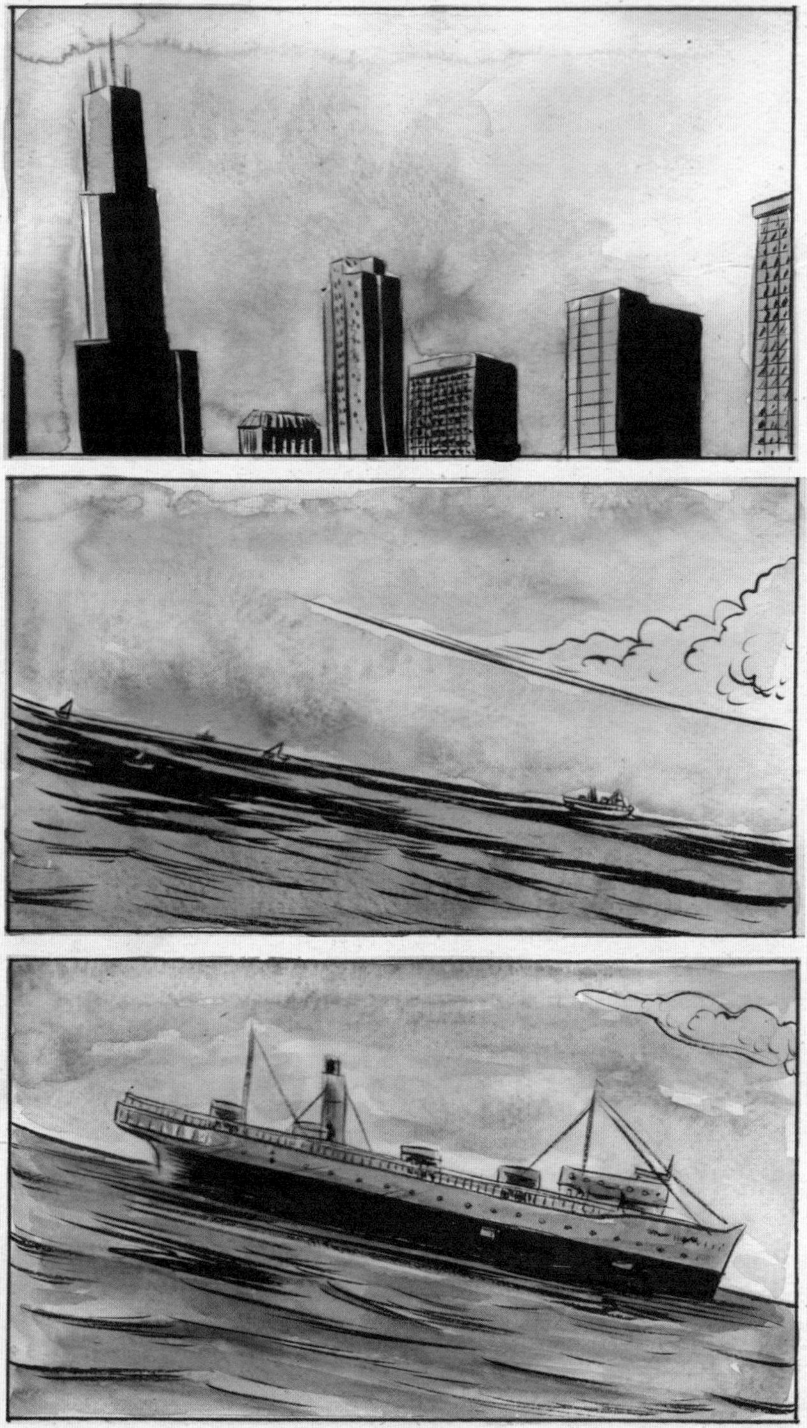

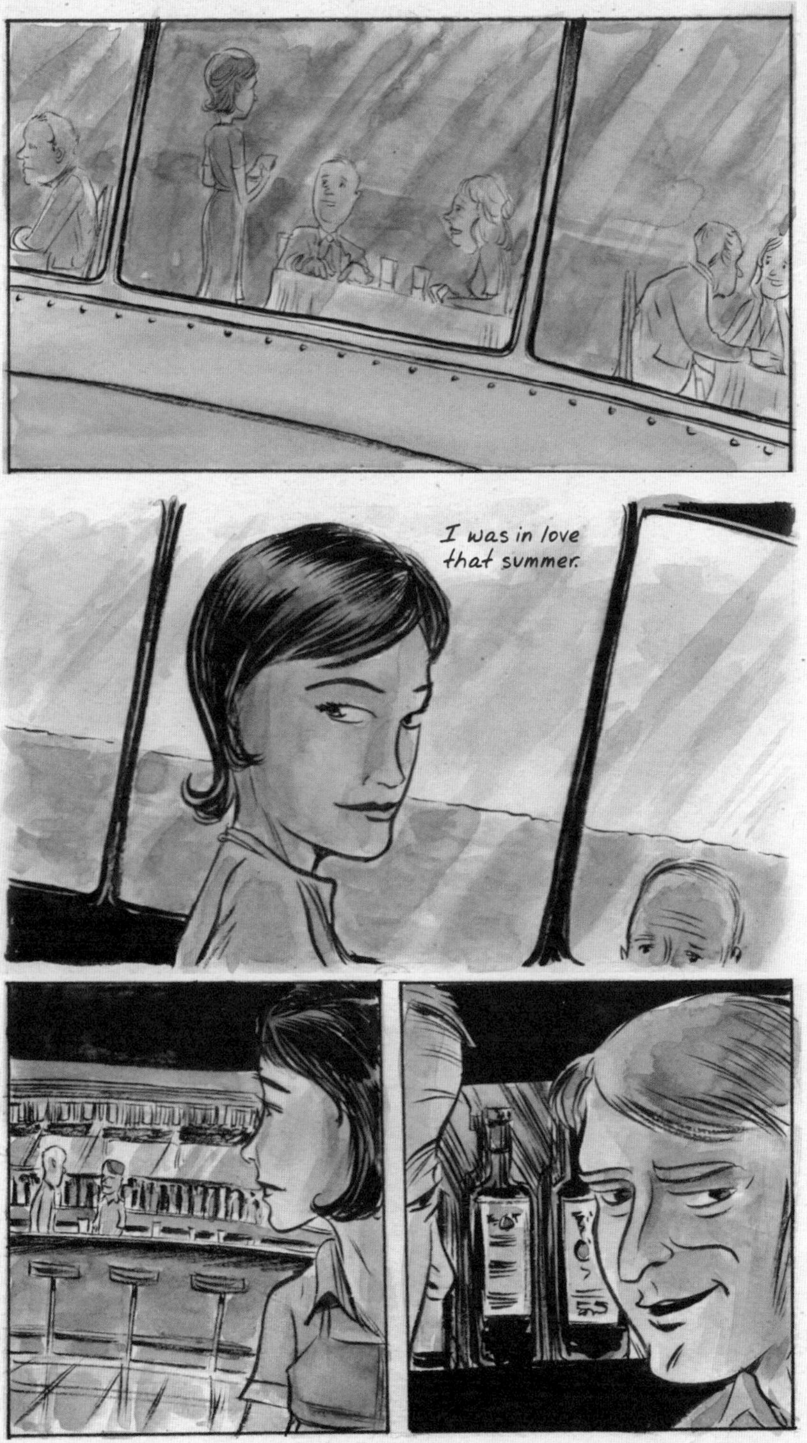
I was in love
that summer.

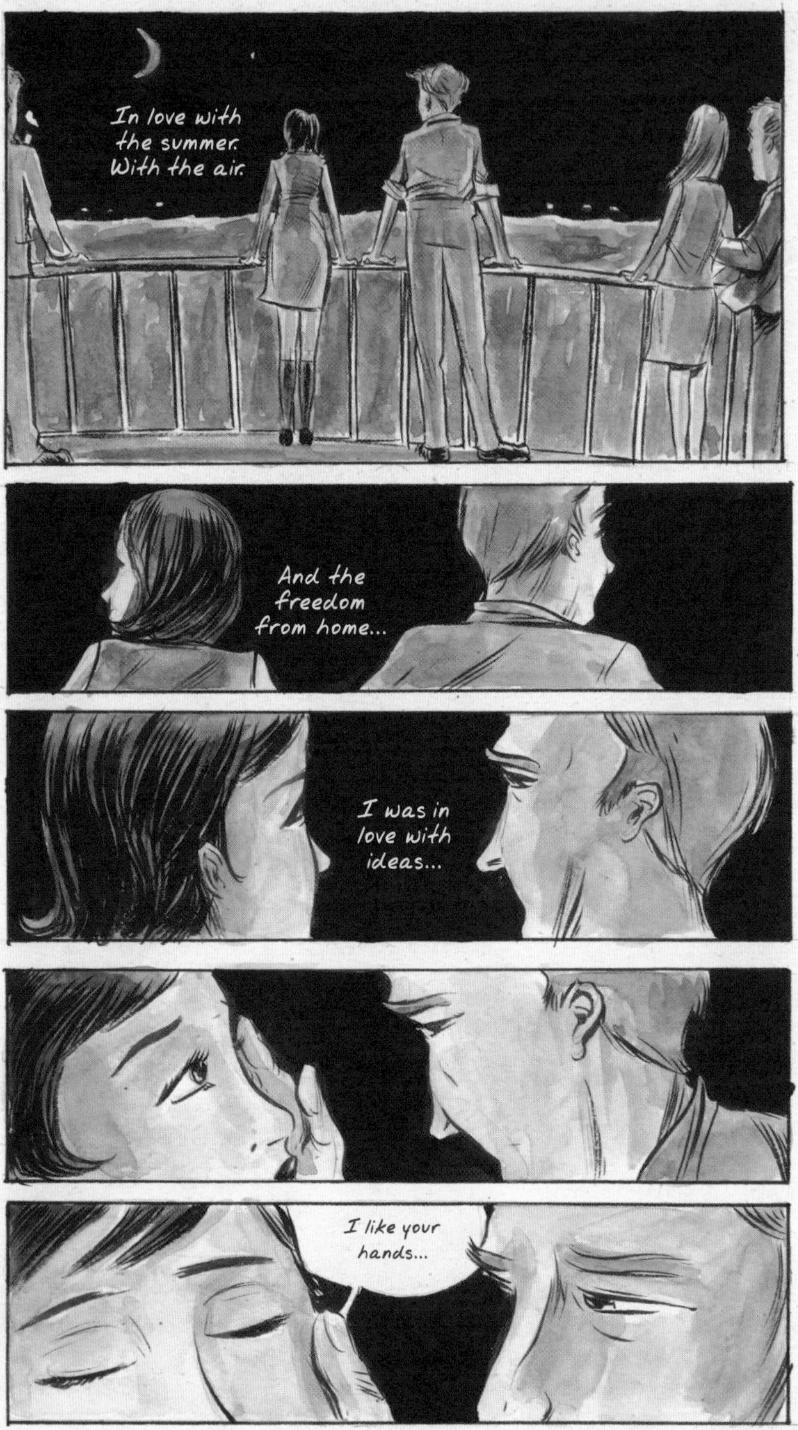
In love with the summer. With the air.
And the freedom from home...
I was in love with ideas...
I like your hands...

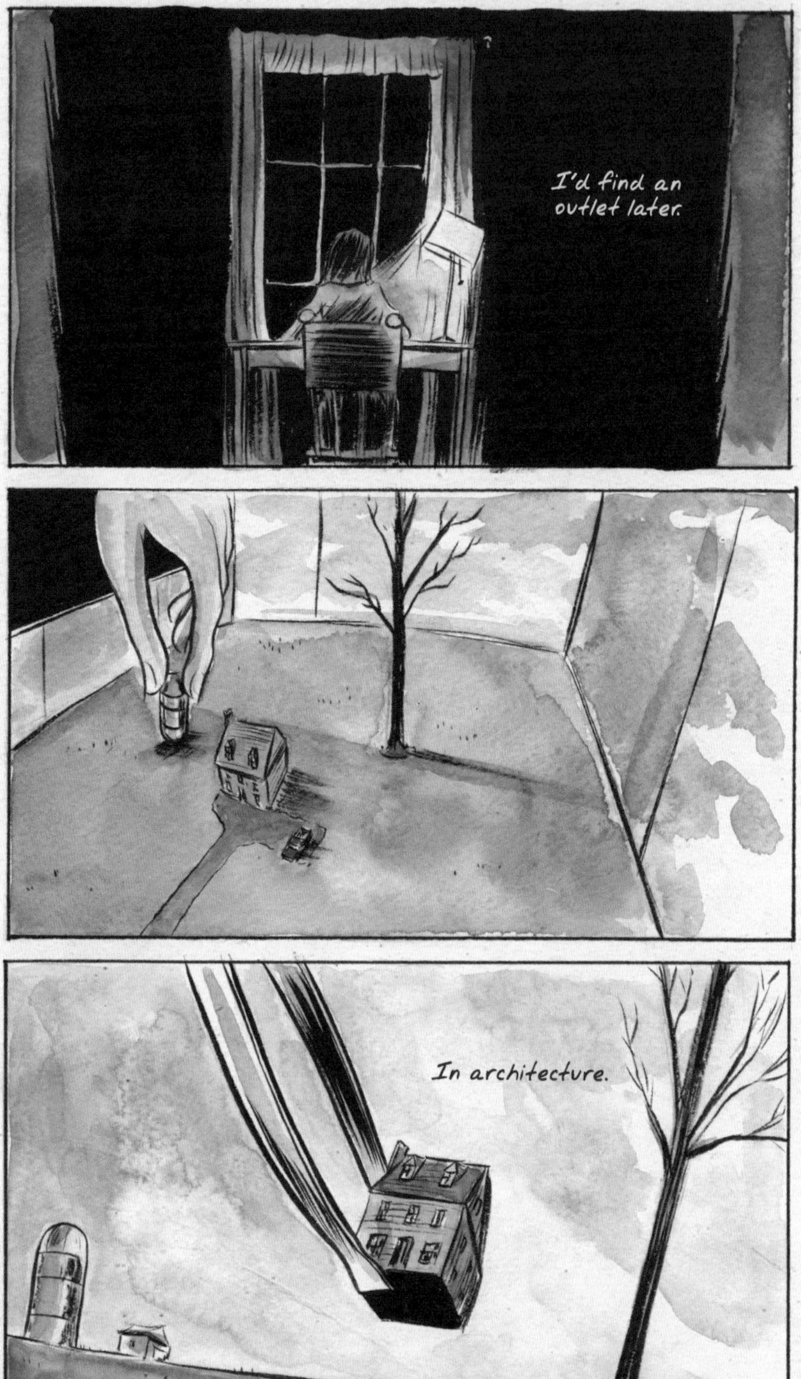
I'd find an outlet later.
In architecture.

57

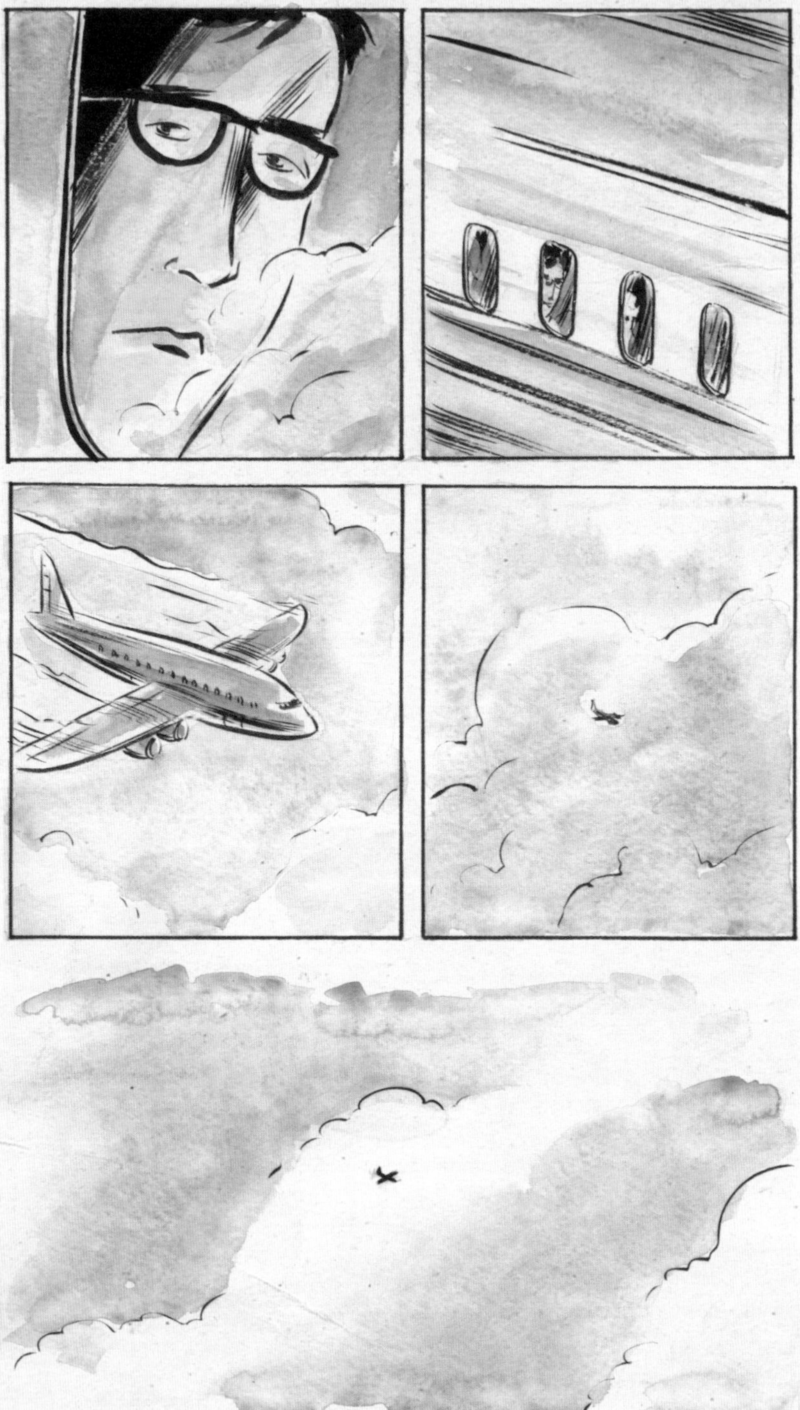

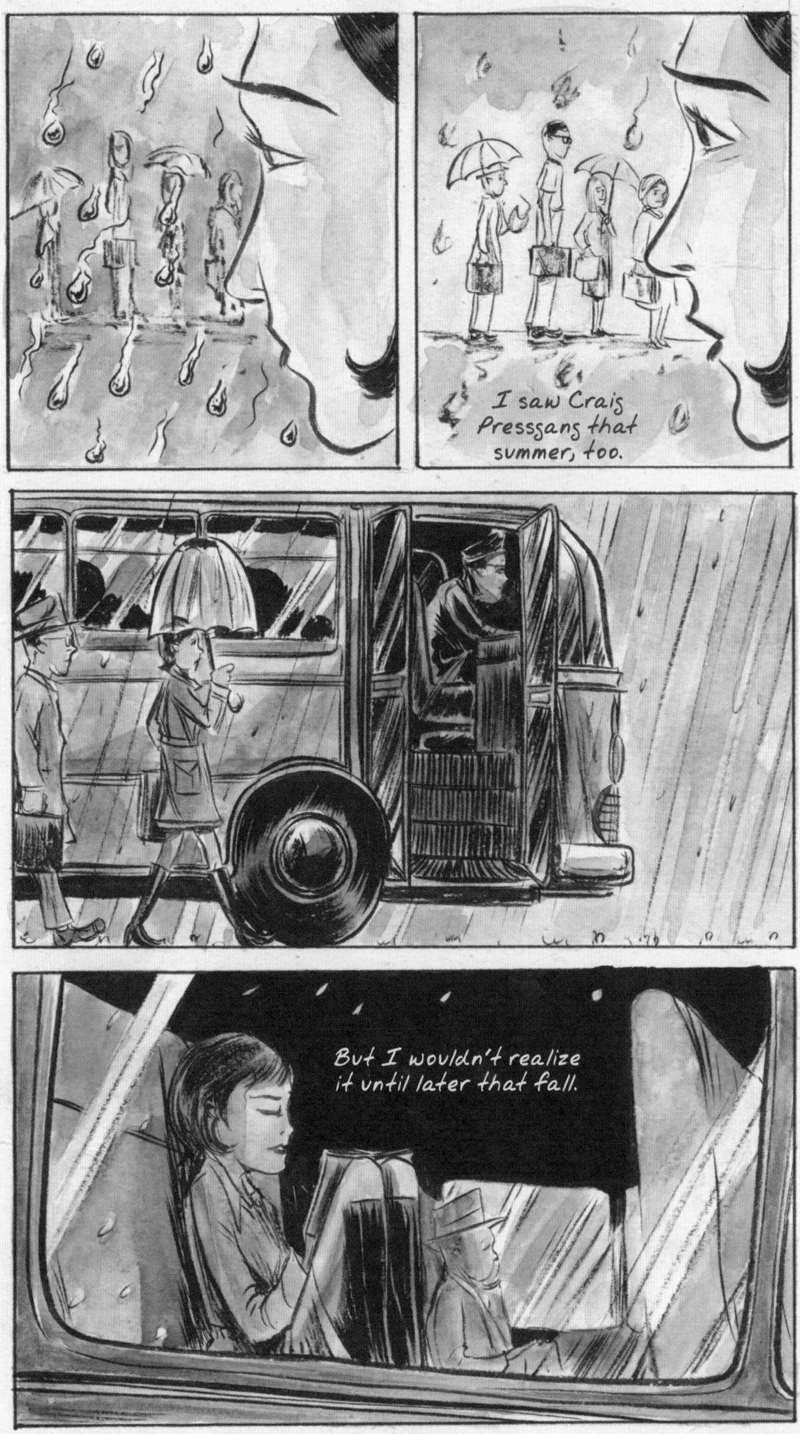
I saw Craig Pressgang that summer, too.
But I wouldn't realize it until later that fall.

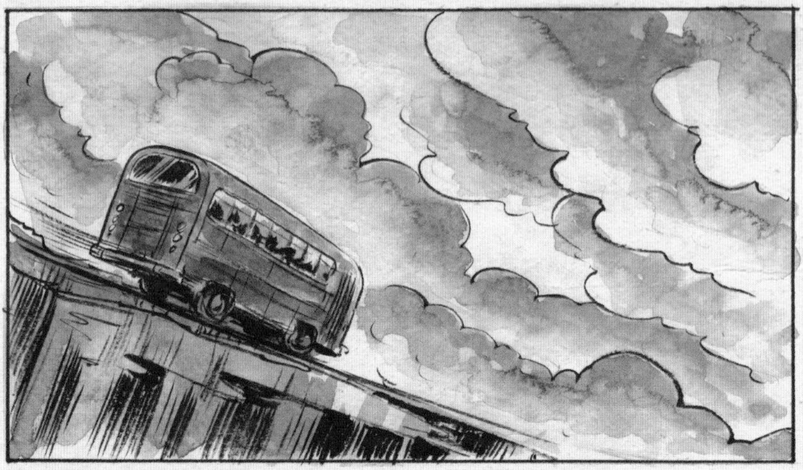

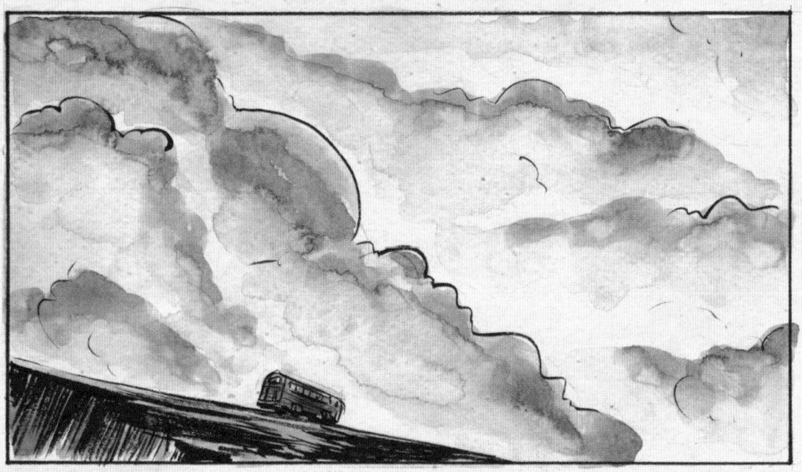

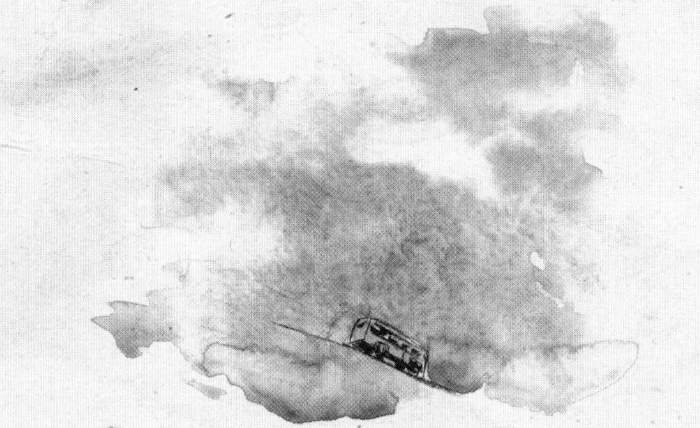

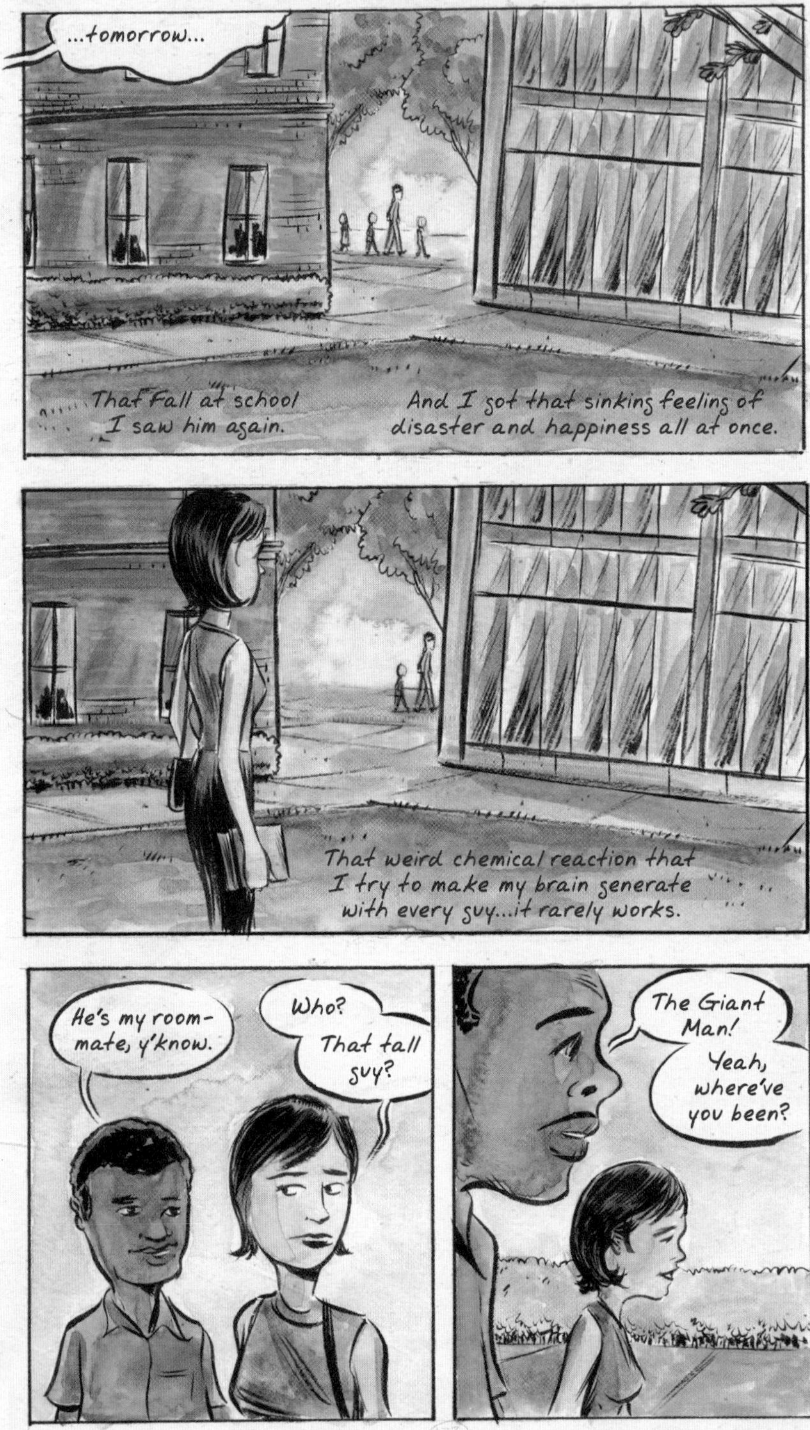
...tomorrow...
That Fall at school I saw him again.
And I got that sinking feeling of disaster and happiness all at once.
That weird chemical reaction that I try to make my brain generate with every guy...it rarely works.
He's my room-mate, y'know.
Who?
That tall guy?
The Giant Man!
Yeah, where've you been?

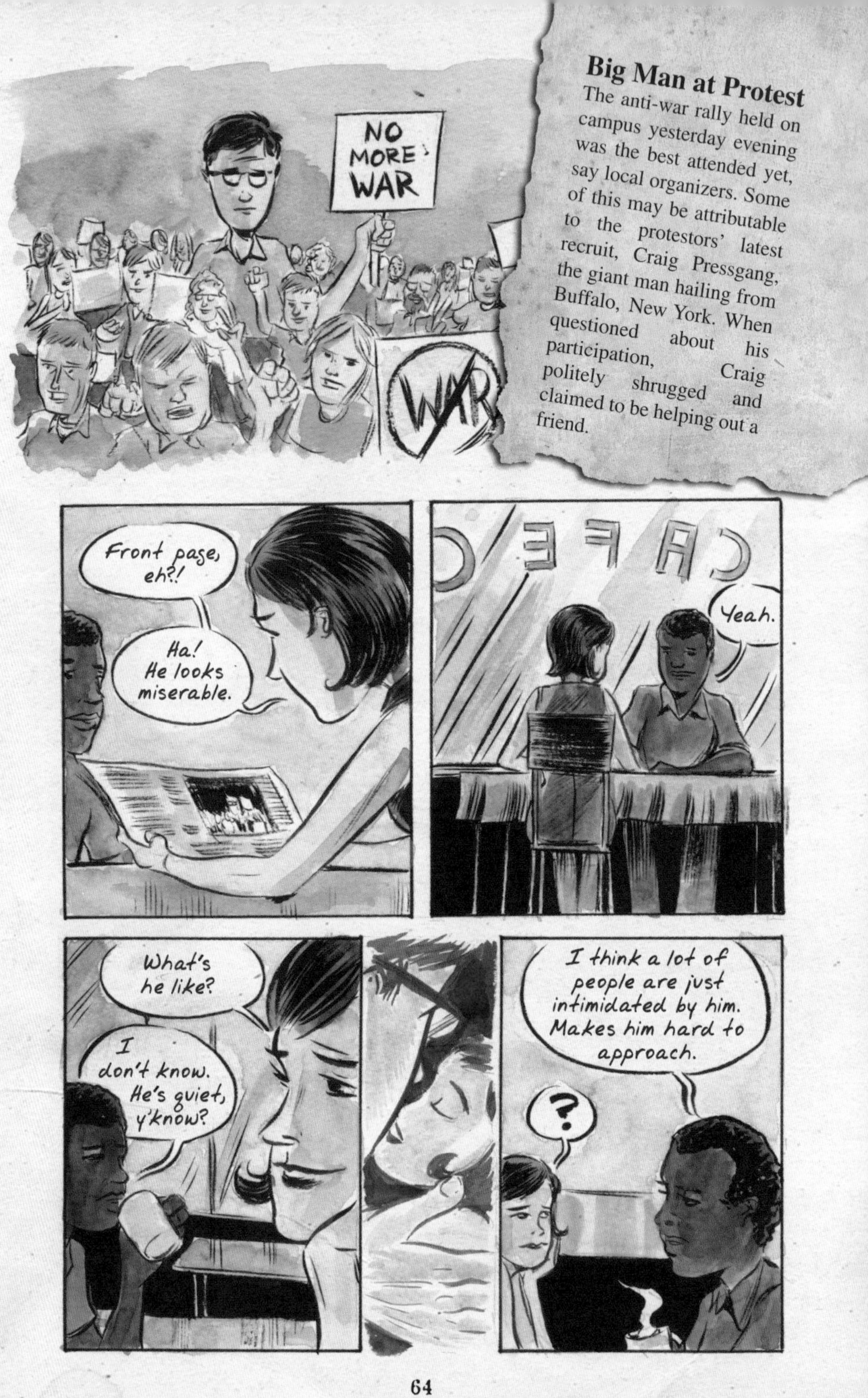
NO MORE WAR
WAR
Big Man at Protest
The anti-war rally held on campus yesterday evening was the best attended yet, say local organizers. Some of this may be attributable to the protestors' latest recruit, Craig Pressgang, the giant man hailing from Buffalo, New York. When questioned about his participation, Craig politely shrugged and claimed to be helping out a friend.
Front page, eh?!
Ha! He looks miserable.
CAFE
Yeah.
What's he like?
I don't know. He's quiet, y'know?
I think a lot of people are just intimidated by him. Makes him hard to approach.
?

In the late 1960s, young Craig became a straight-A student and often participated in friendly rallies to promote local events and causes.

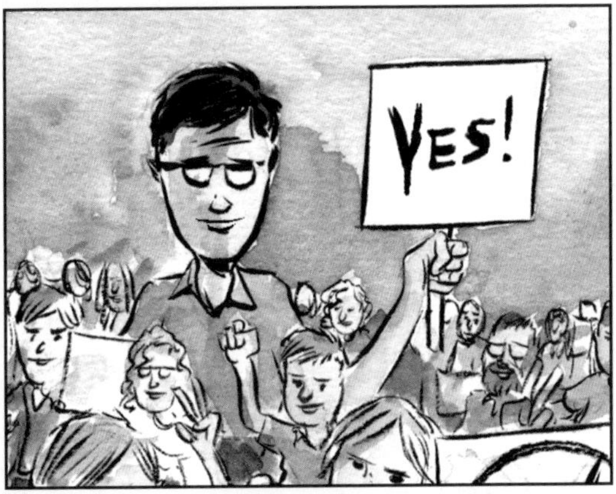
YES!

He lent his unique talents and affable personality to many great causes and helped everyone he knew. Those closest to him agreed: he was outgoing, personable, and "just another one of the guys."

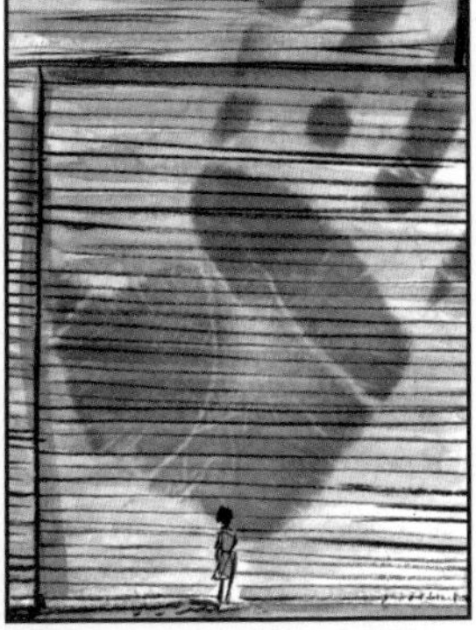

Craig would go on to graduate with honors. He received a degree in business, and he even found time to take some art classes. He especially enjoyed creating art, having the most fun and success with his famous "hand prints."

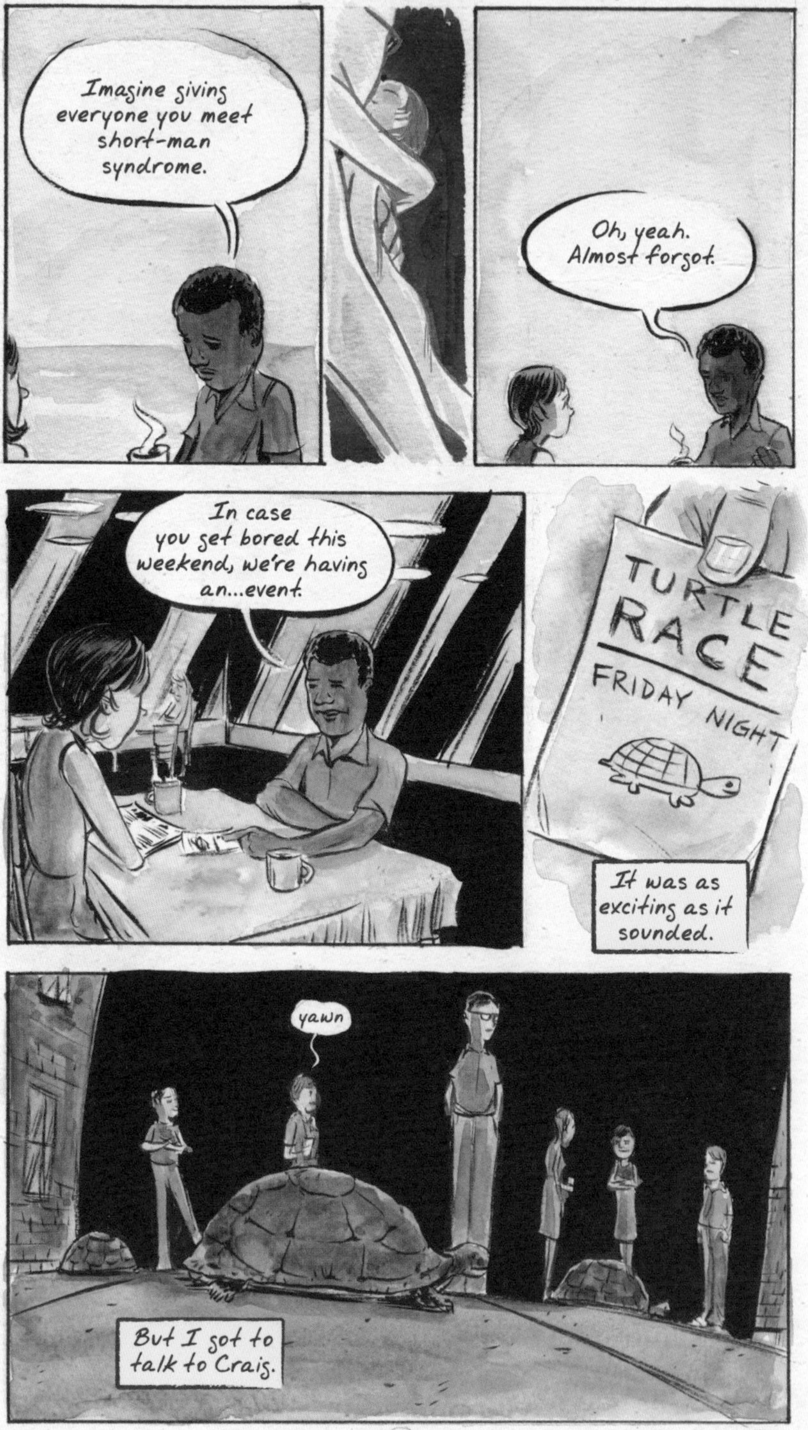

Imagine giving everyone you meet short-man syndrome.
Oh, yeah. Almost forgot.
In case you get bored this weekend, we're having an...event.
TURTLE RACE
FRIDAY NIGHT
It was as exciting as it sounded.
yawn
But I got to talk to Craig.

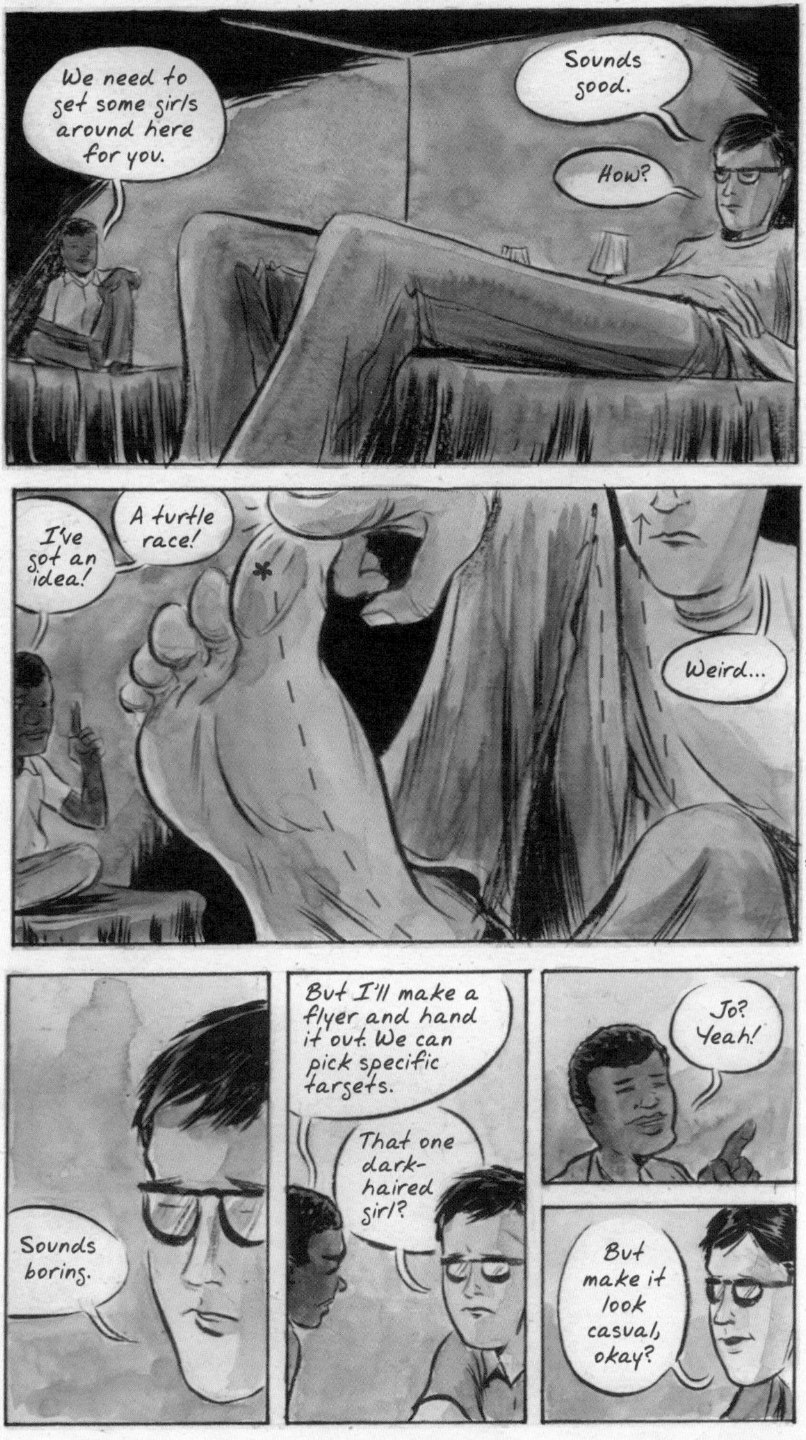
We need to get some girls around here for you.
Sounds good.
How?
I've got an idea!
A turtle race!
*
Weird...
Sounds boring.
But I'll make a flyer and hand it out. We can pick specific targets.
That one dark-haired girl?
Jo? Yeah!
But make it look casual, okay?

* Elapsed time: 2 seconds

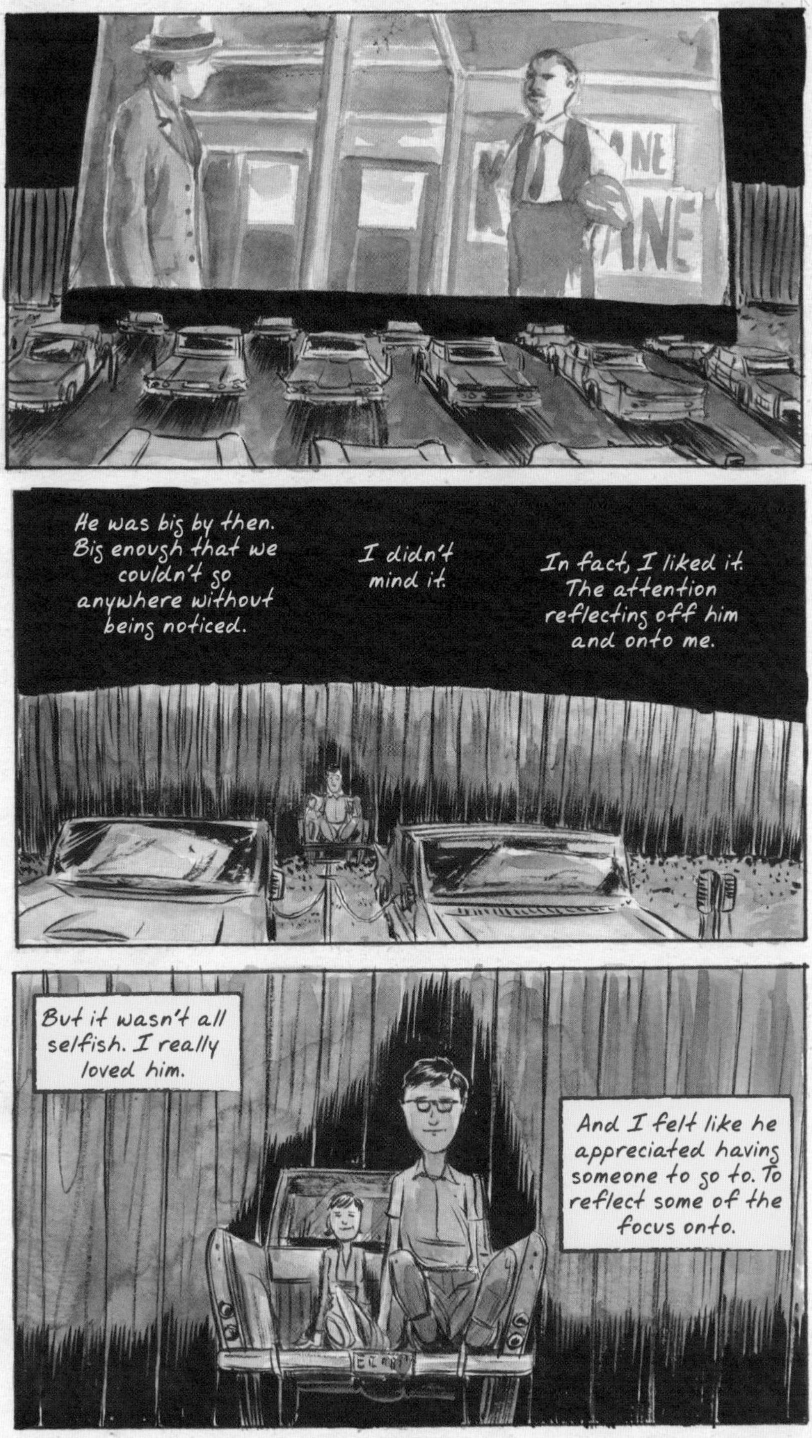
ONE
ANE
He was big by then. Big enough that we couldn't go anywhere without being noticed.
I didn't mind it.
In fact, I liked it. The attention reflecting off him and onto me.
But it wasn't all selfish. I really loved him.
And I felt like he appreciated having someone to go to. To reflect some of the focus onto.

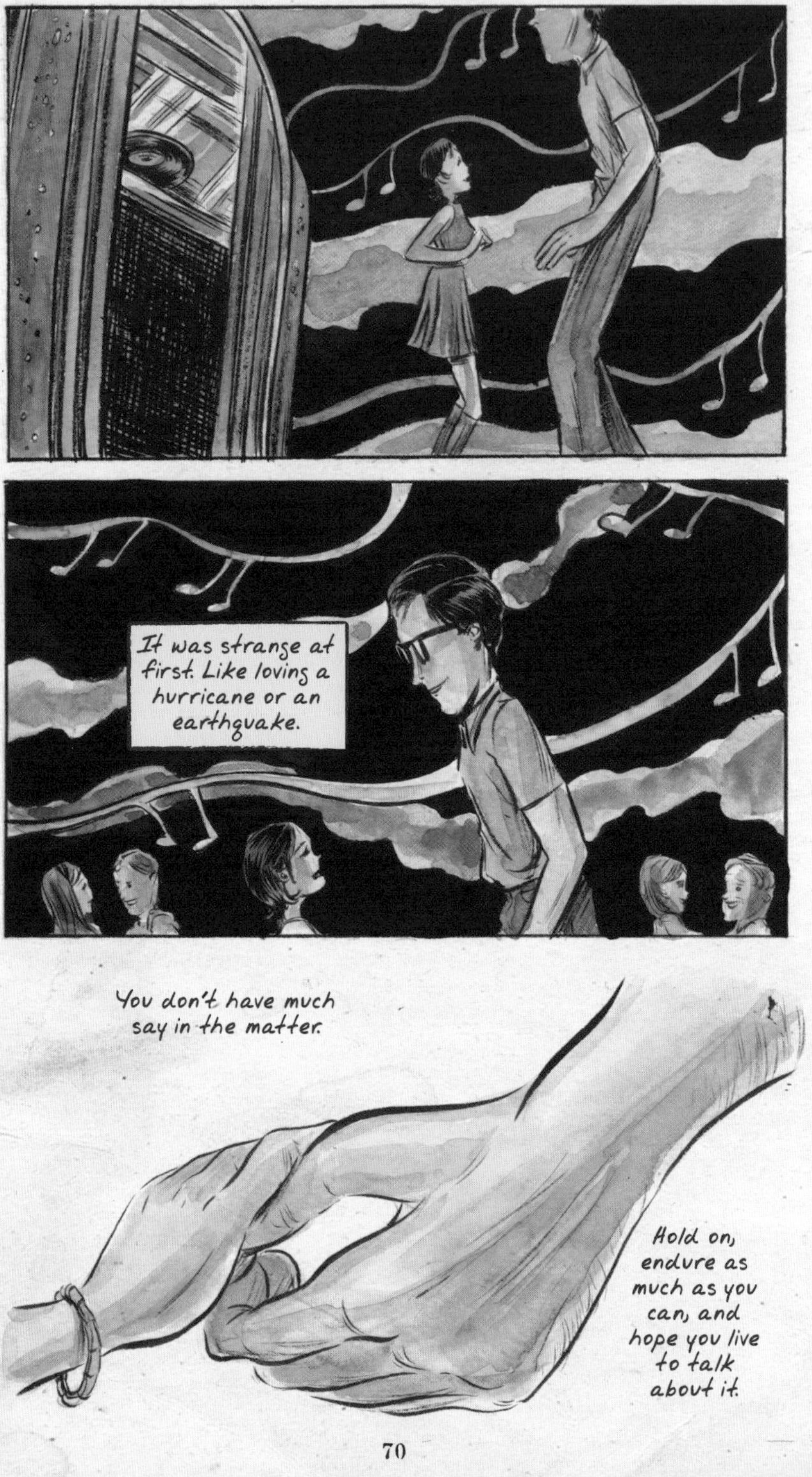
It was strange at first. Like loving a hurricane or an earthquake.
You don't have much say in the matter.
Hold on, endure as much as you can, and hope you live to talk about it.

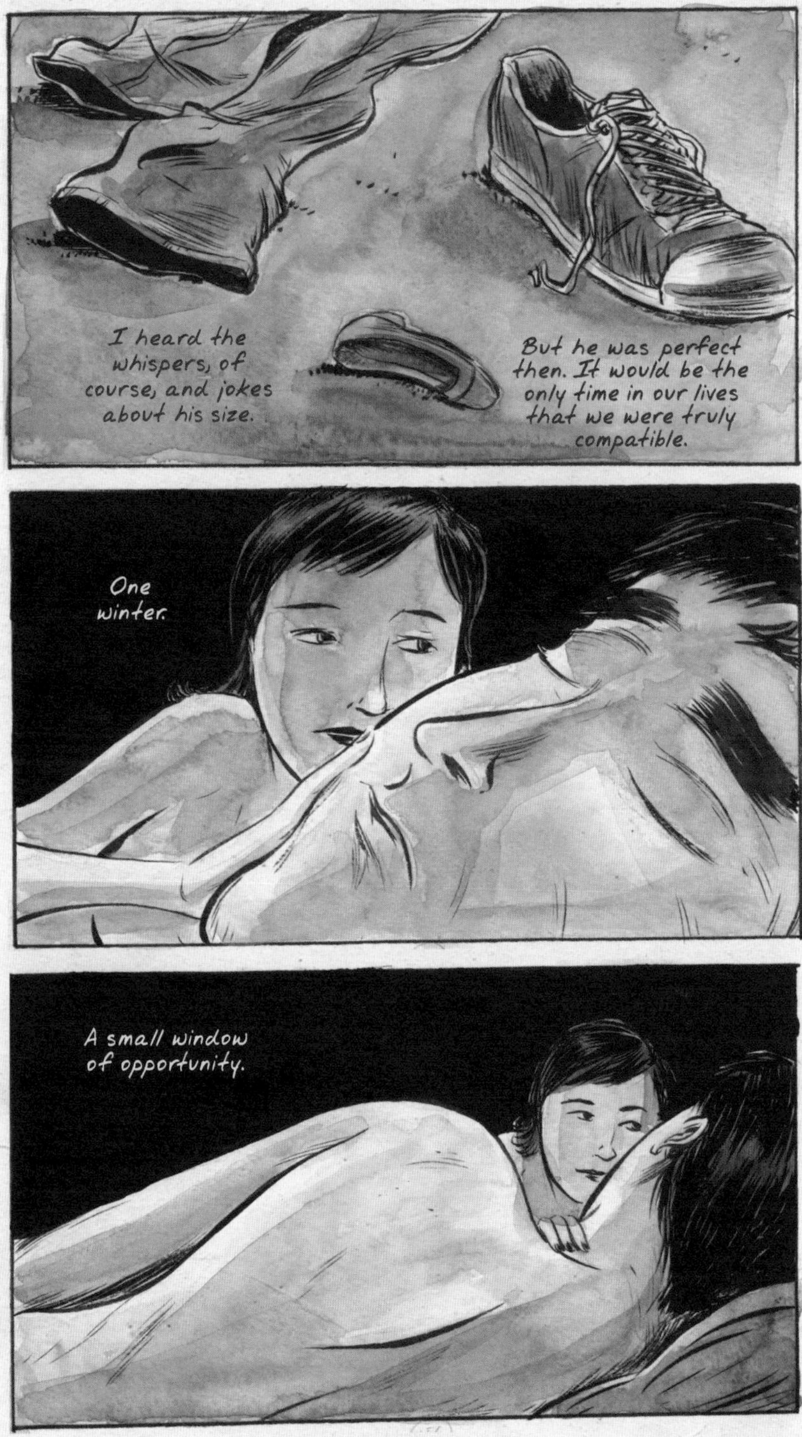
I heard the whispers, of course, and jokes about his size.
But he was perfect then. It would be the only time in our lives that we were truly compatible.
One winter.
A small window of opportunity.

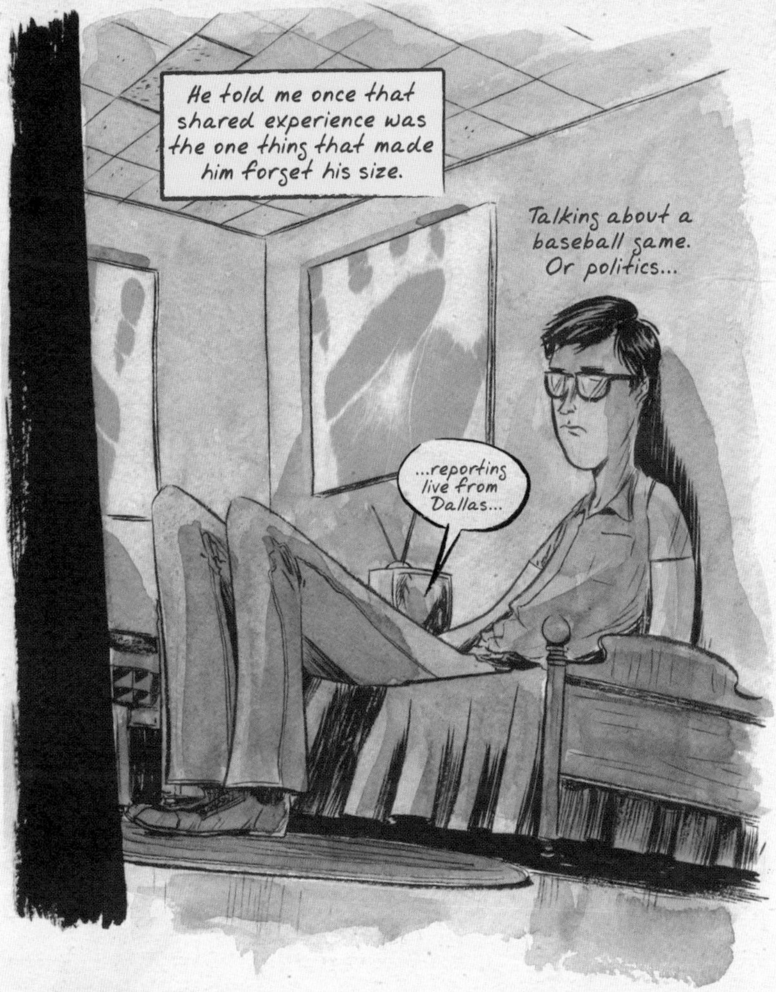
He told me once that shared experience was the one thing that made him forget his size.
Talking about a baseball game. Or politics...
...reporting live from Dallas...

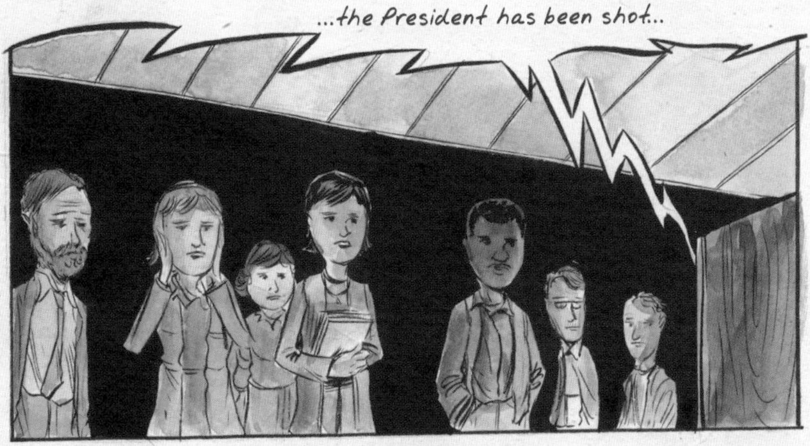
...the President has been shot...

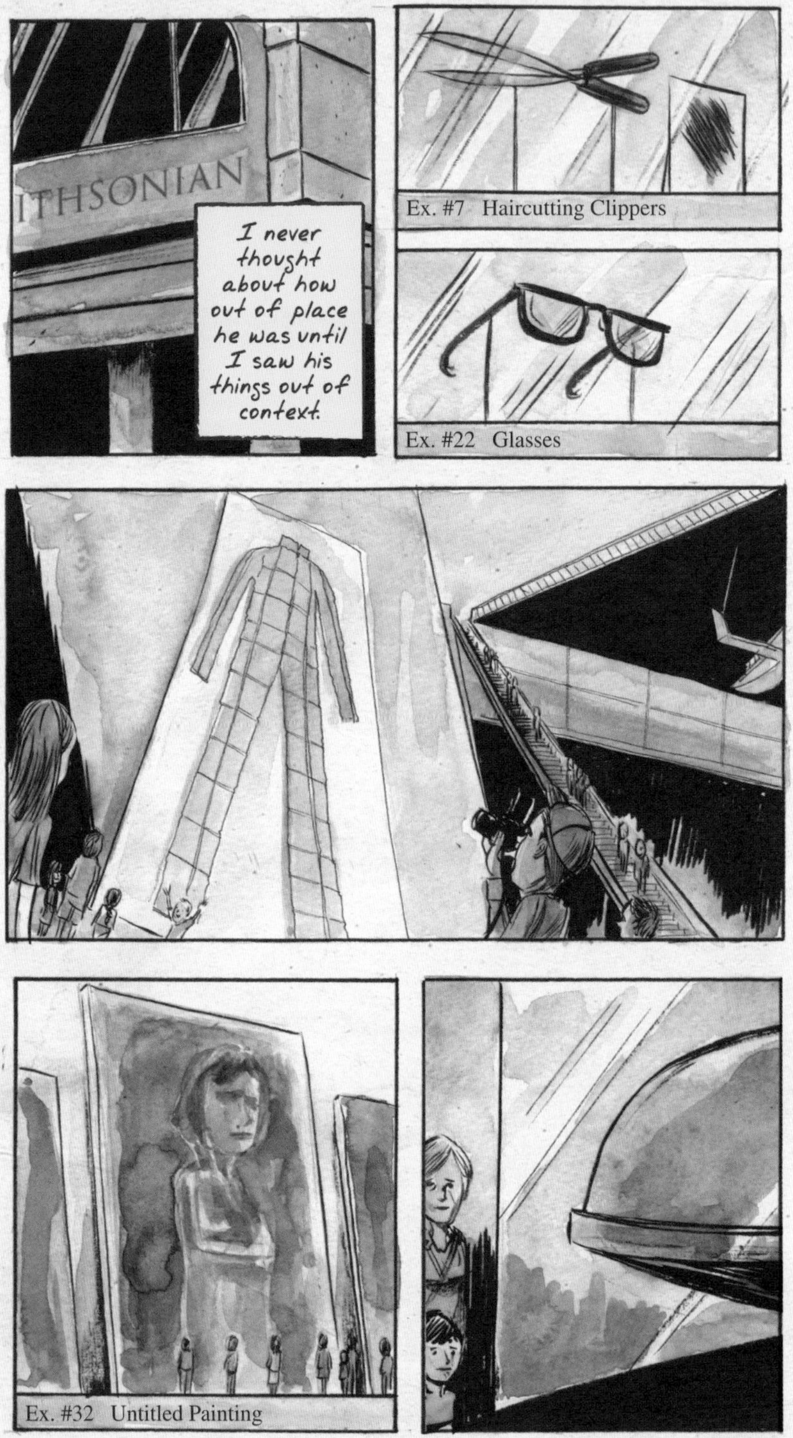
ITHSONIAN
I never thought about how out of place he was until I saw his things out of context.
Ex. #7 Haircutting Clippers
Ex. #22 Glasses
Ex. #32 Untitled Painting

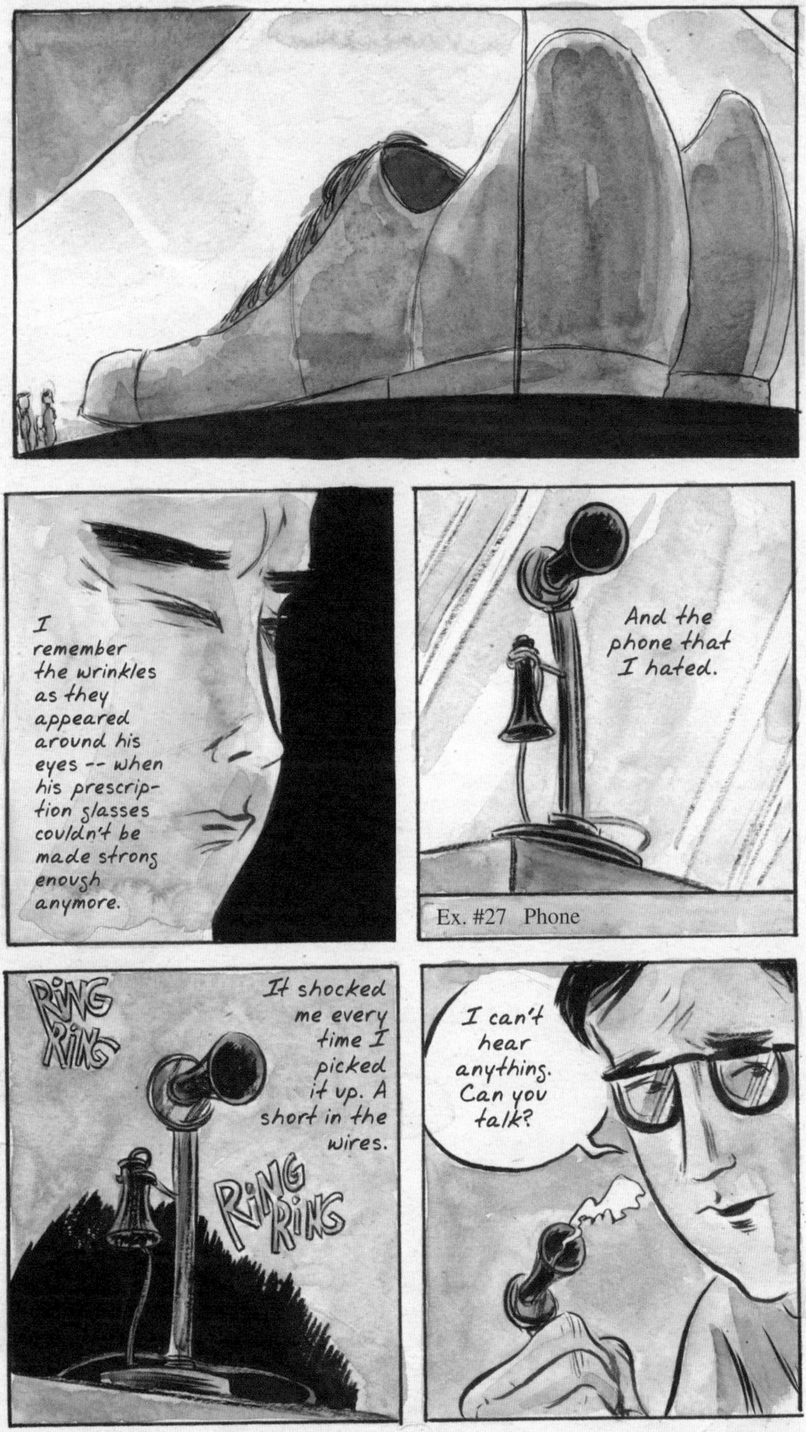
I remember the wrinkles as they appeared around his eyes -- when his prescription glasses couldn't be made strong enough anymore.
And the phone that I hated.
Ex. #27 Phone
RING RING
It shocked me every time I picked it up. A short in the wires.
RING RING
I can't hear anything. Can you talk?

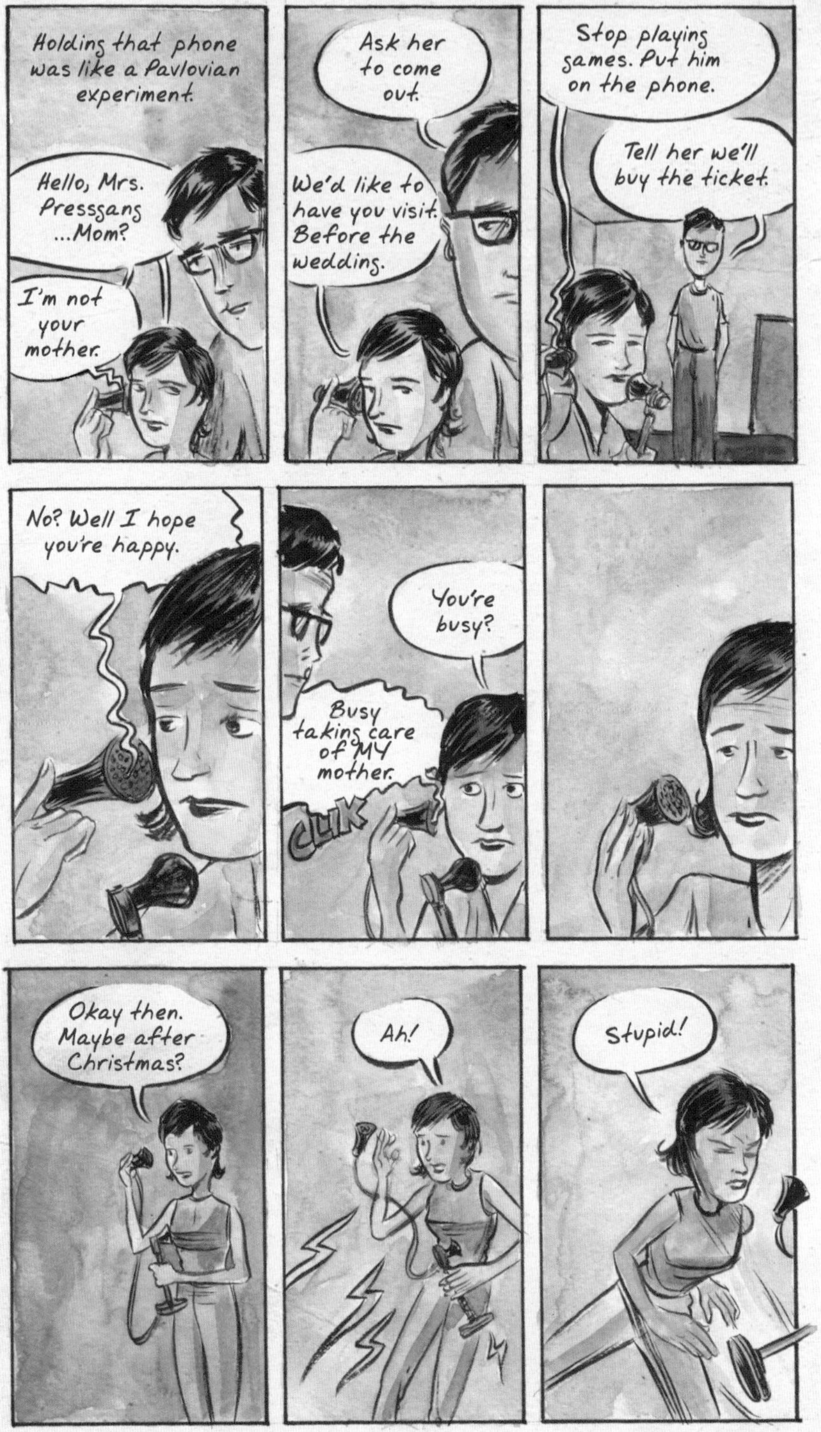
Holding that phone was like a Pavlovian experiment.
Hello, Mrs. Presssans ...Mom?
I'm not your mother.
Ask her to come out.
We'd like to have you visit. Before the wedding.
Stop playing games. Put him on the phone.
Tell her we'll buy the ticket.
No? Well I hope you're happy.
You're busy?
Busy taking care of MY mother.
CLIK
Okay then. Maybe after Christmas?
Ah!
Stupid!

GIANT takes you away from the everyday

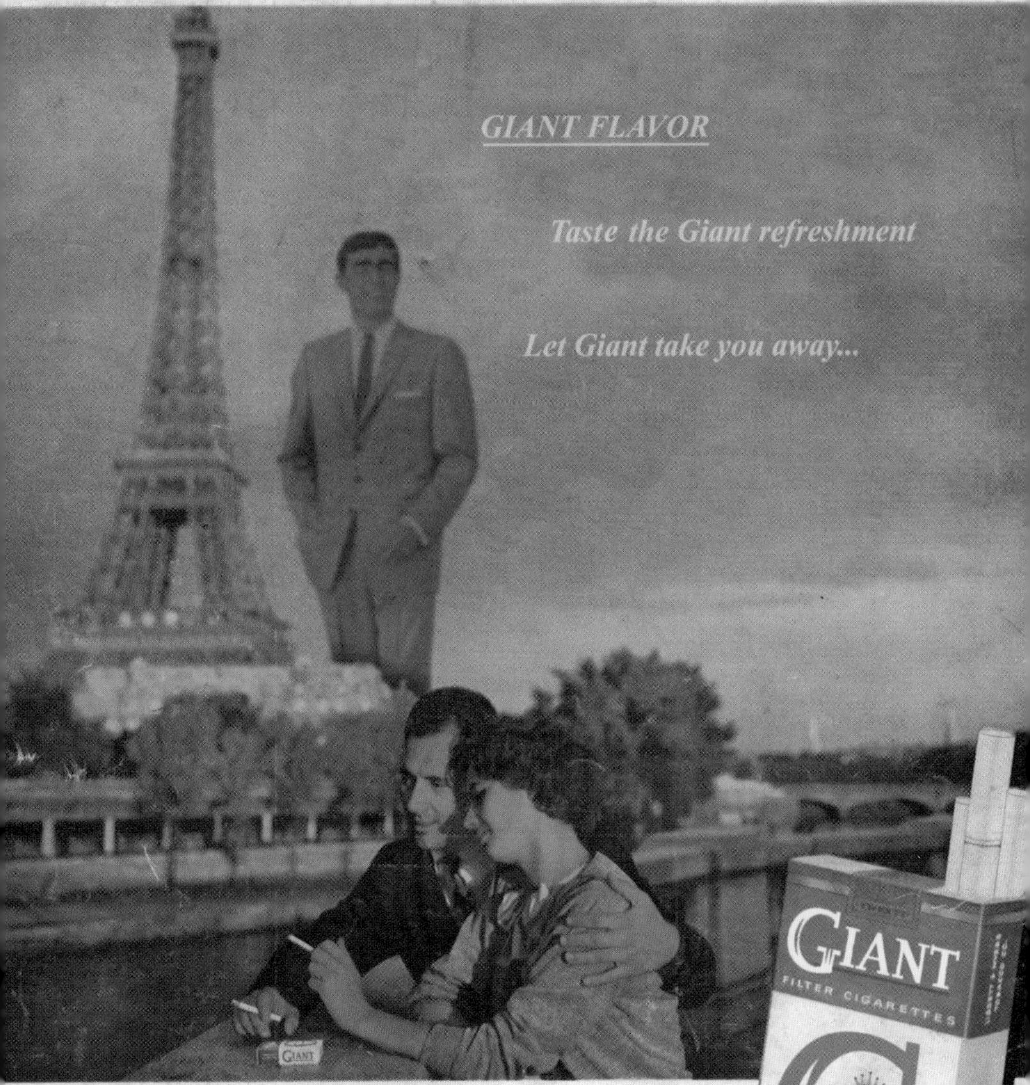
GIANT FLAVOR
Taste the Giant refreshment
Let Giant take you away...
GIANT
FILTER CIGARETTES
WITH
Menthol Mist

"But you don't smoke," she says.
He replies: "I know, I know. It's more of a trade, really. I endorse them, and they hire someone to manufacture my clothes. I get to keep the suit from the photo shoot." She didn't like it but went along with it anyway. He wasn't going to stop growing. That much was clear. So every hour, every day he spent doing something else, was time she—they—would never get back.

He interrupted her thought and continued talking in his low baritone. "I wonder if they could make me a giant cigarette. That'd be kind of funny. They'd probably call the fire department on me."

She gave him a wan smile. Well, at least she'd finally get to see Paris.

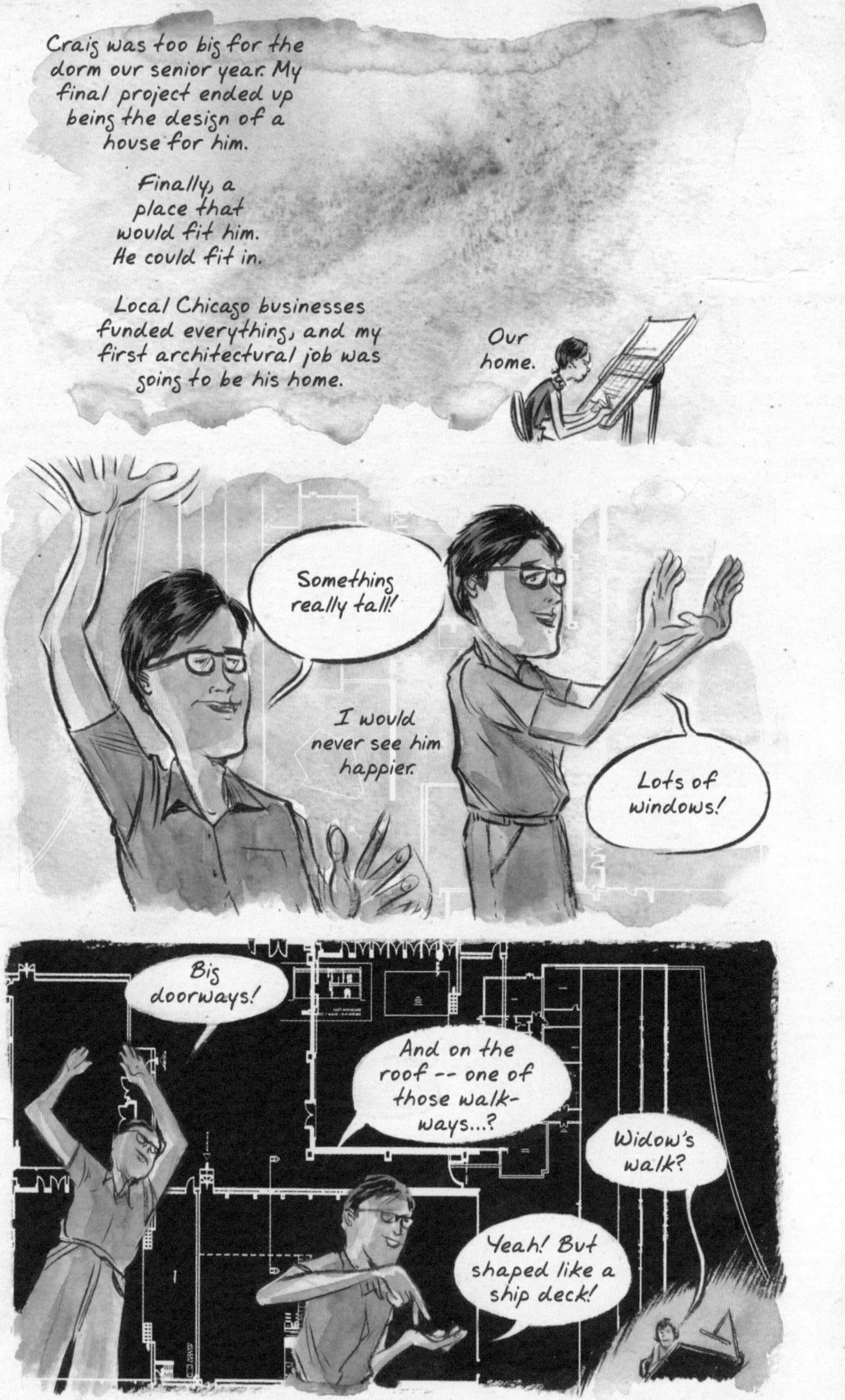

Craig was too big for the dorm our senior year. My final project ended up being the design of a house for him.
Finally, a place that would fit him. He could fit in.
Local Chicago businesses funded everything, and my first architectural job was going to be his home.
Our home.
Something really tall!
I would never see him happier.
Lots of windows!
Big doorways!
And on the roof -- one of those walk-ways...?
Widow's walk?
Yeah! But shaped like a ship deck!

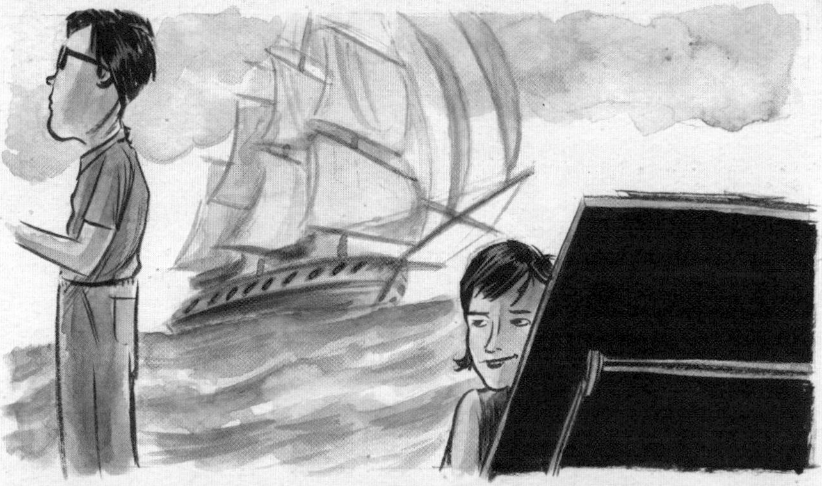

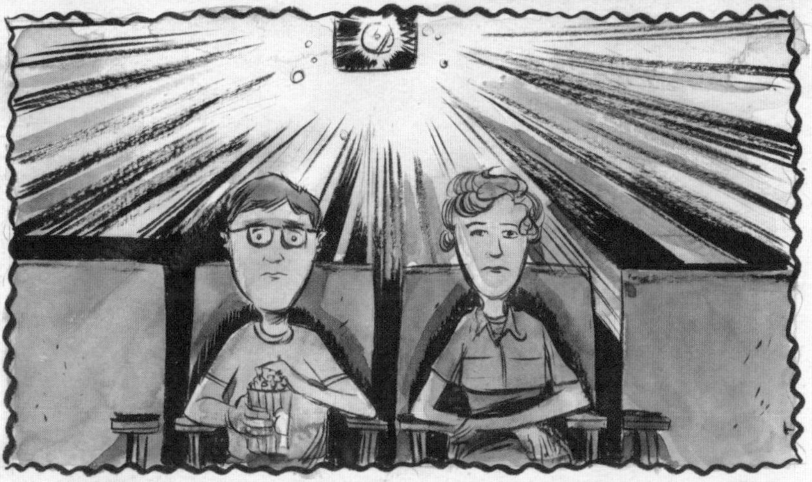

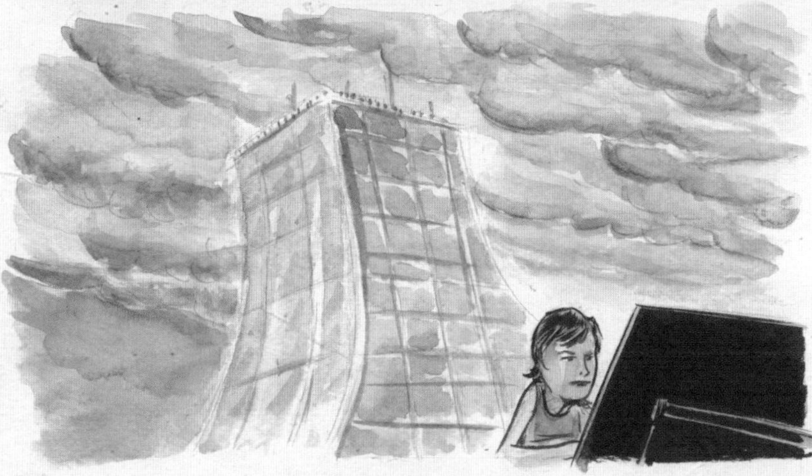

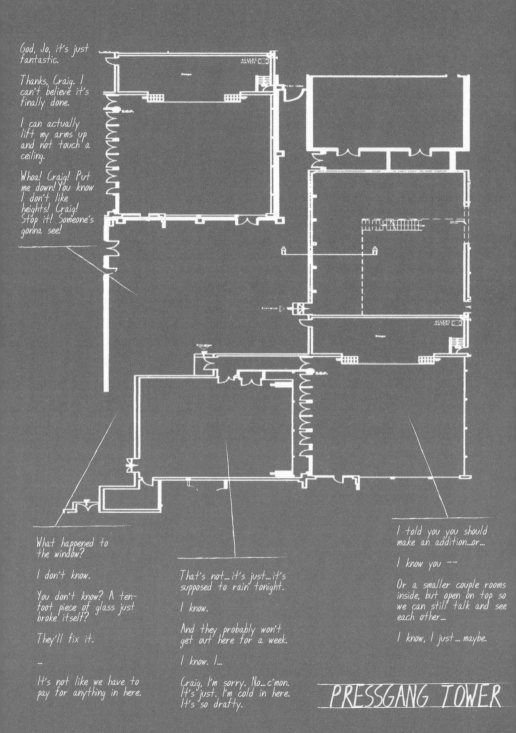

God, Jo, it's just
fantastic.

Thanks, Craig. I
can't believe it's
finally done.

I can actually
lift my arms up
and not touch a
ceiling.

Whoa! Craig! Put
me down! You know
I don't like
heights! Craig!
Stop it! Someone's
gonna see!

What happened to
the window?

I don't know.

You don't know? A ten-
foot piece of glass just
broke itself?

They'll fix it.

...

It's not like we have to
pay for anything in here.

That's not...it's just...it's
supposed to rain tonight.

I know.

And they probably won't
get out here for a week.

I know. I...

Craig, I'm sorry. No...c'mon.
It's just. I'm cold in here.
It's so drafty.

I told you you should
make an addition...or...

I know you --

Or a smaller couple rooms
inside, but open on top so
we can still talk and see
each other...

I know, I just... maybe.

PRESSGANG TOWER

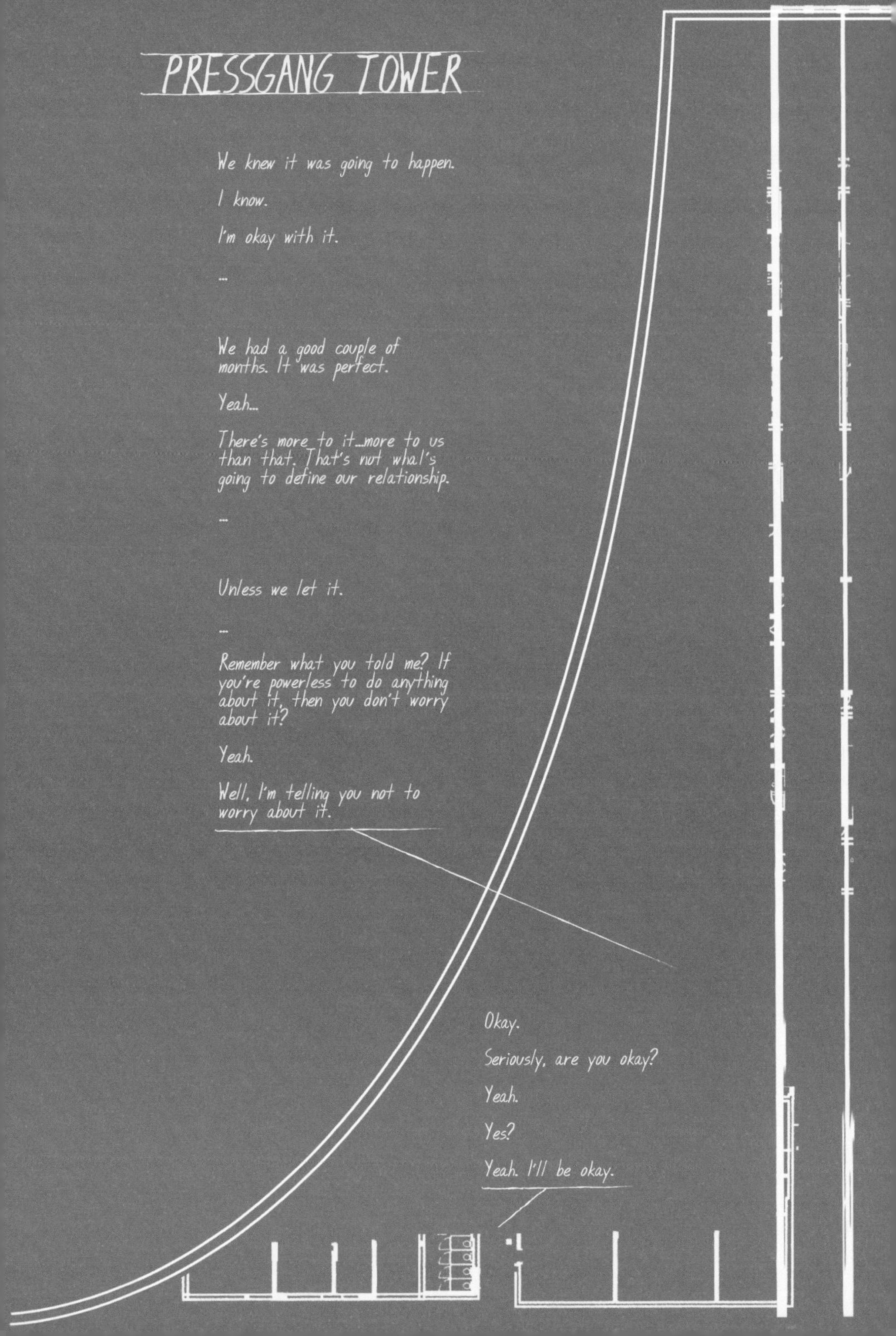
PRESSGANG TOWER
We knew it was going to happen.
I know.
I'm okay with it.
...
We had a good couple of months. It was perfect.
Yeah...
There's more to it...more to us than that. That's not what's going to define our relationship.
...
Unless we let it.
...
Remember what you told me? If you're powerless to do anything about it, then you don't worry about it?
Yeah.
Well, I'm telling you not to worry about it.
Okay.
Seriously, are you okay?
Yeah.
Yes?
Yeah. I'll be okay.

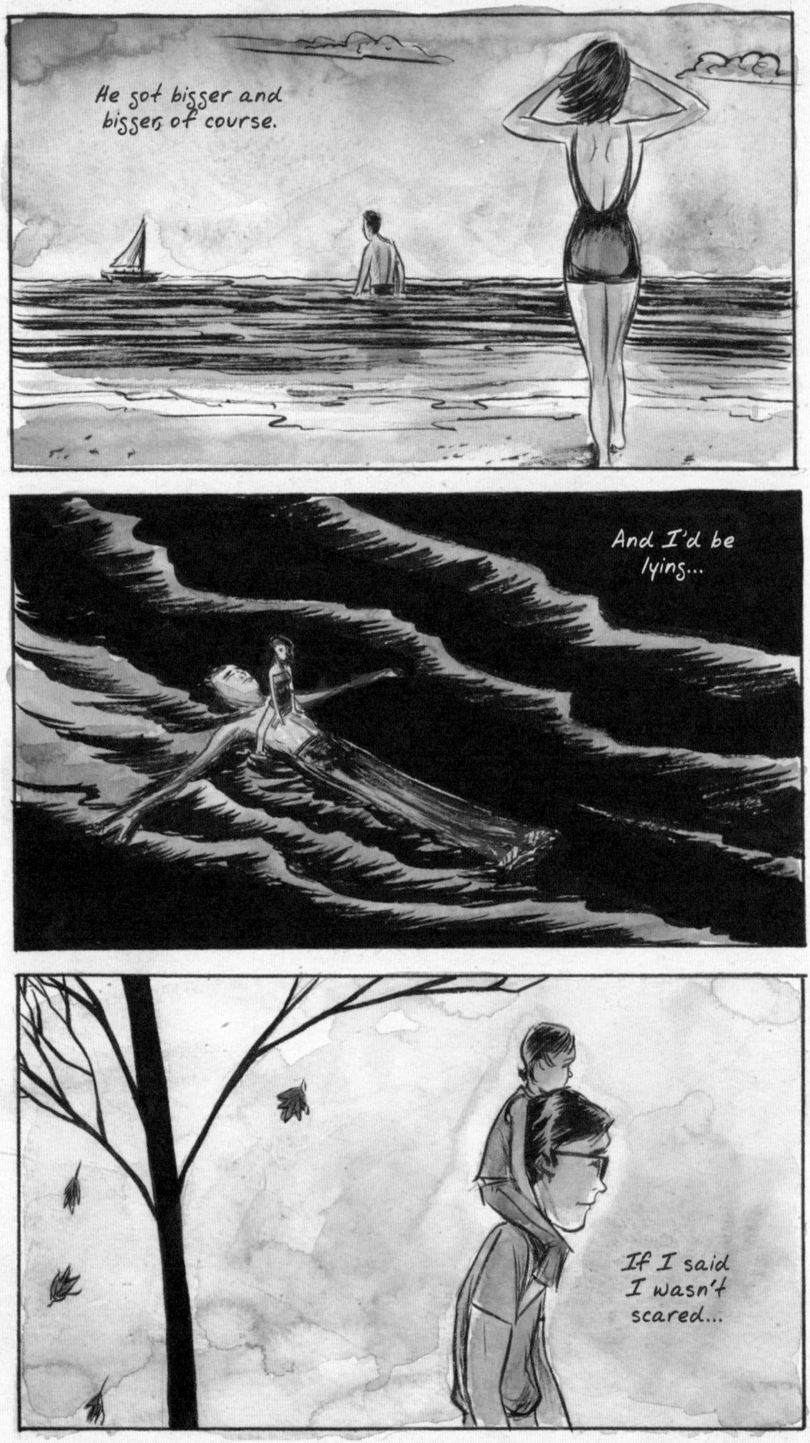
He got bigger and bigger of course.
And I'd be lying...
If I said I wasn't scared...

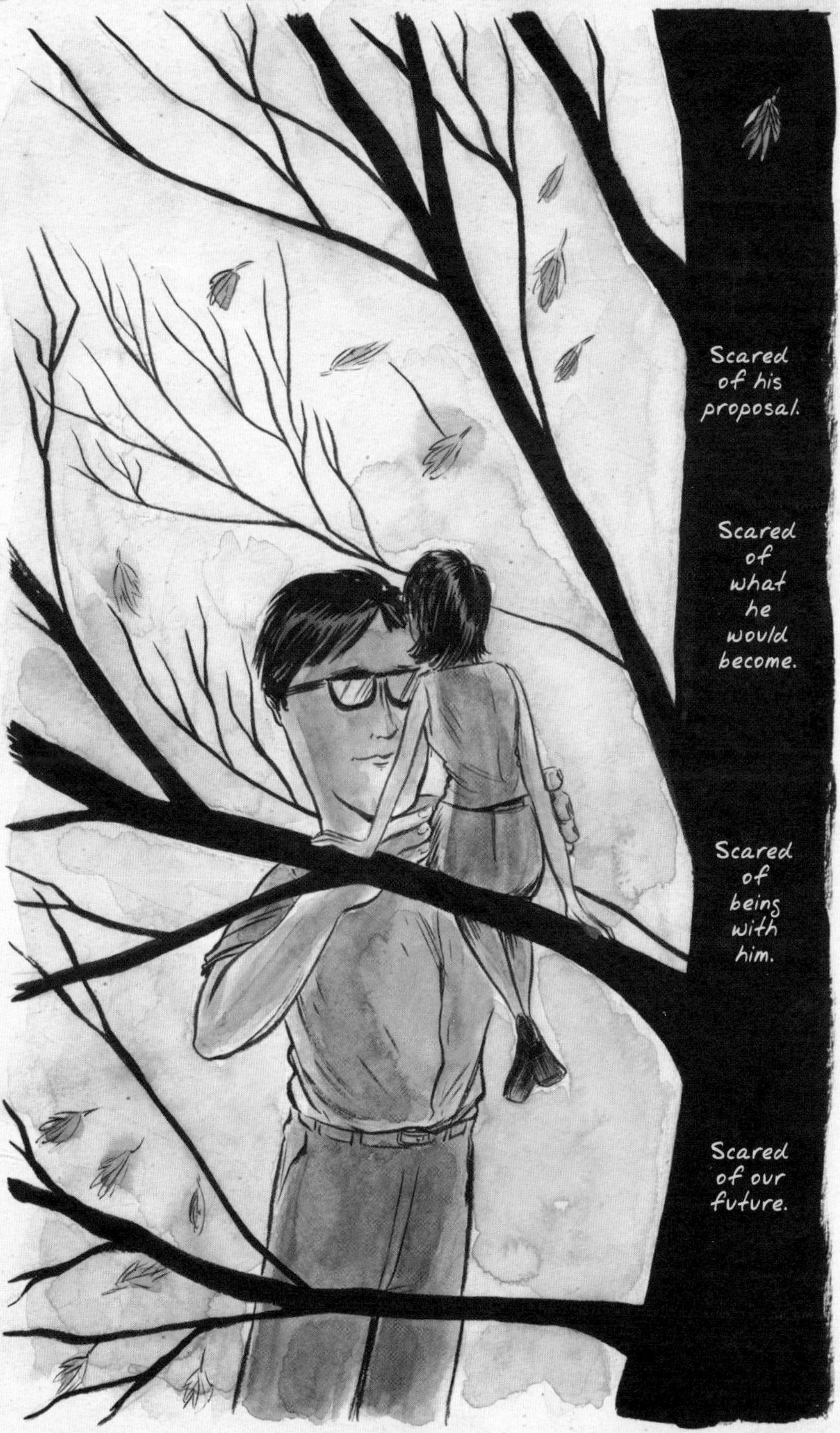
Scared
of his
proposal.
Scared
of
what
he
would
become.
Scared
of
being
with
him.
Scared
of our
future.

But
we
did
it.

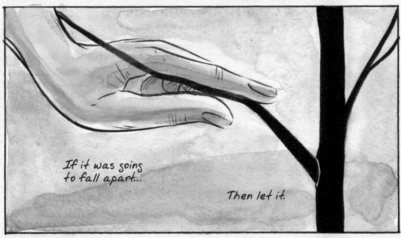

If it was going
to fall apart...

Then let it.

Who else did
he have?

started out as small as any child. But as he grew, so did his art. Some of his larger pieces stand at three stories tall and use over 1,000 gallons of paint.

The sheer size of Craig's larger still-lifes and outdoor scenes makes them not only cost-prohibitive to the average art enthusiast, but also exhibition-prohibitive. Most of Craig's larger works are being stored in government facilities and by the Smithsonian Institute in Washington, D.C.

This is not to say that Craig's art does not sell. The demand for his signature hand-print canvases is still high. The size of these pieces varies depending on the year they were created, with his earlier hand prints, measuring a comparatively modest four feet wide, fetching the highest prices among collectors. When asked about this phenomenon, the

(continued on following page)

A family gathers at one of Craig's outdoor exhibits.

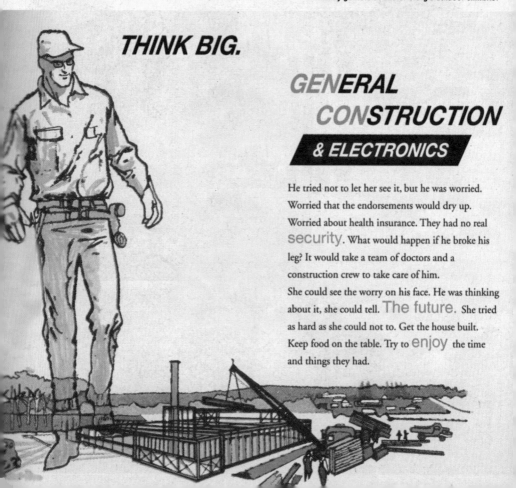

THINK BIG.

GENERAL
CONSTRUCTION
& ELECTRONICS

He tried not to let her see it, but he was worried. Worried that the endorsements would dry up. Worried about health insurance. They had no real security. What would happen if he broke his leg? It would take a team of doctors and a construction crew to take care of him.

She could see the worry on his face. He was thinking about it, she could tell. The future. She tried as hard as she could not to. Get the house built. Keep food on the table. Try to enjoy the time and things they had.

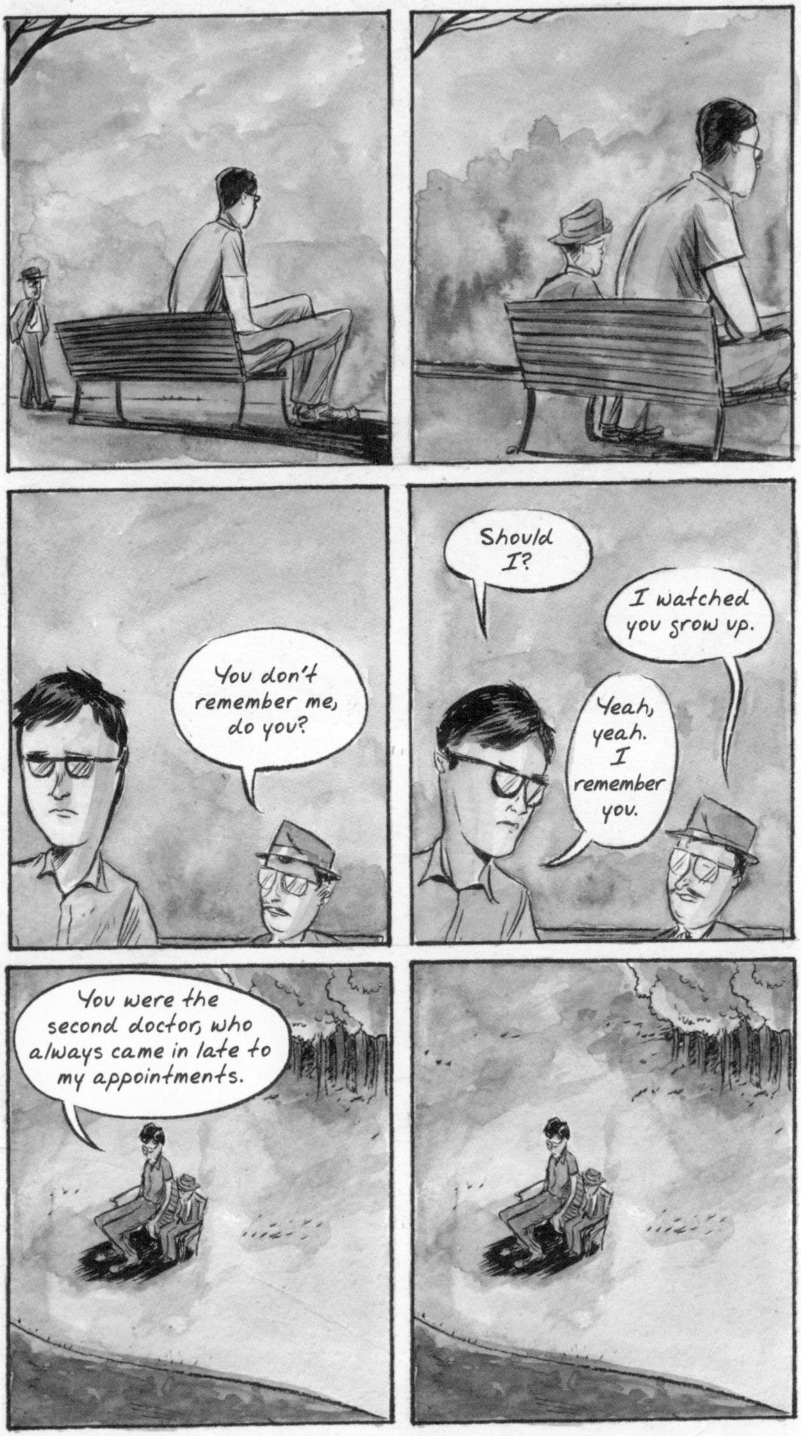
You don't remember me, do you?
Should I?
I watched you grow up.
Yeah, yeah. I remember you.
You were the second doctor, who always came in late to my appointments.

We need to do a few tests.

What's new.

We have new technology. We might be able to find a way to help you.

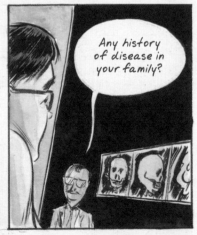

Any history of disease in your family?

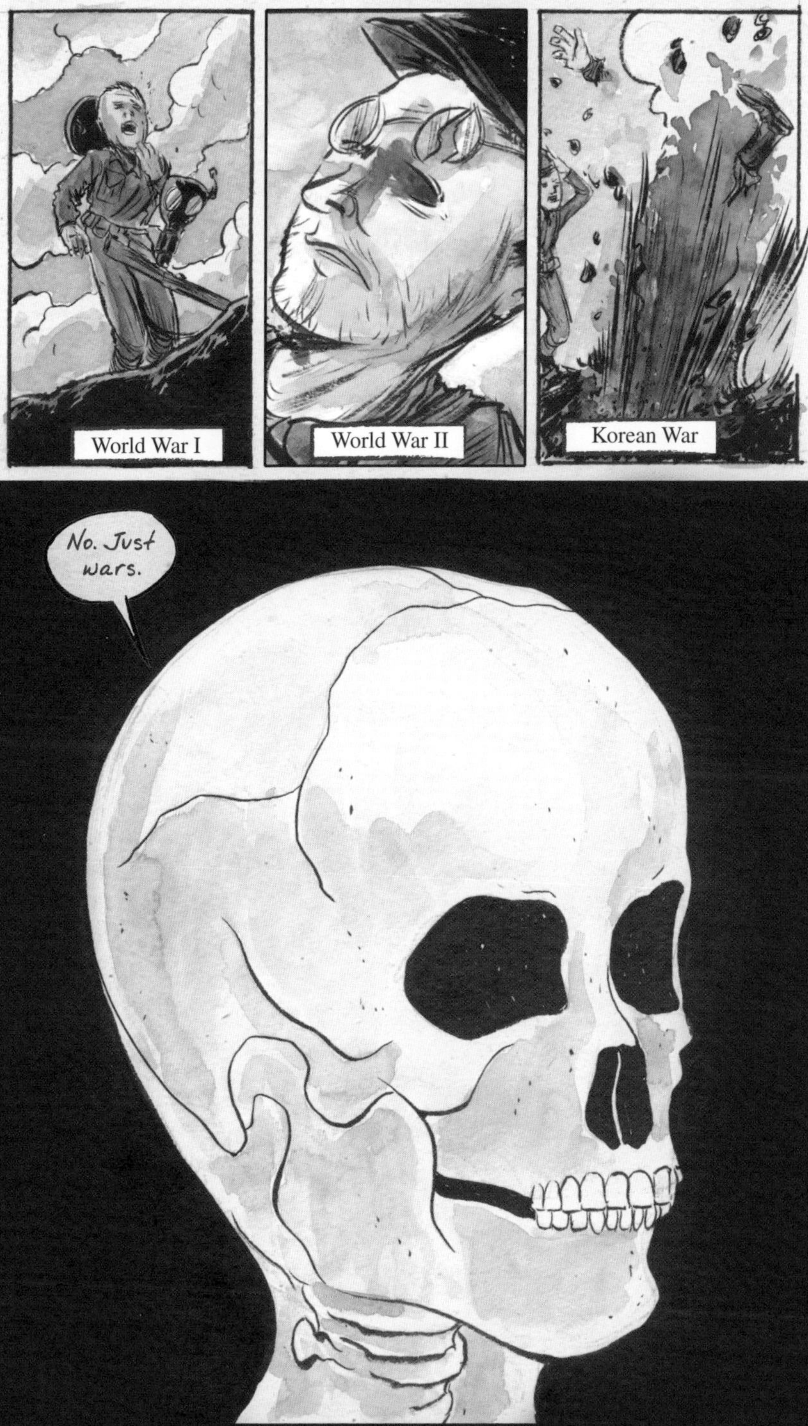
World War I
World War II
Korean War
No. Just wars.

Your pitu-
itary gland
is being
stimulated
by a tumor.

As it grows,
so do you.

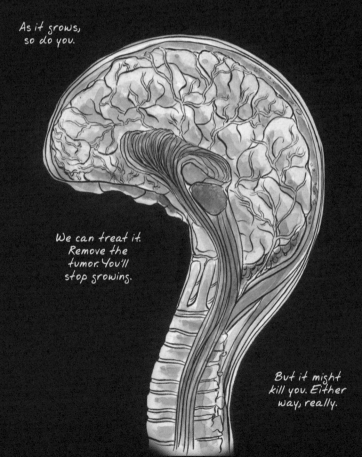

We can treat it.
Remove the
tumor. You'll
stop growing.

But it might
kill you. Either
way, really.

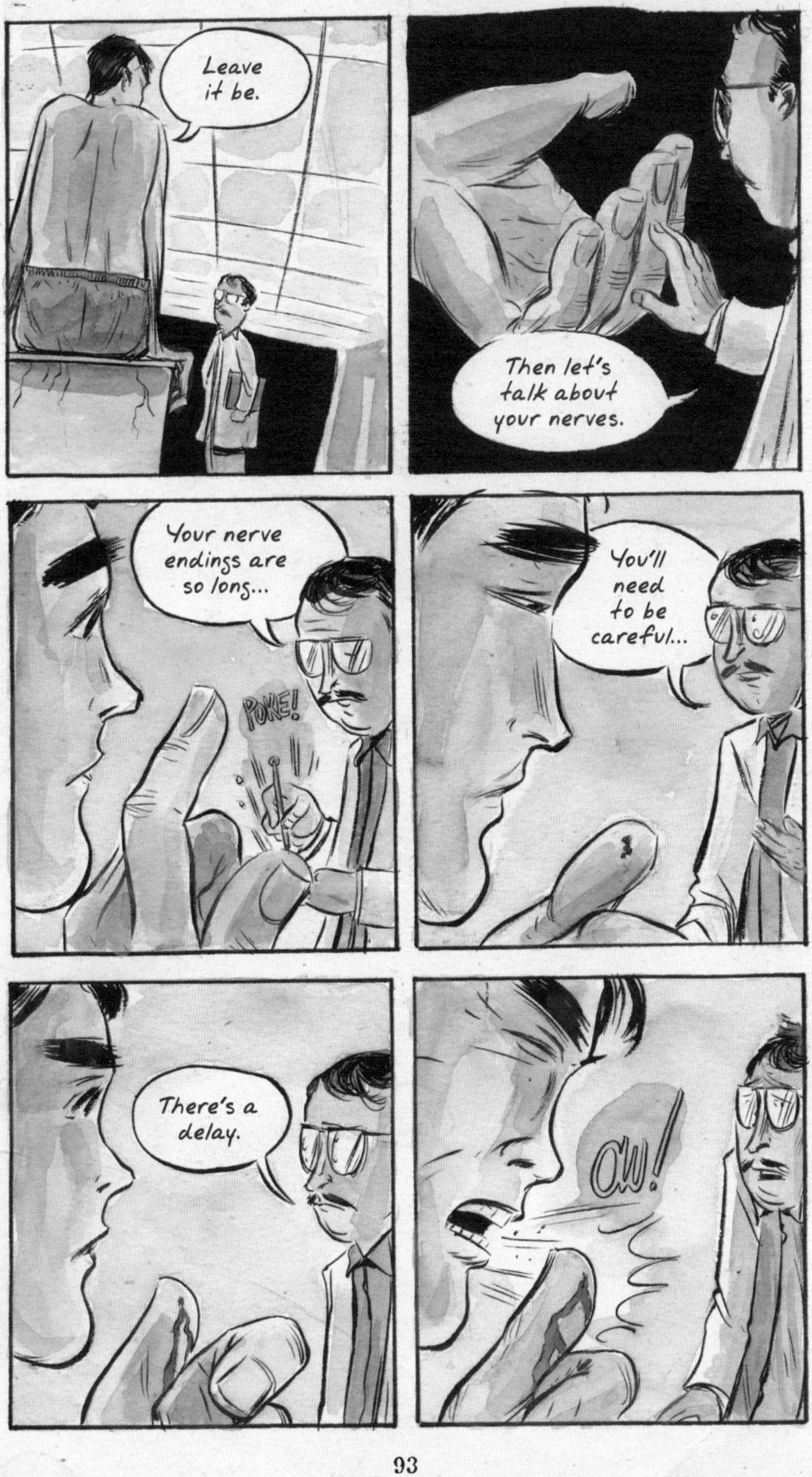
Leave it be.
Then let's talk about your nerves.
Your nerve endings are so long...
POKE!
You'll need to be careful...
There's a delay.
OW!

Robert Wadlow was the tallest Cub Scout—on a boating trip, they wouldn't let him in the boat.

"If you fell in, we wouldn't be able to get you back in the boat," the Cub Scout leader warned.

The other boys laughed and
enjoyed the boat ride.

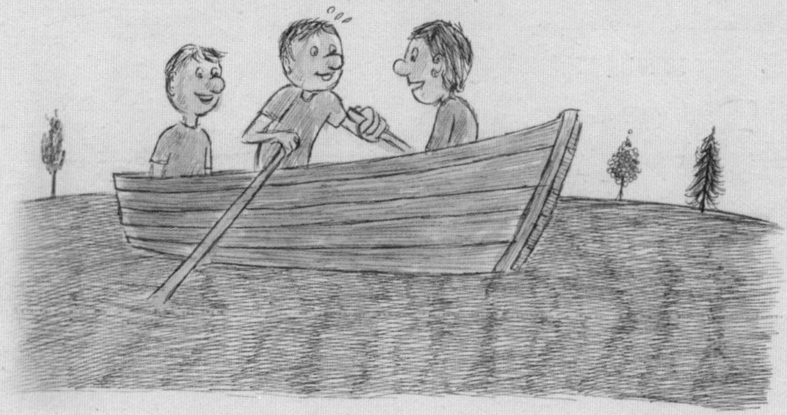

They didn't notice that
Robert had disappeared.

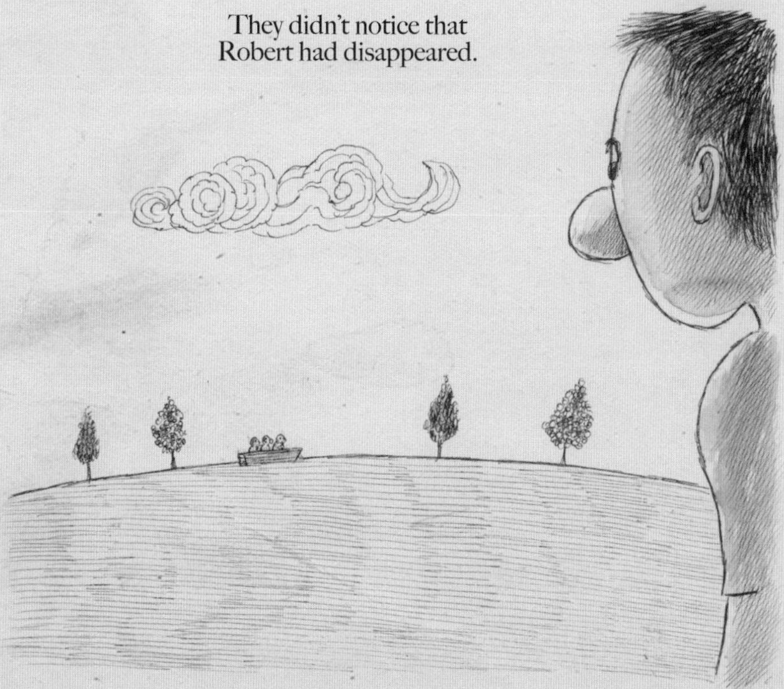

Slowly, Robert crept up behind the
boat, careful not to make a noise.

And then he stood up to his full height!

They had underestimated
Robert's size. He could
easily stand in the lake.

After that, he always got a
ride on the boat.

Take care of yourself.

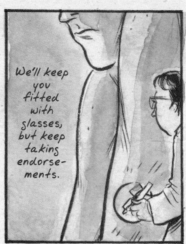

We'll keep you fitted with glasses, but keep taking endorsements.

This suit should grow with you to approximately three stories tall. After that, we'll hopefully have engineered a new one.

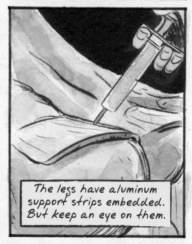

The legs have aluminum support strips embedded. But keep an eye on them.

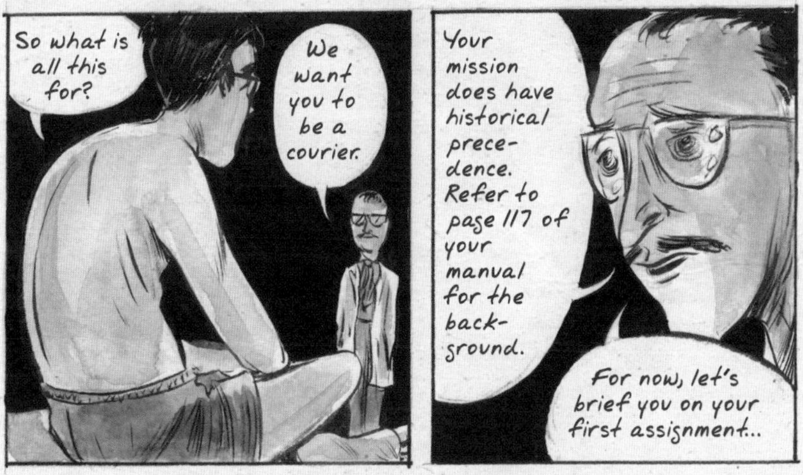
So what is all this for?
We want you to be a courier.
Your mission does have historical prece-dence. Refer to page 117 of your manual for the back-ground.
For now, let's brief you on your first assignment...

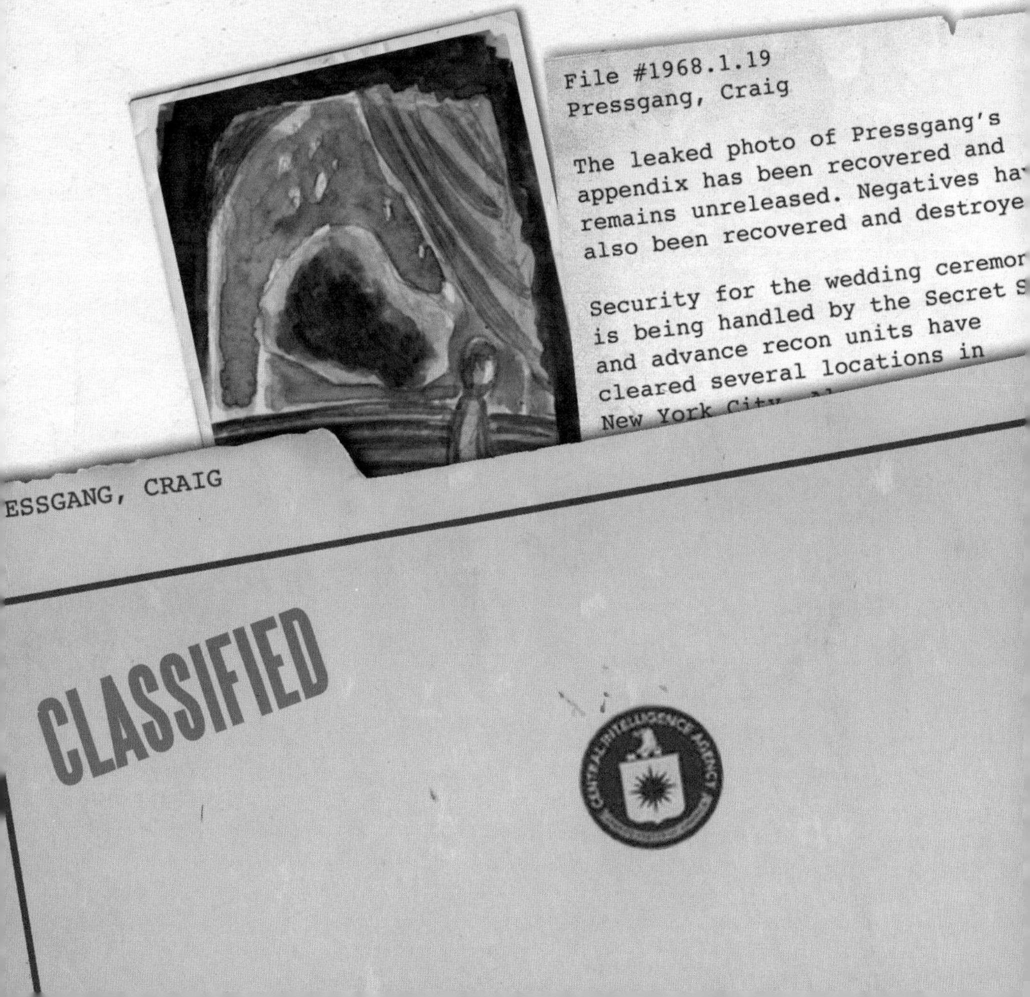
File #1968.1.19
Pressgang, Craig
The leaked photo of Pressgang's
appendix has been recovered and
remains unreleased. Negatives ha
also been recovered and destroye
Security for the wedding ceremor
is being handled by the Secret S
and advance recon units have
cleared several locations in
ESSGANG, CRAIG
CLASSIFIED

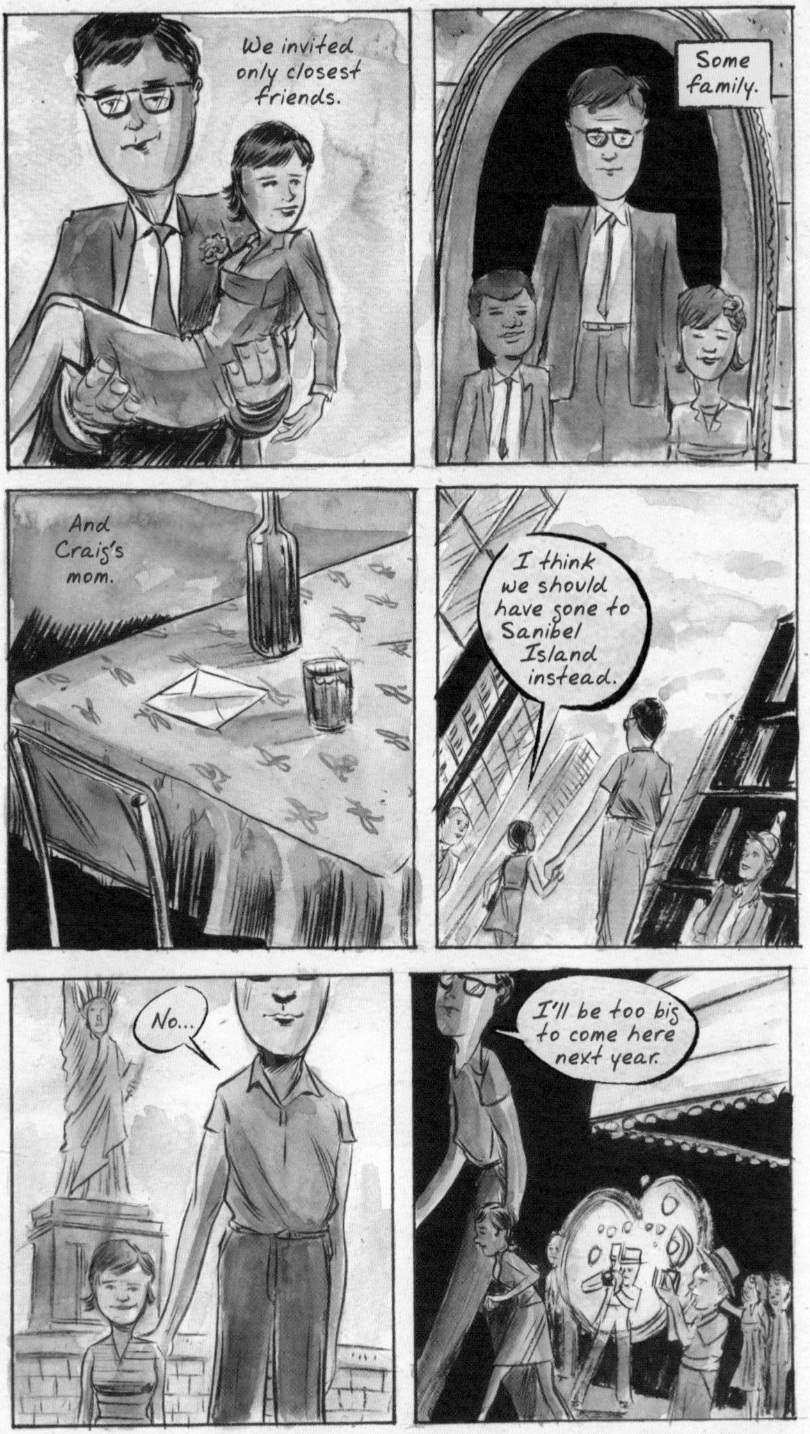
We invited only closest friends.
Some family.
And Craig's mom.
I think we should have gone to Sanibel Island instead.
No...
I'll be too big to come here next year.

Soon after graduating from college, Craig married the love of his life and college sweetheart, Jo. They went on to become the darlings of America! The dream couple in a dream home, living the American dream!

Craig was intent on showing the world that being large wasn't a handicap, but an advantage. And that if you work hard enough and long enough, eventually anything is possible!

Little did anyone know how successful Craig would become. And famous! His famous Tour of the World was about to begin! Soon the name Craig Pressgang would be known in every household!

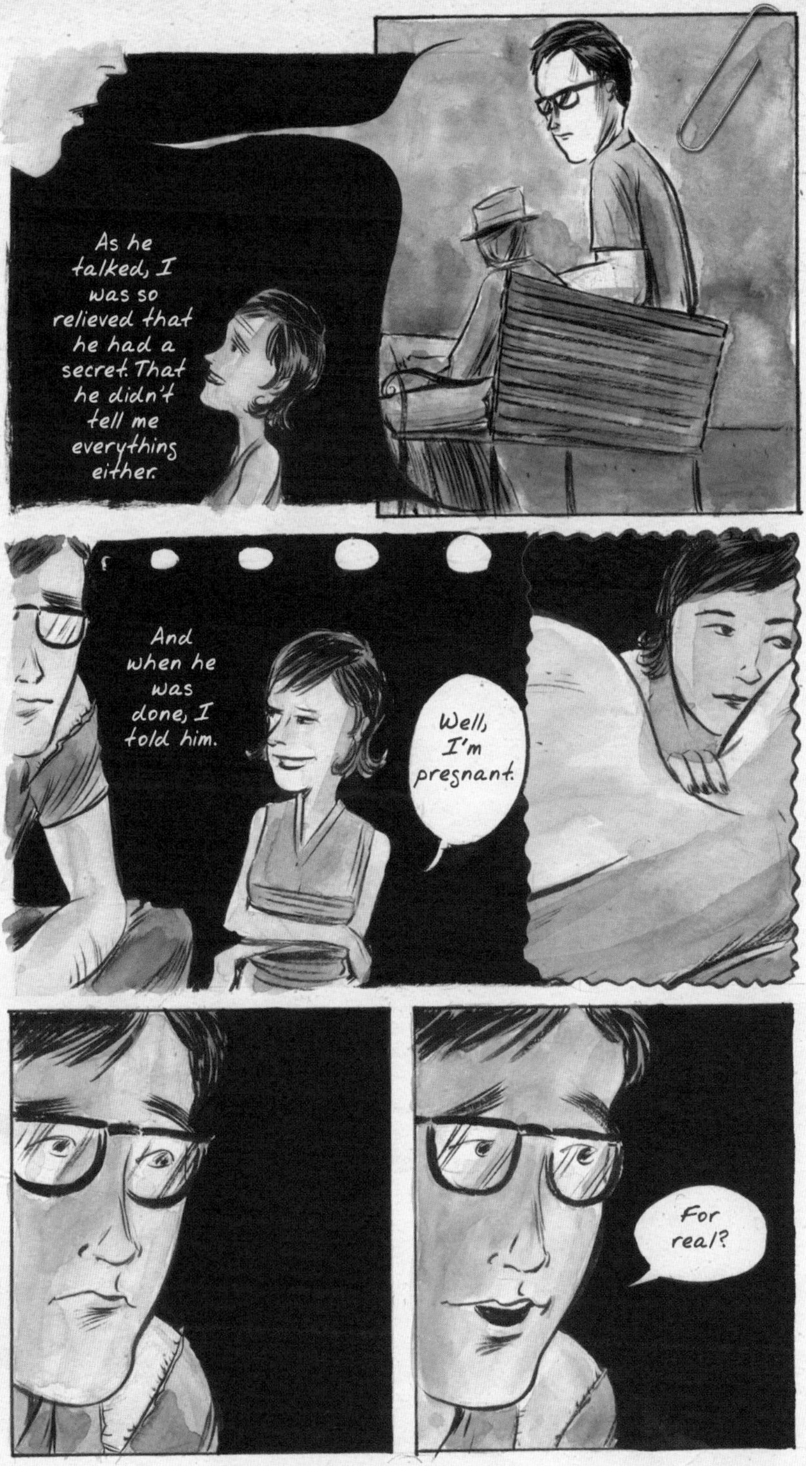
As he talked, I was so relieved that he had a secret. That he didn't tell me everything either.
And when he was done, I told him.
Well, I'm pregnant.
For real?

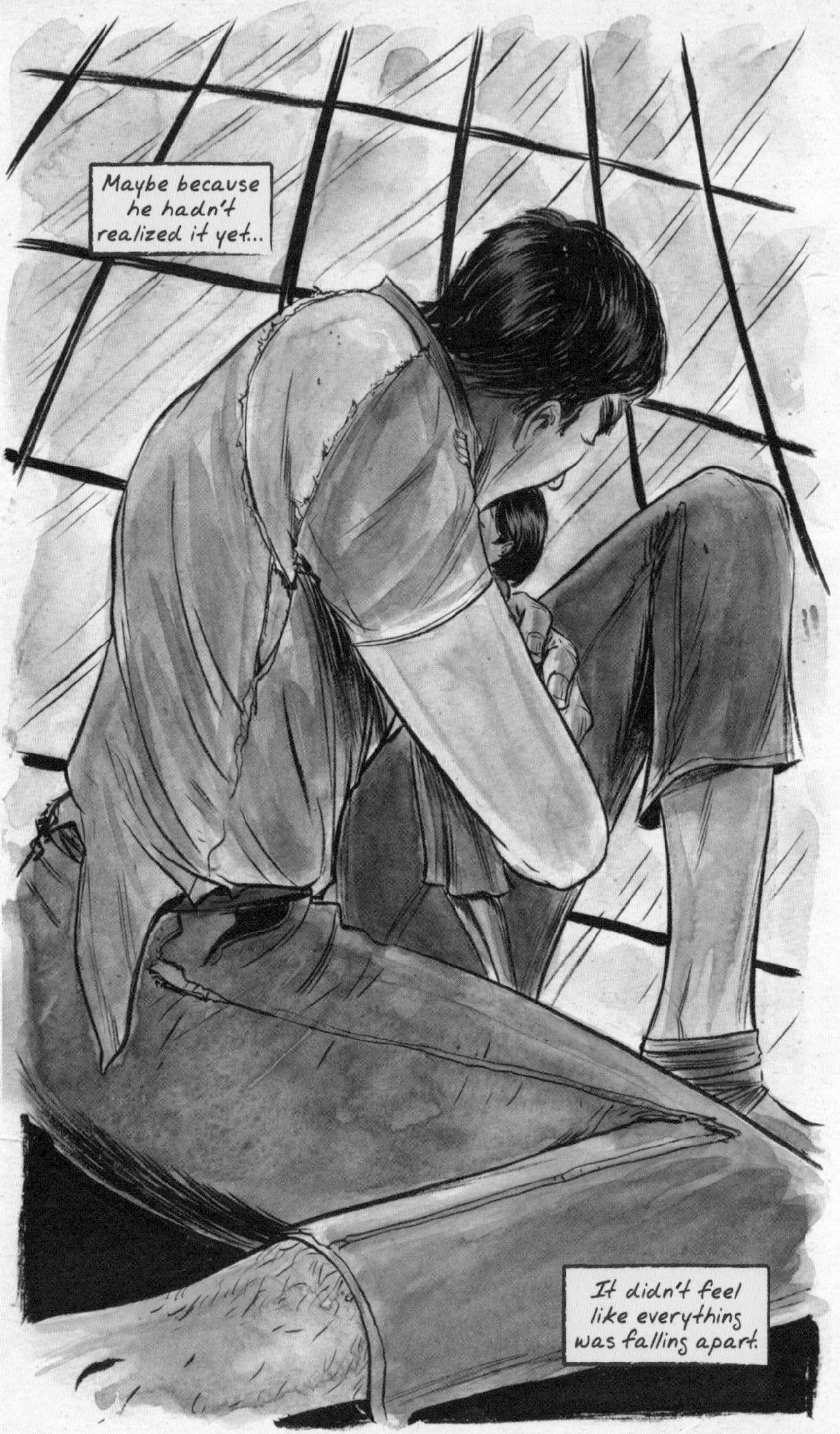
Maybe because he hadn't realized it yet...
It didn't feel like everything was falling apart.

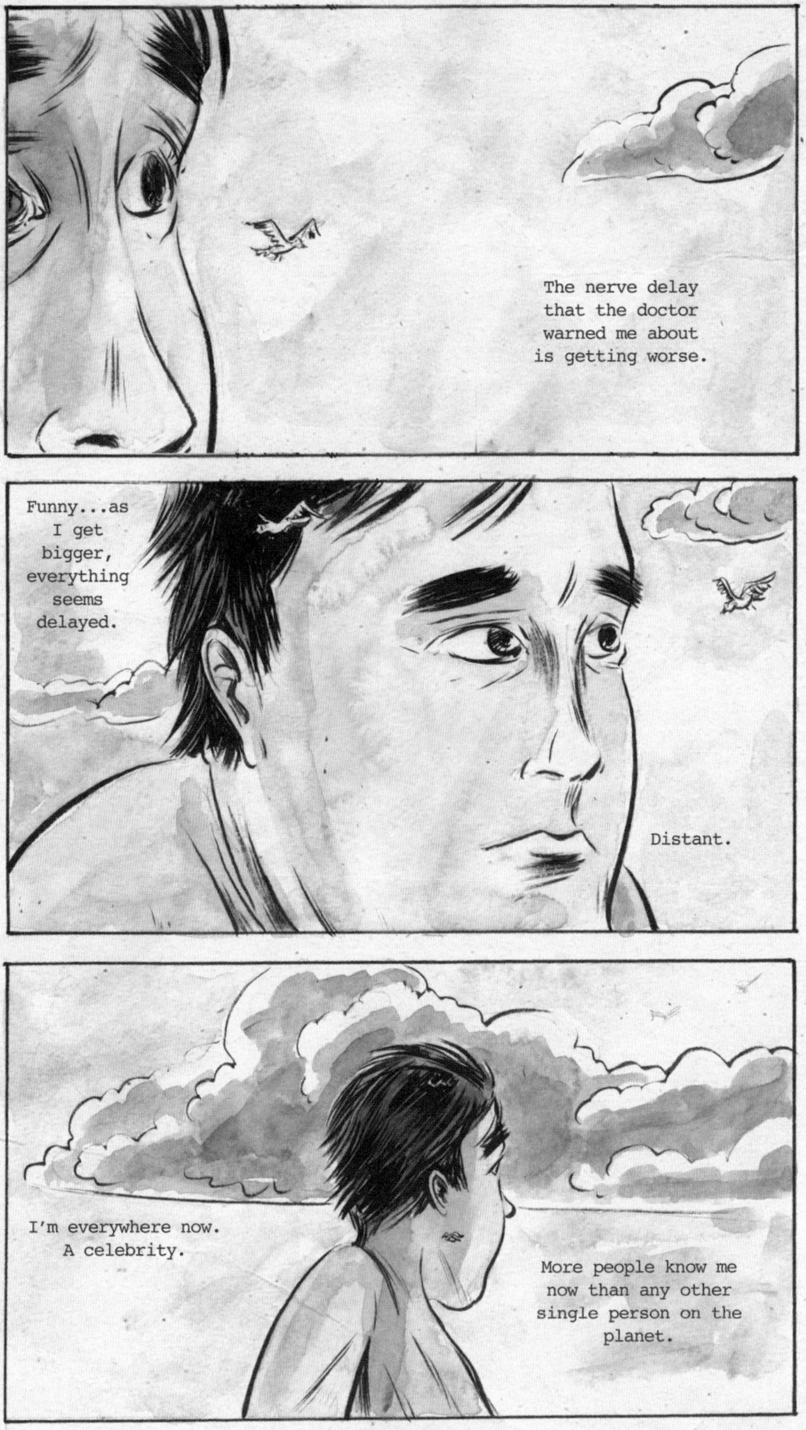
The nerve delay that the doctor warned me about is getting worse.
Funny...as I get bigger, everything seems delayed.
Distant.
I'm everywhere now. A celebrity.
More people know me now than any other single person on the planet.

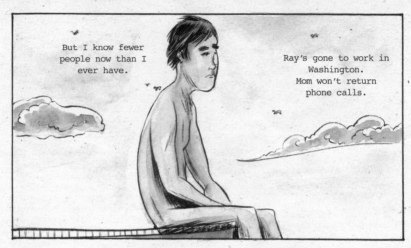

But I know fewer people now than I ever have.

Ray's gone to work in Washington. Mom won't return phone calls.

I end up holding onto Jo. But even that thread is starting to disappear.

I don't have an eye for detail now. Everything's fuzzy.

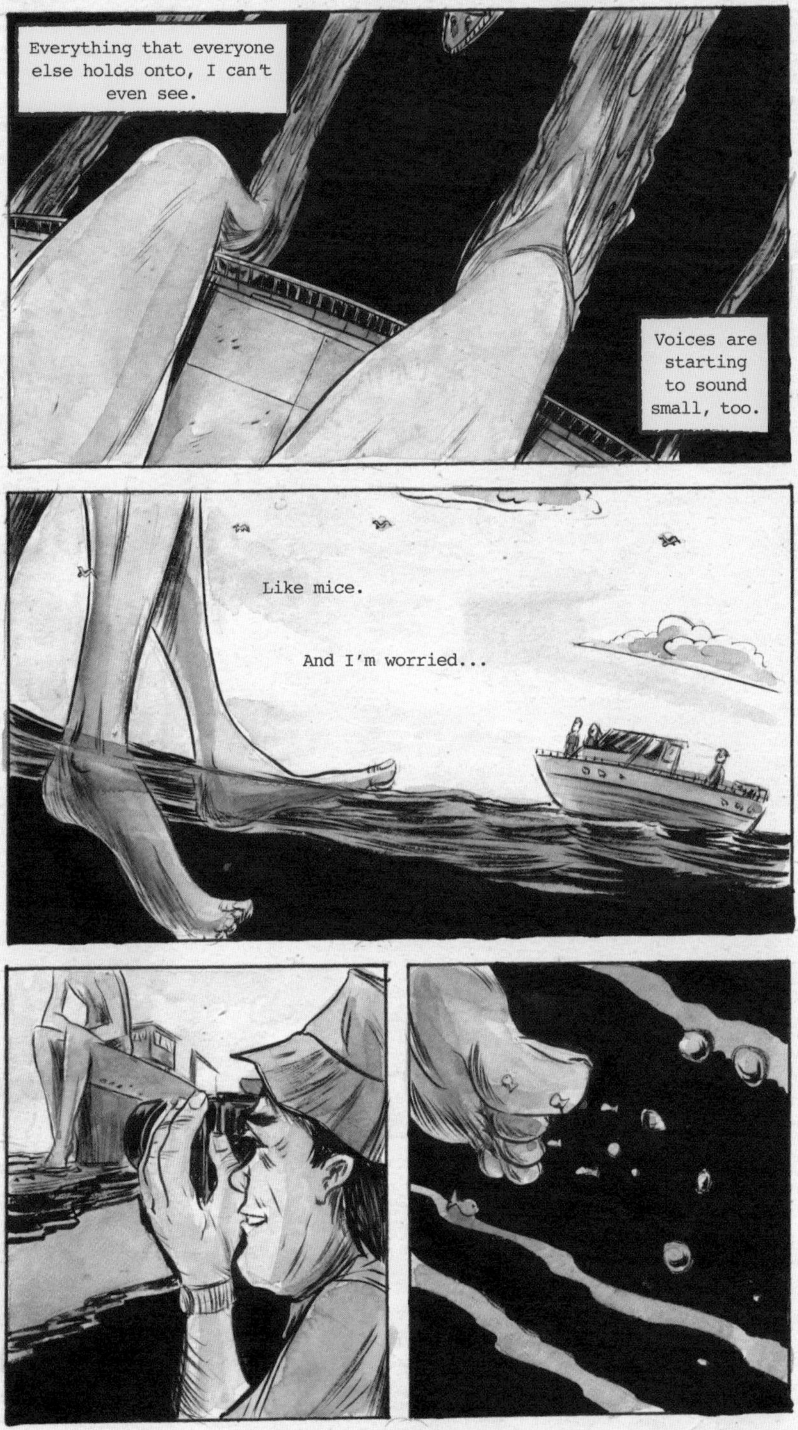
Everything that everyone else holds onto, I can't even see.
Voices are starting to sound small, too.
Like mice.
And I'm worried...

I worry that
it's spreading.

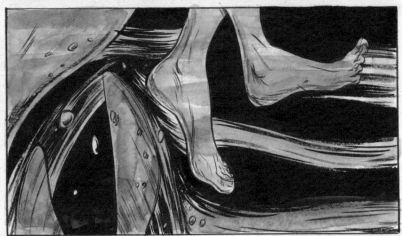

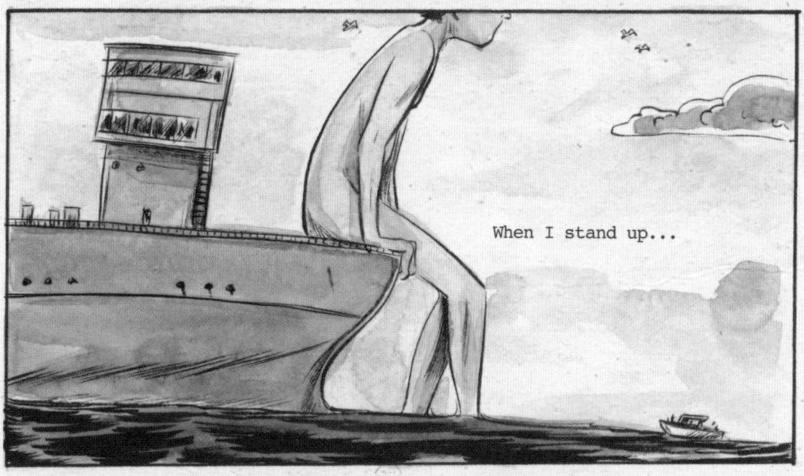
When I stand up...

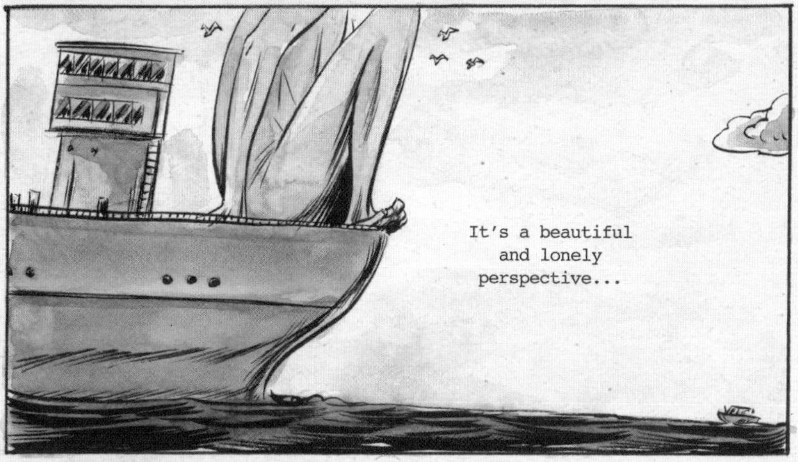
It's a beautiful
and lonely
perspective...

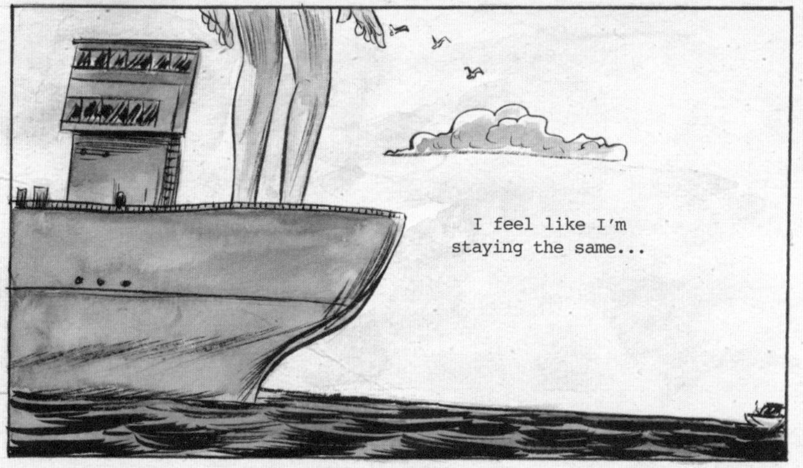
I feel like I'm
staying the same...

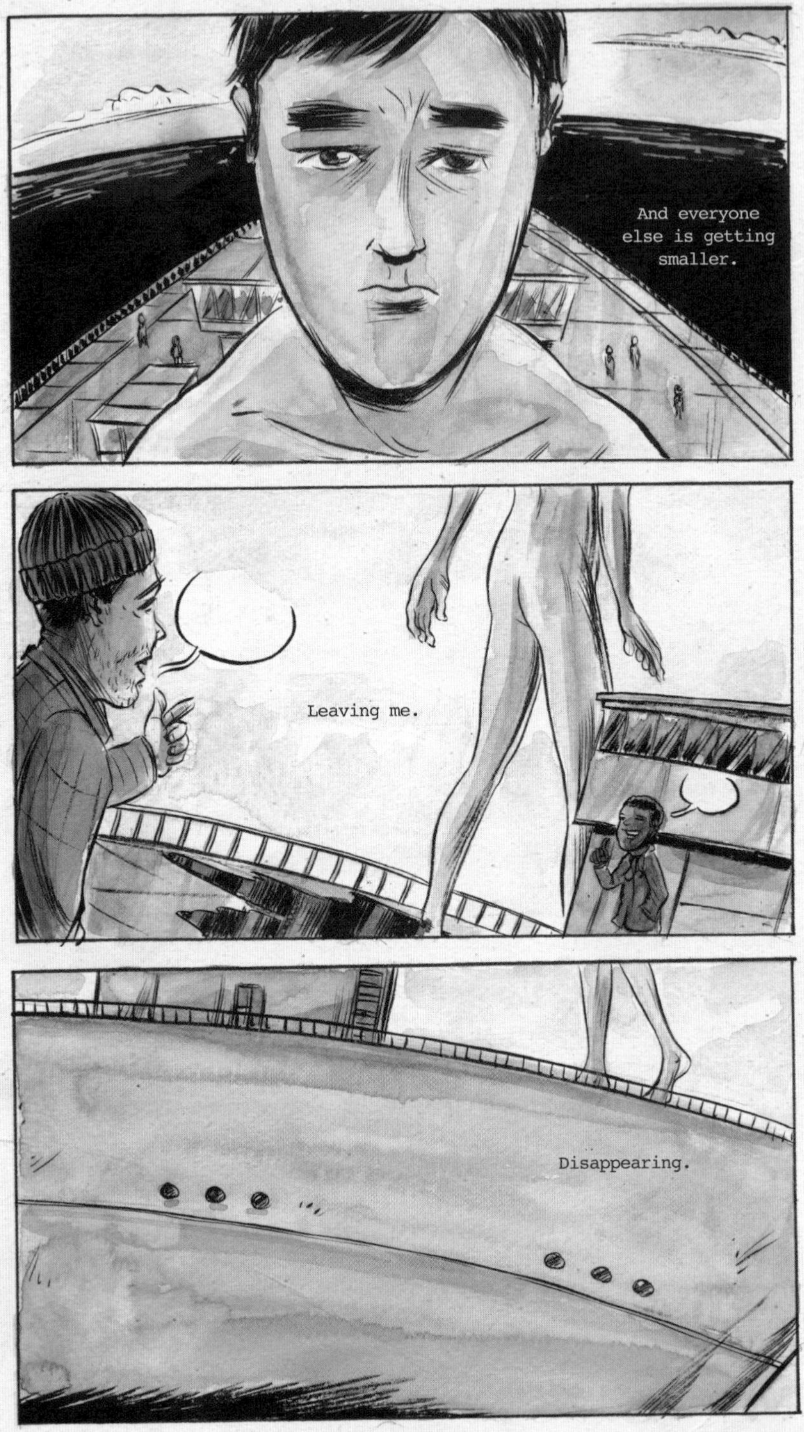
And everyone else is getting smaller.
Leaving me.
Disappearing.

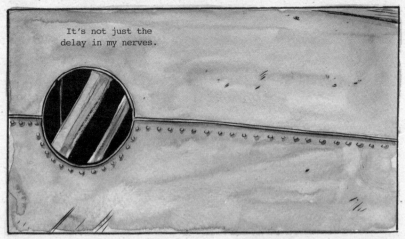

It's not just the
delay in my nerves.

I look at
her...

I look at
Jo...

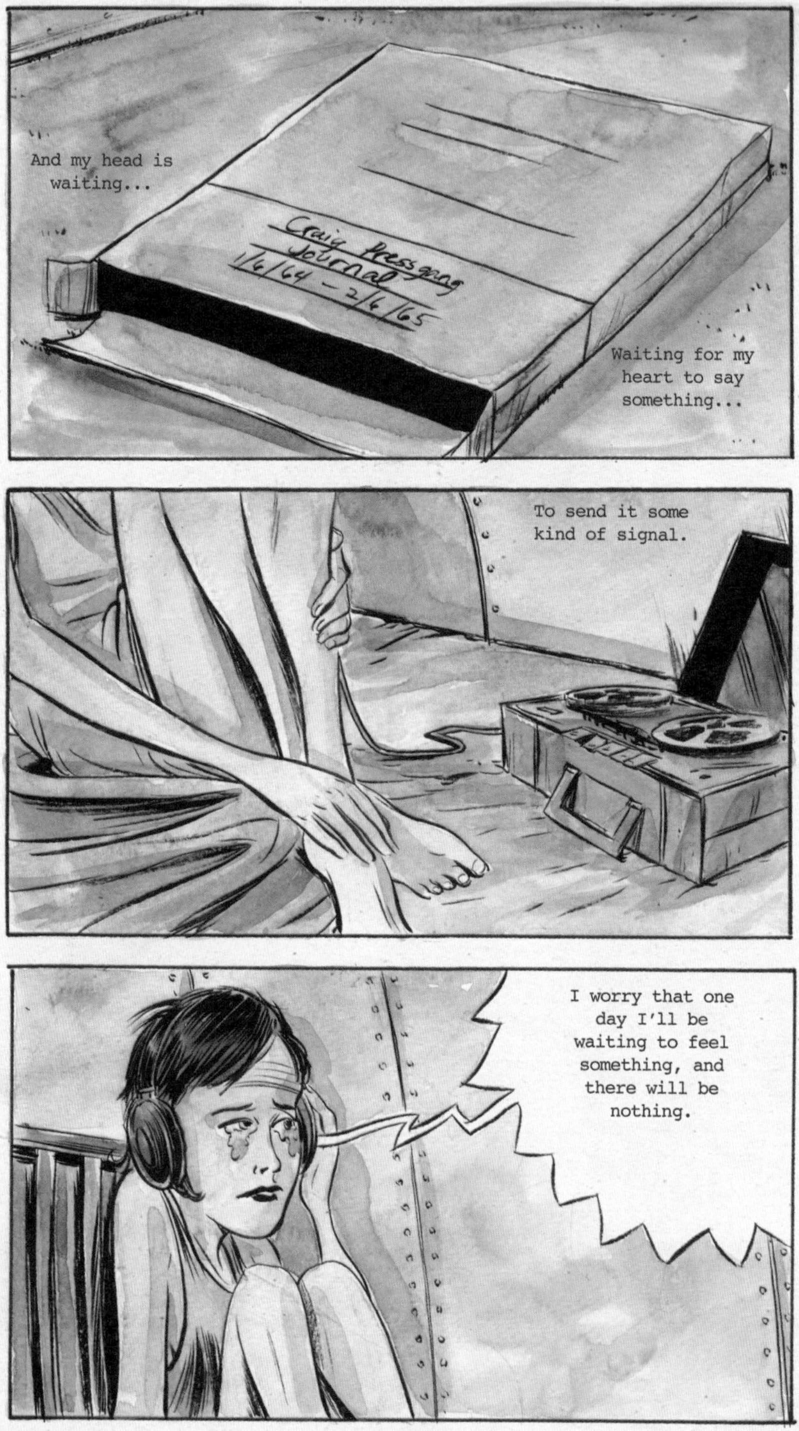
And my head is waiting...
Craig Pressgang Journal 1/6/64 – 2/6/65
Waiting for my heart to say something...
To send it some kind of signal.
I worry that one day I'll be waiting to feel something, and there will be nothing.

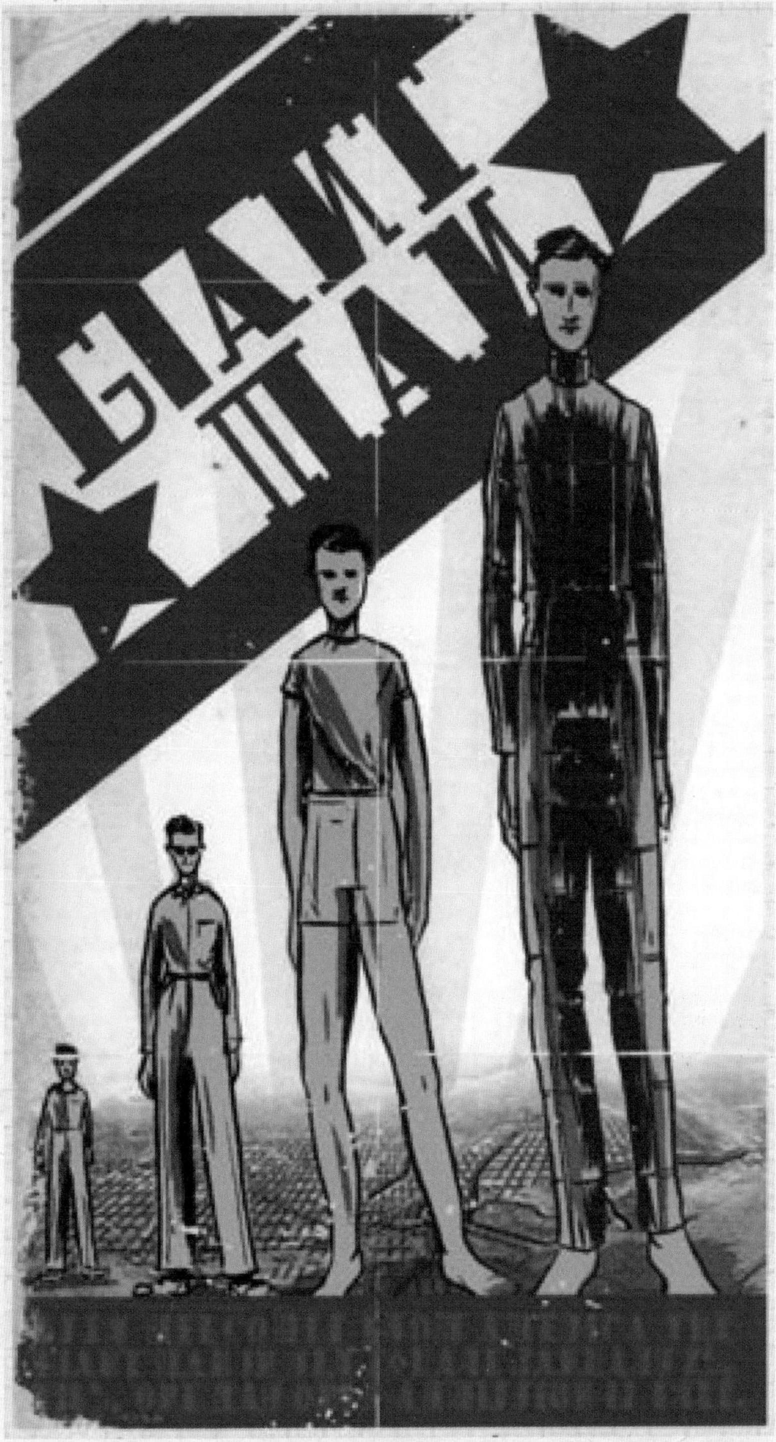

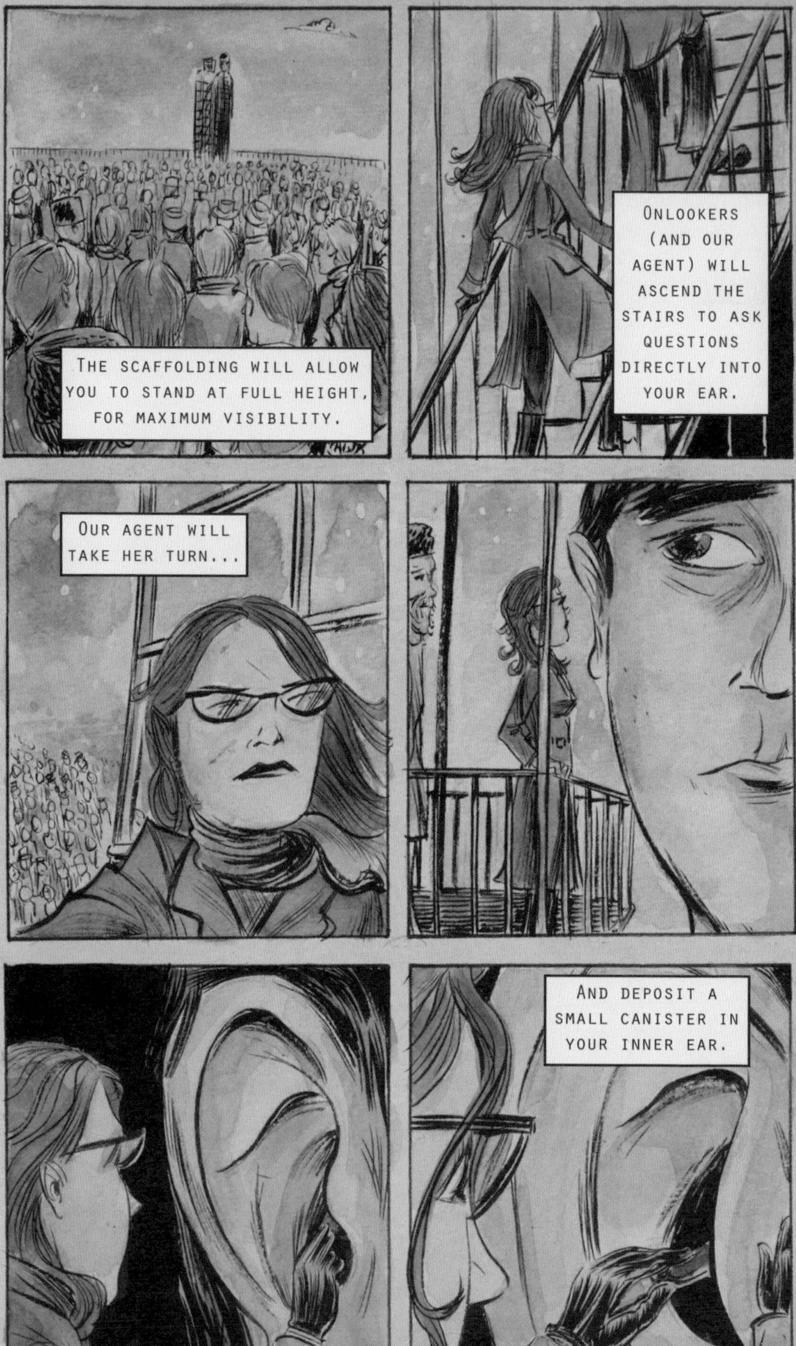
The scaffolding will allow you to stand at full height, for maximum visibility.
Onlookers (and our agent) will ascend the stairs to ask questions directly into your ear.
Our agent will take her turn...
And deposit a small canister in your inner ear.

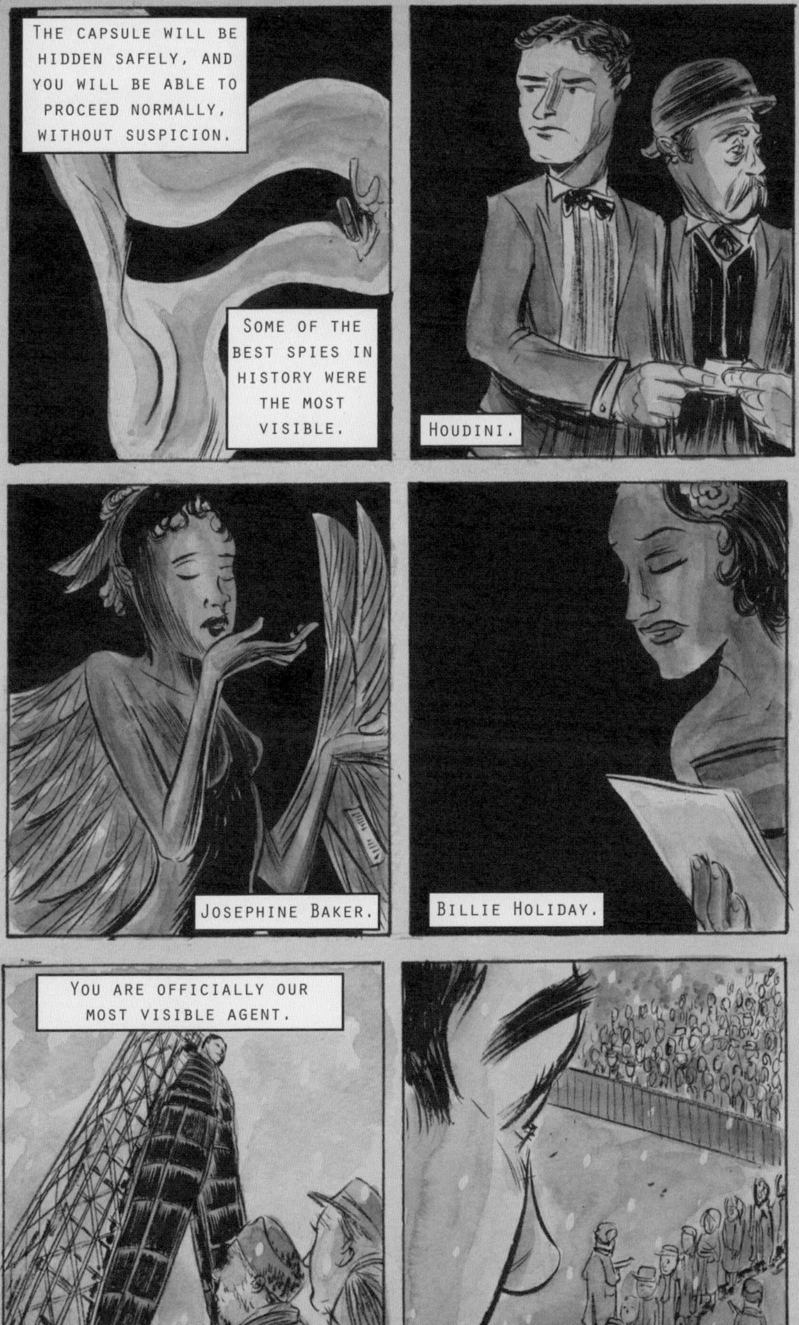
The capsule will be hidden safely, and you will be able to proceed normally, without suspicion.
Some of the best spies in history were the most visible.
Houdini.
Josephine Baker.
Billie Holiday.
You are officially our most visible agent.

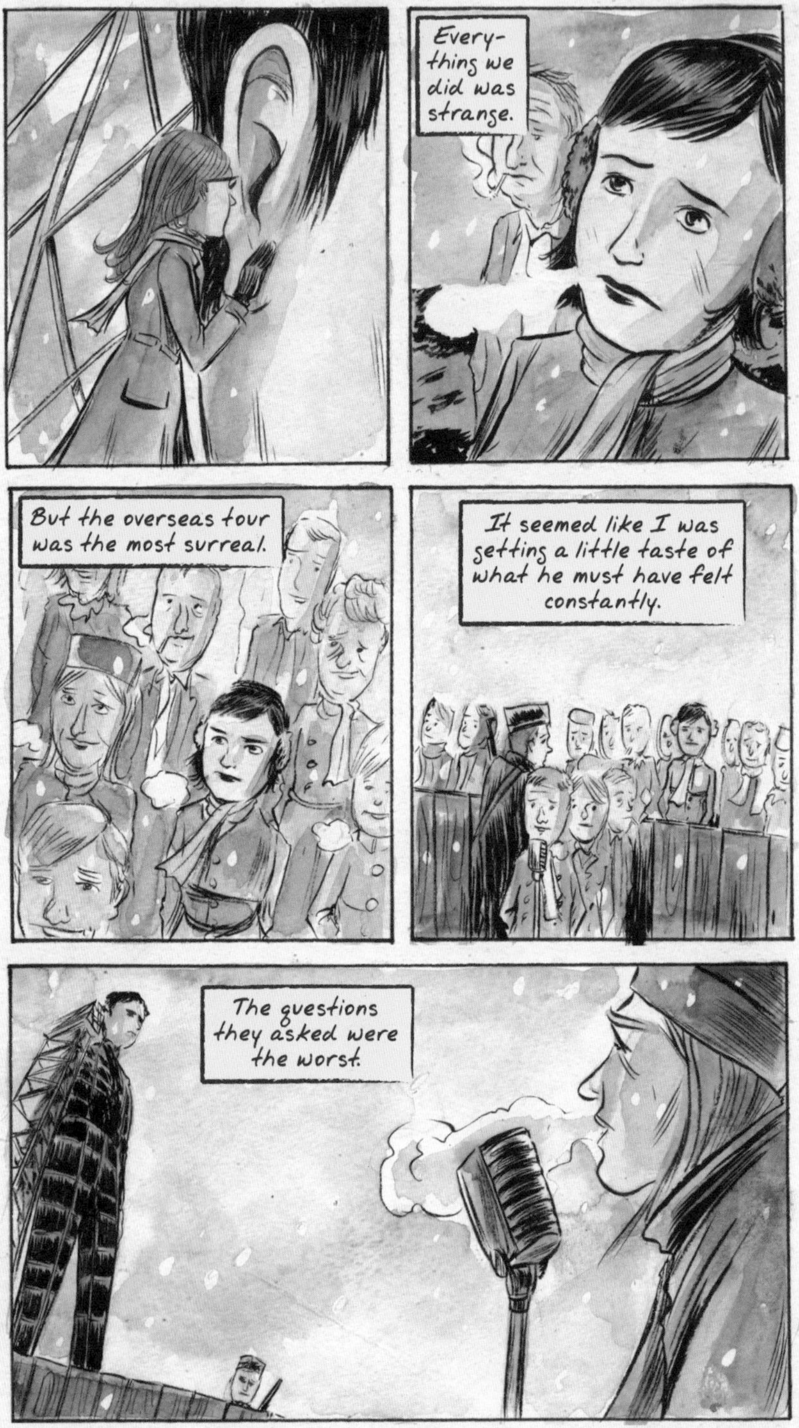

Everything we did was strange.
But the overseas tour was the most surreal.
It seemed like I was getting a little taste of what he must have felt constantly.
The questions they asked were the worst.

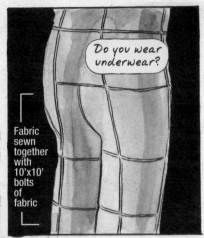

Giant Man in Thanksgiving Parade

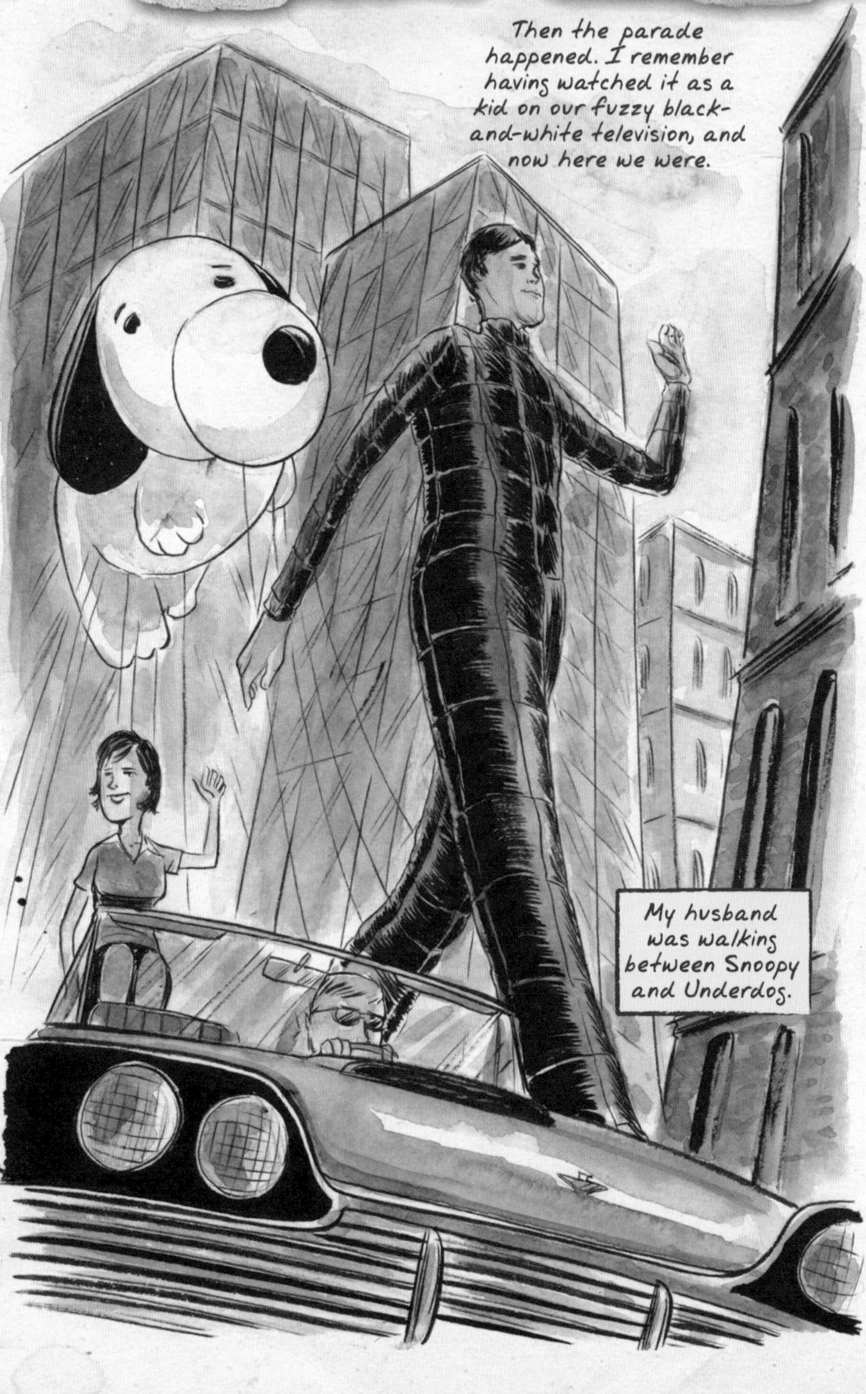

Then the parade happened. I remember having watched it as a kid on our fuzzy black-and-white television, and now here we were.
My husband was walking between Snoopy and Underdog.

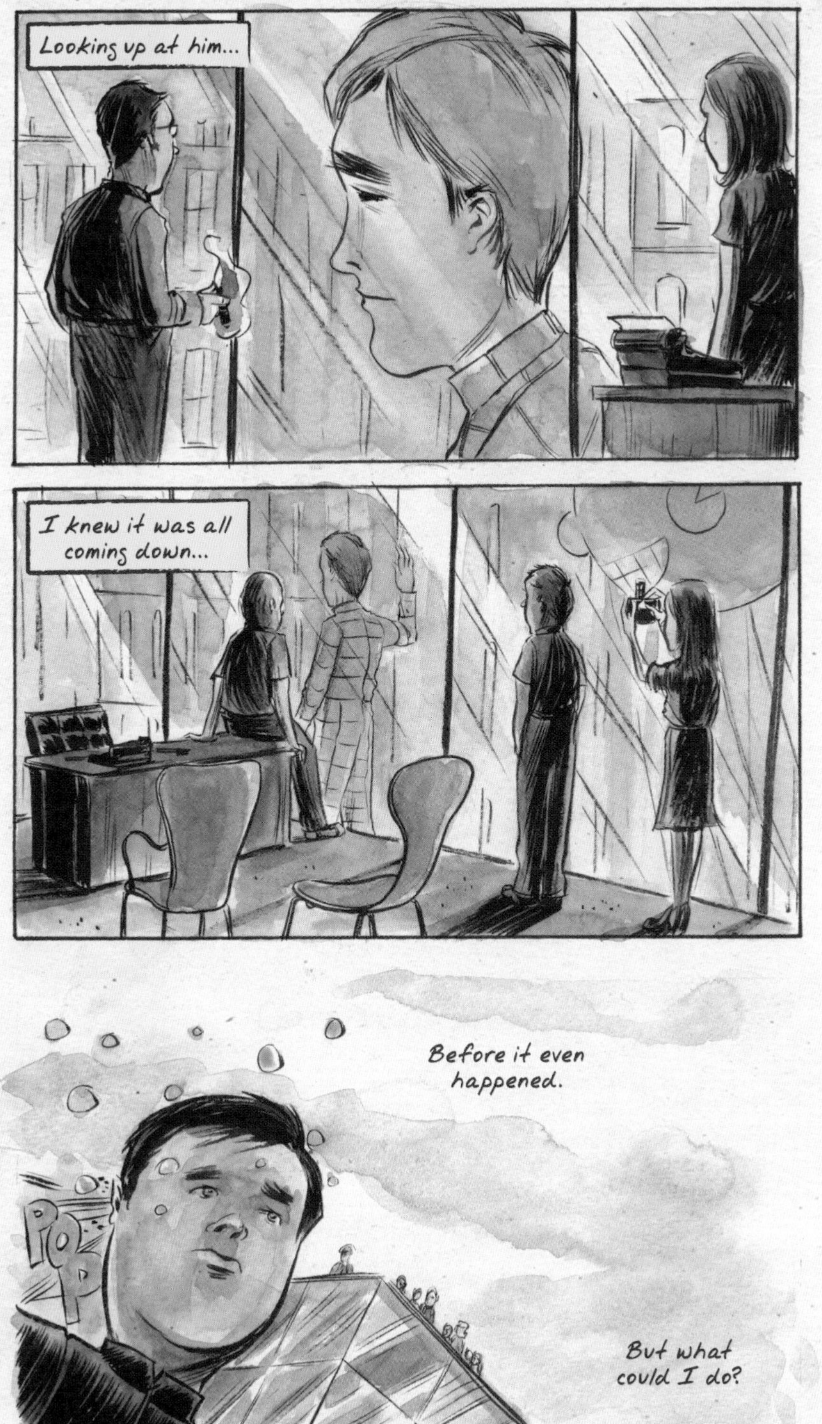
Looking up at him...
I knew it was all coming down...
Before it even happened.
POP
But what could I do?

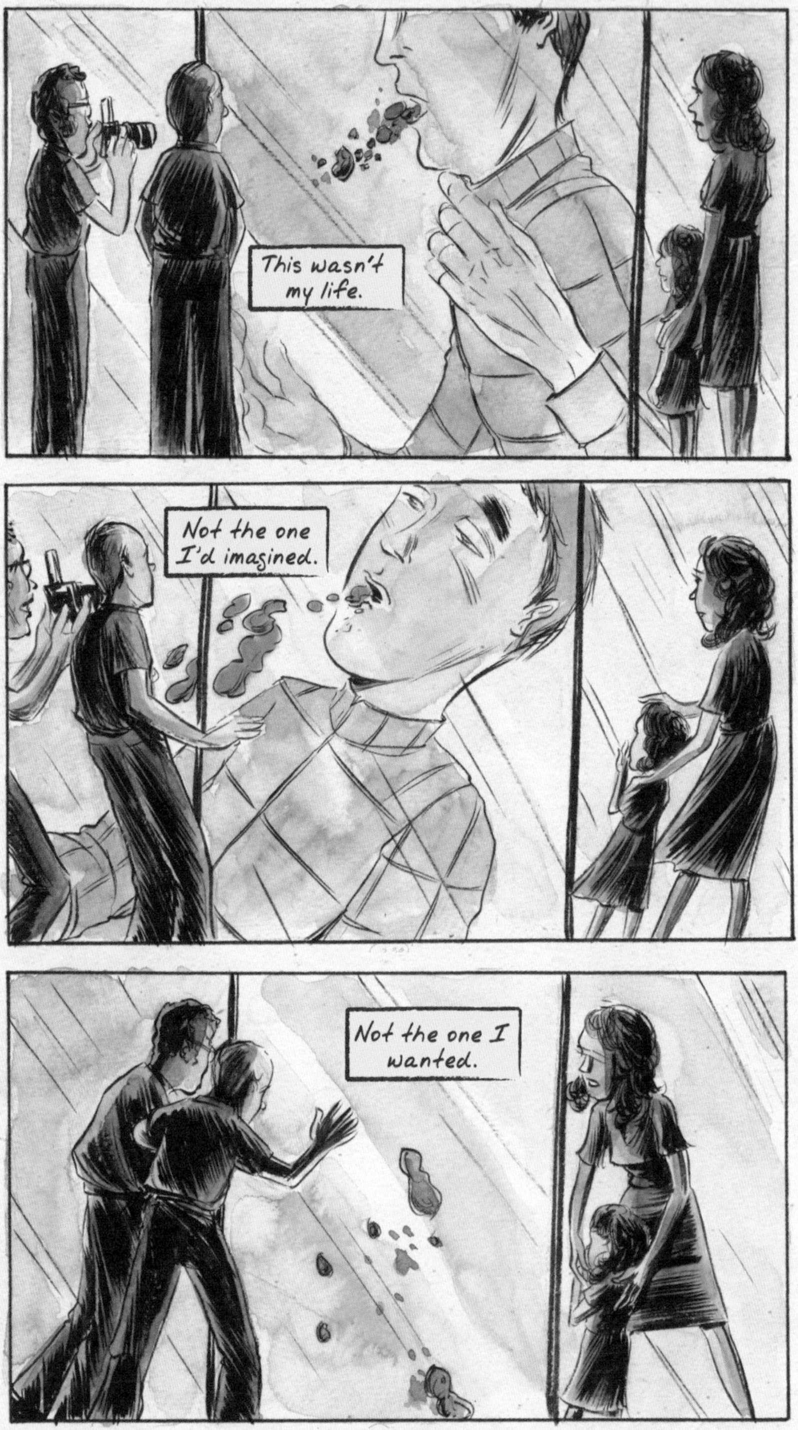
This wasn't my life.
Not the one I'd imagined.
Not the one I wanted.

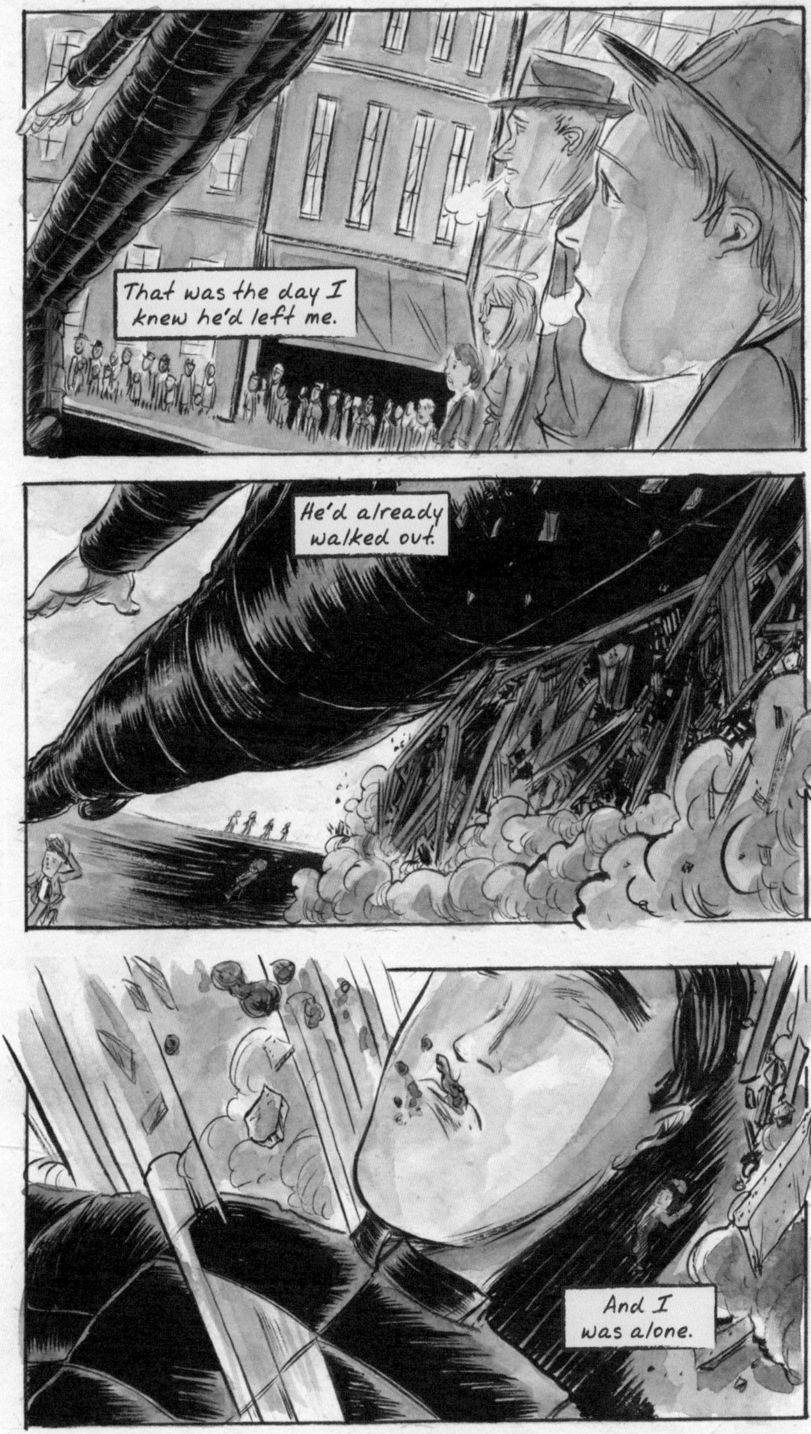
That was the day I knew he'd left me.
He'd already walked out.
And I was alone.

Disaster!

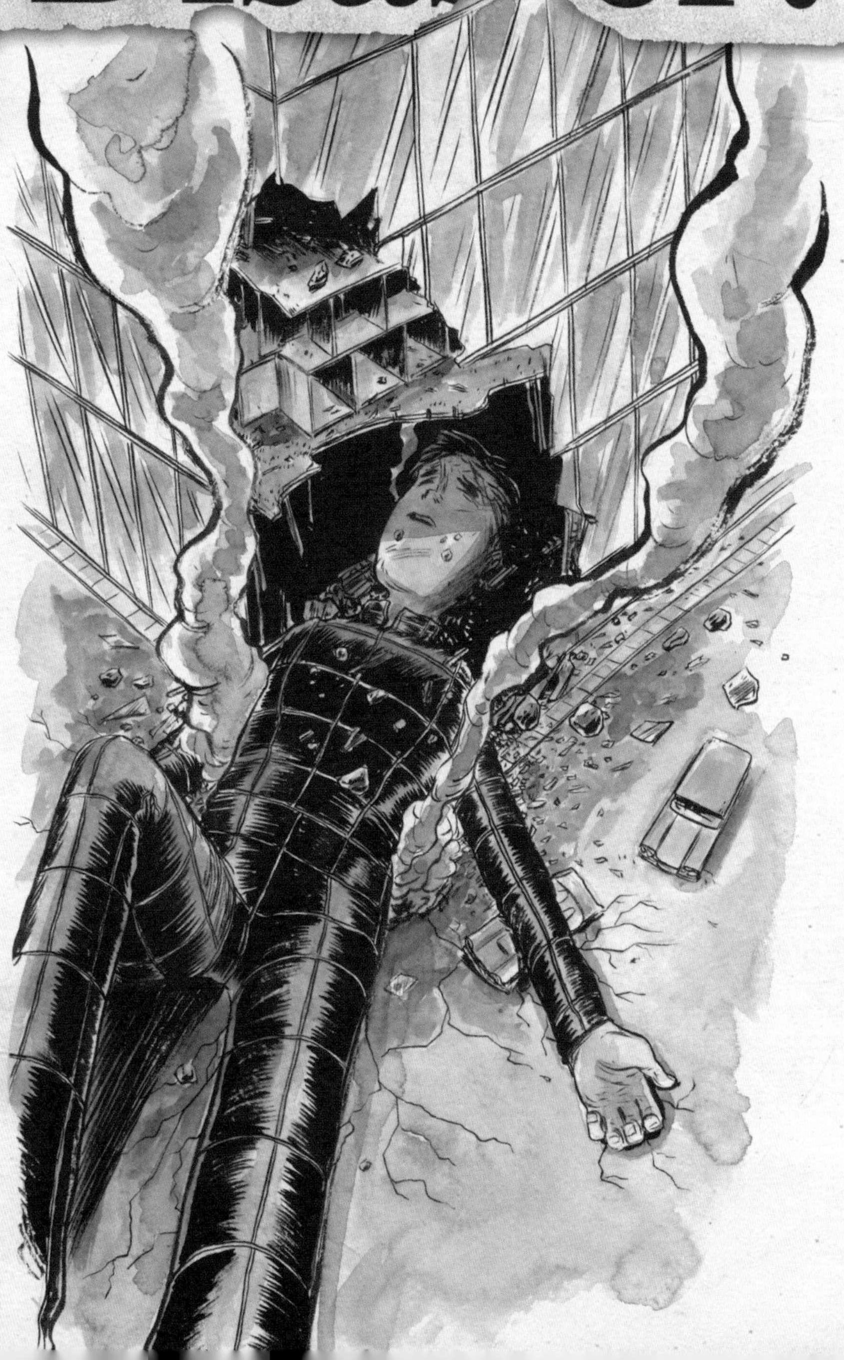

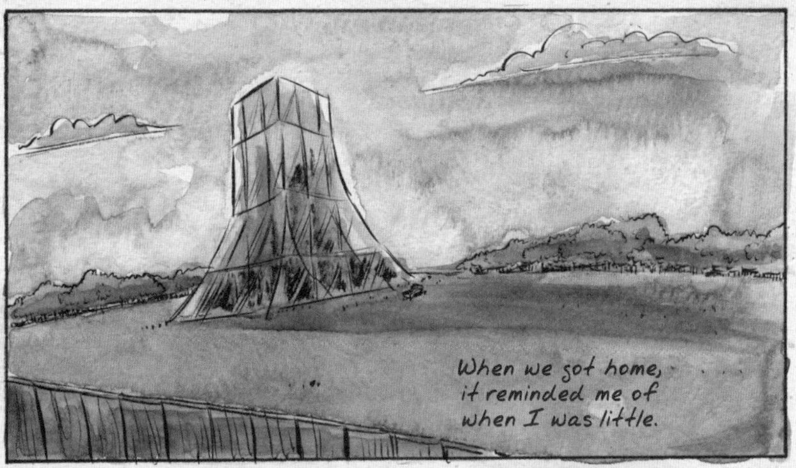
When we got home, it reminded me of when I was little.

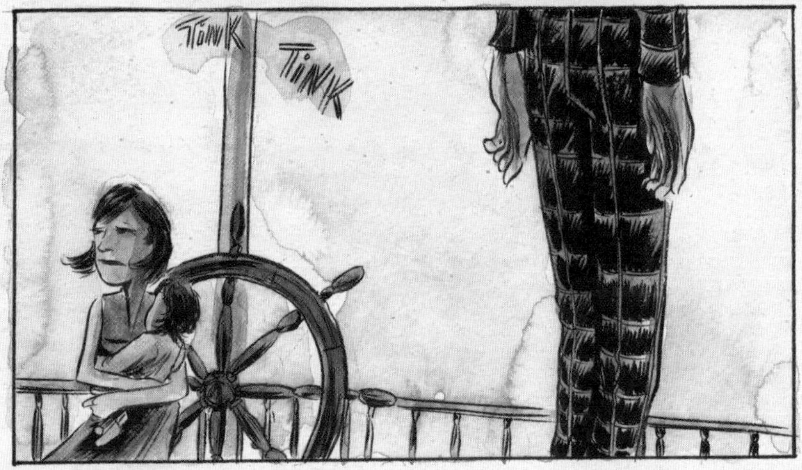
TINK
TINK

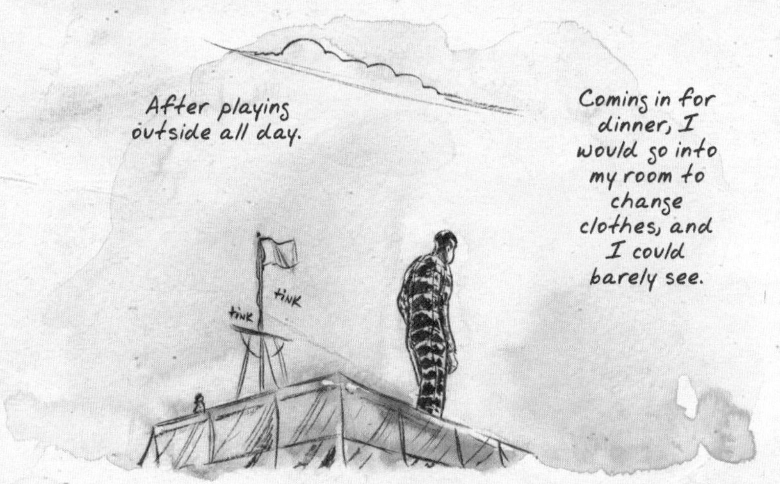
After playing outside all day.
Coming in for dinner, I would go into my room to change clothes, and I could barely see.
tink
tink

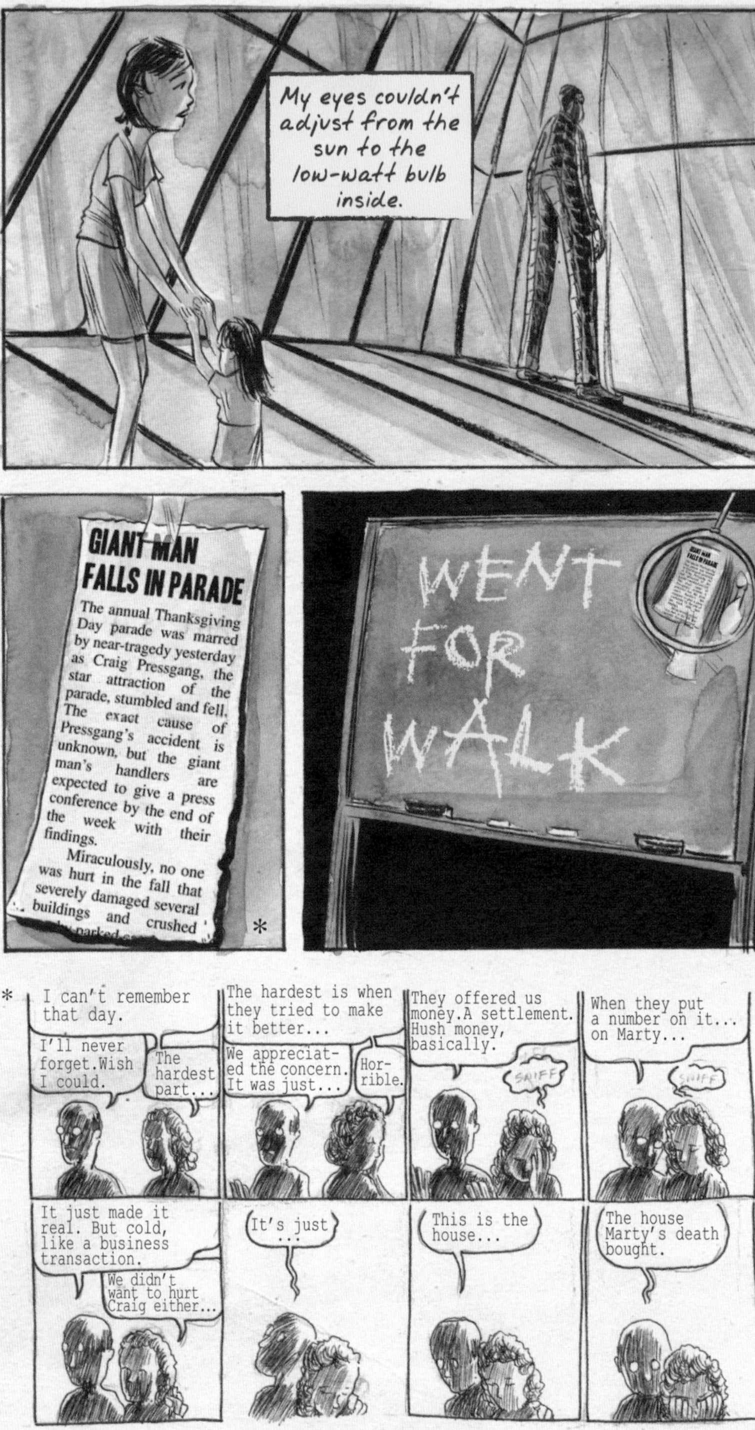
My eyes couldn't adjust from the sun to the low-watt bulb inside.
GIANT MAN FALLS IN PARADE
The annual Thanksgiving Day parade was marred by near-tragedy yesterday as Craig Pressgang, the star attraction of the parade, stumbled and fell. The exact cause of Pressgang's accident is unknown, but the giant man's handlers are expected to give a press conference by the end of the week with their findings.
Miraculously, no one was hurt in the fall that severely damaged several buildings and crushed
*
WENT FOR WALK
* I can't remember that day.
I'll never forget. Wish I could.
The hardest part...
The hardest is when they tried to make it better...
We appreciated the concern. It was just...
Horrible.
They offered us money. A settlement. Hush money, basically.
SNIFF
When they put a number on it... on Marty...
SNIFF
It just made it real. But cold, like a business transaction.
We didn't want to hurt Craig either...
It's just ...
This is the house...
The house Marty's death bought.

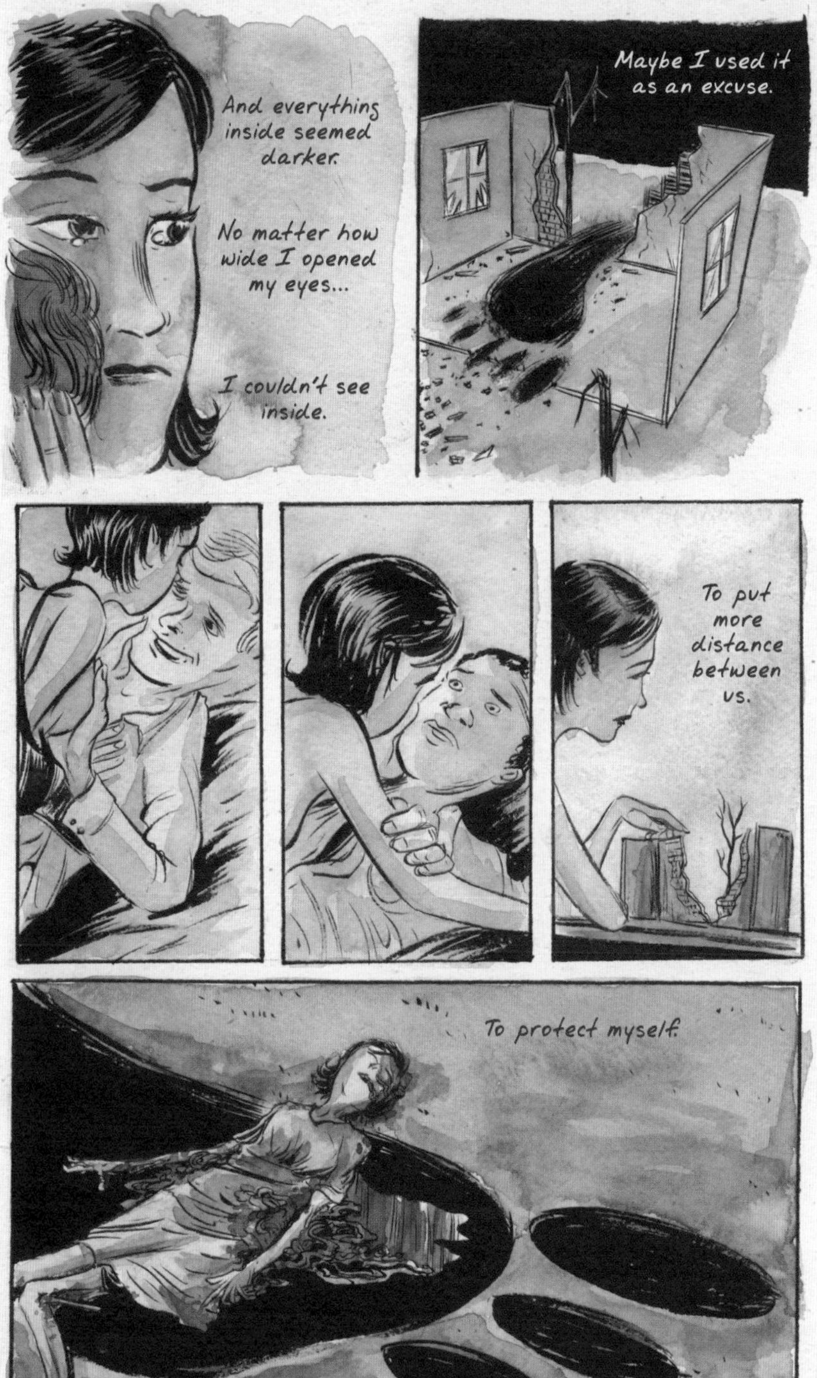
And everything inside seemed darker.
No matter how wide I opened my eyes...
I couldn't see inside.
Maybe I used it as an excuse.
To put more distance between us.
To protect myself.

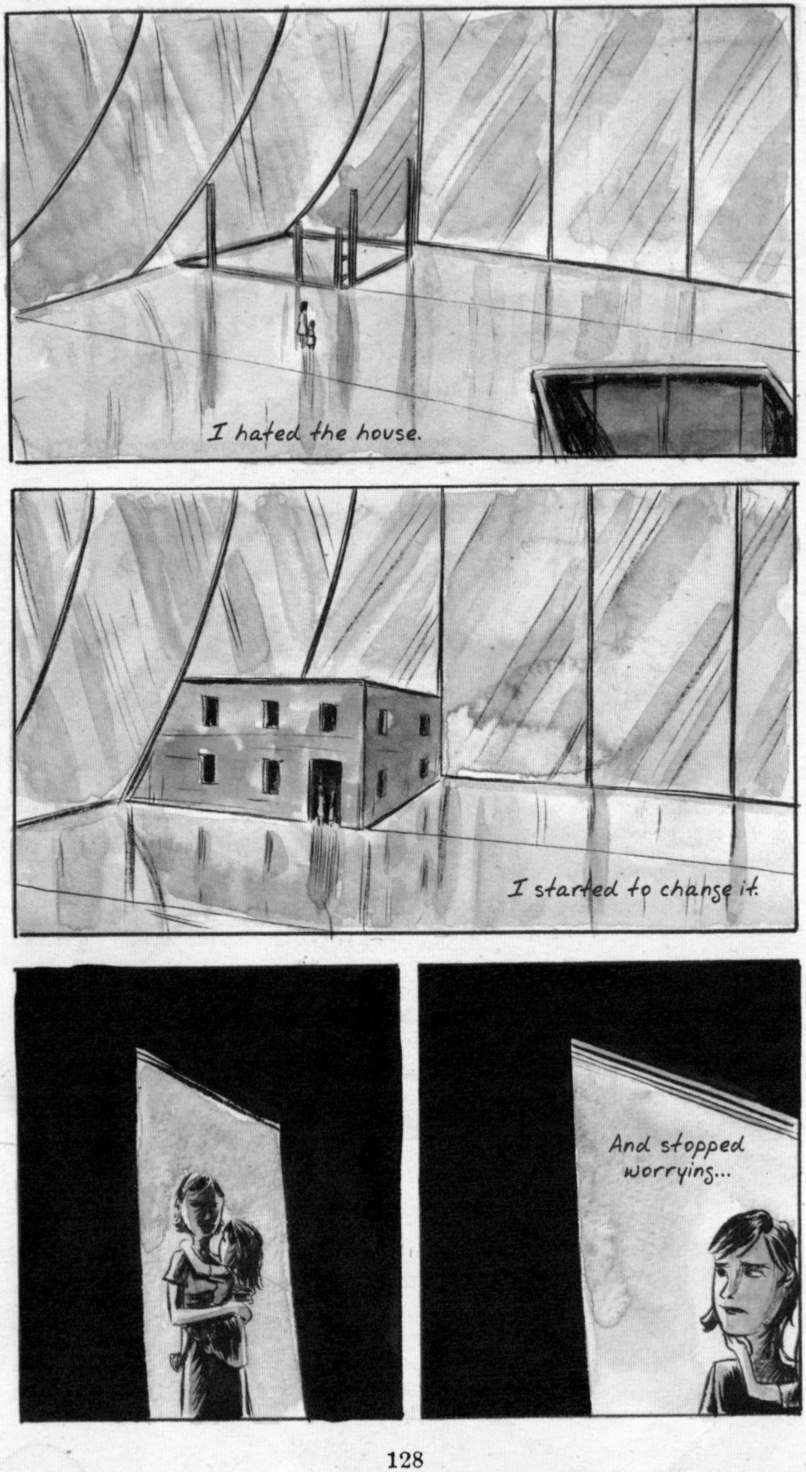
I hated the house.
I started to change it.
And stopped worrying...

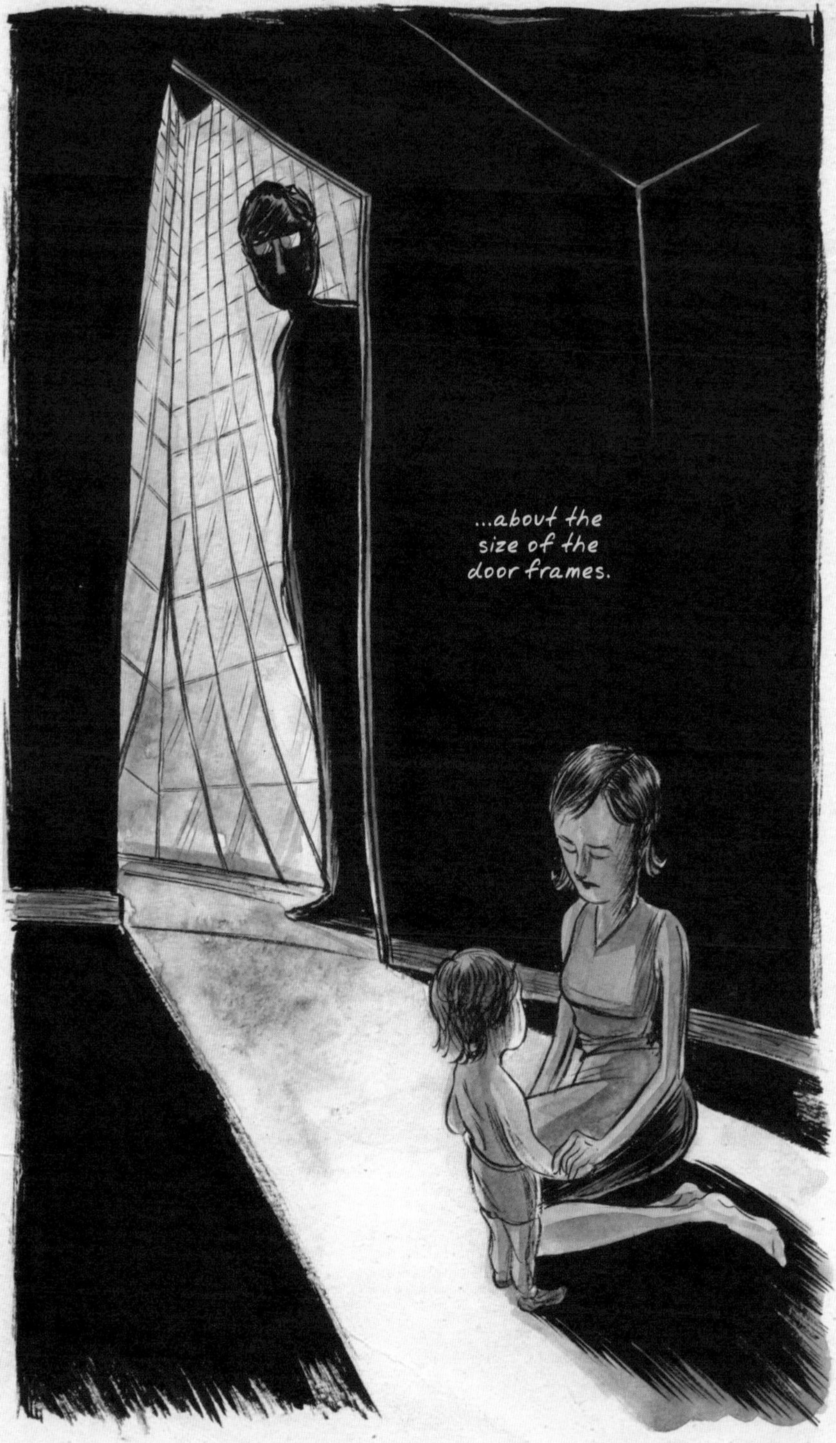
...about the
size of the
door frames.

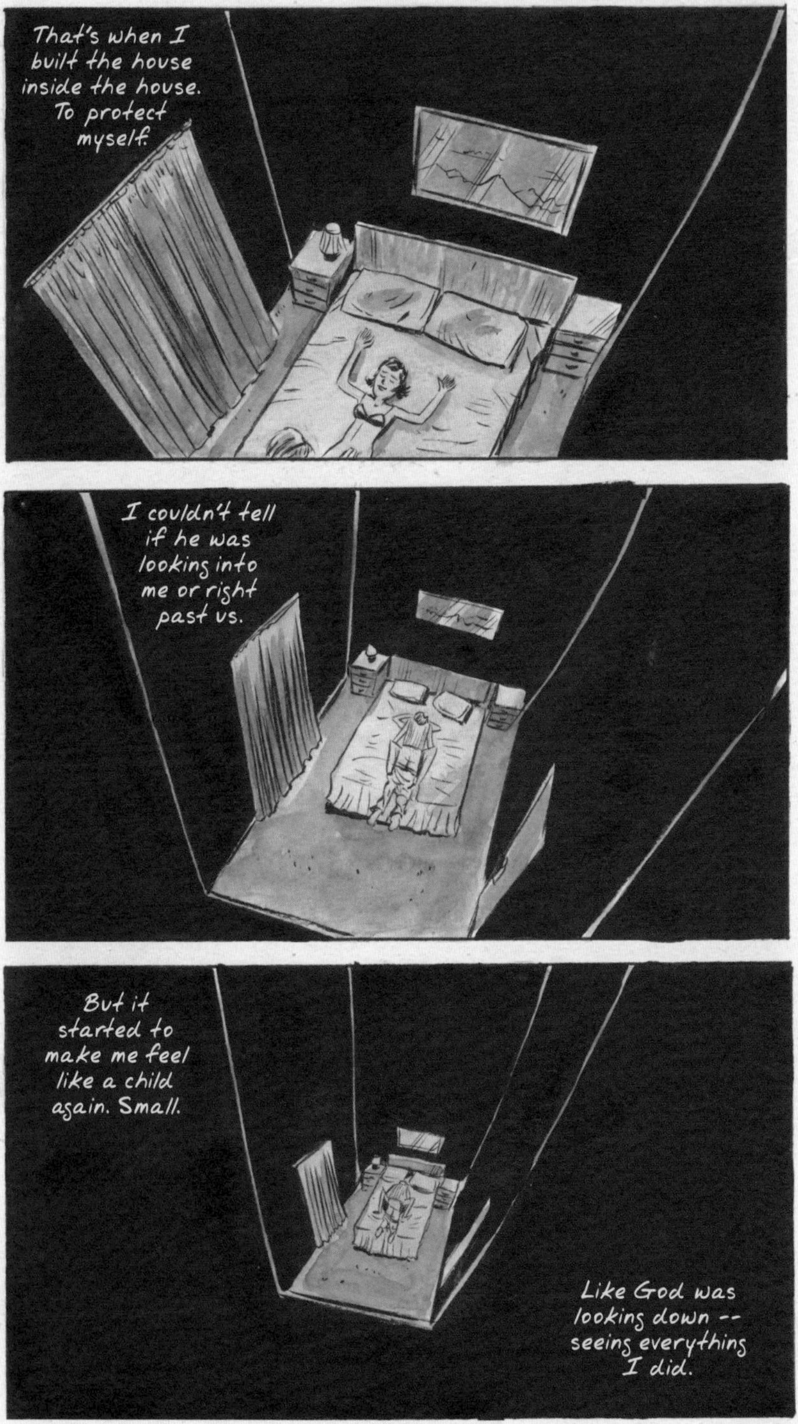
That's when I built the house inside the house. To protect myself.
I couldn't tell if he was looking into me or right past us.
But it started to make me feel like a child again. Small.
Like God was looking down -- seeing everything I did.

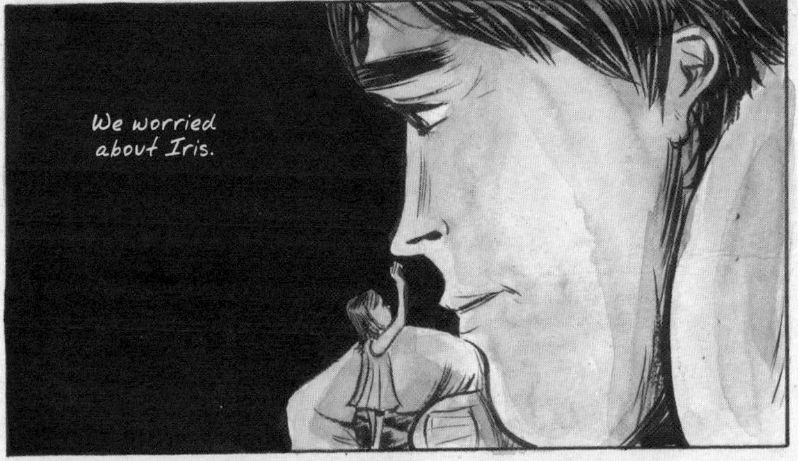
We worried about Iris.

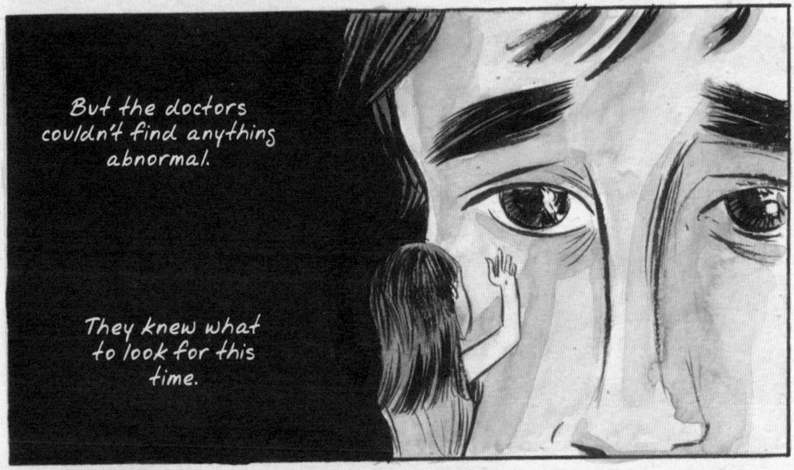
But the doctors couldn't find anything abnormal.
They knew what to look for this time.

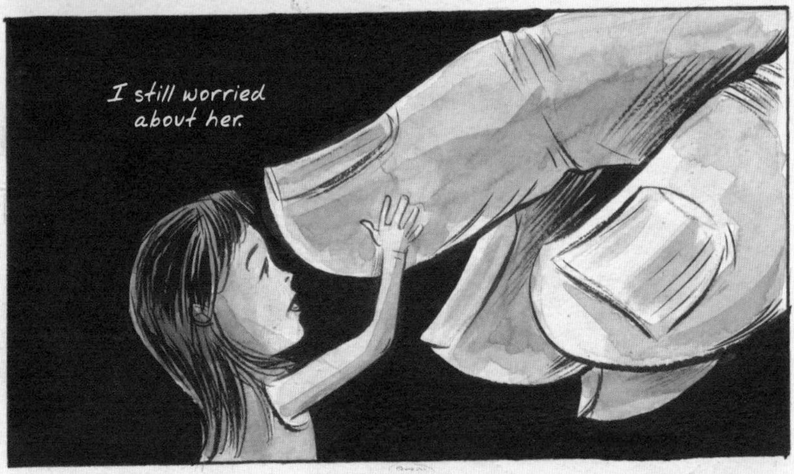
I still worried about her.

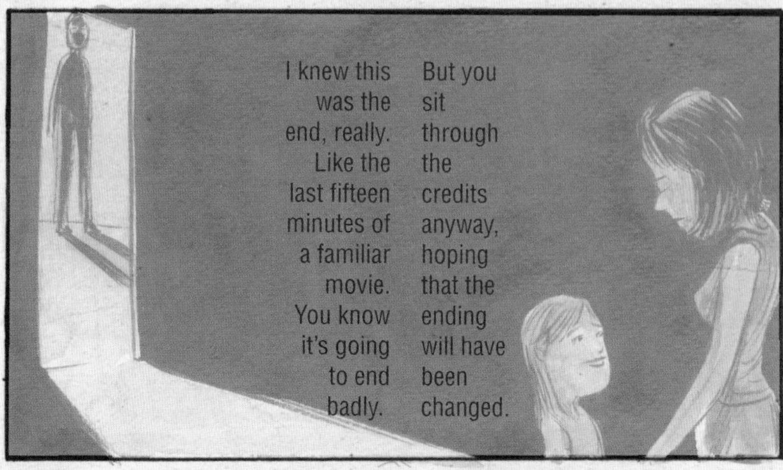
I knew this was the end, really. Like the last fifteen minutes of a familiar movie. You know it's going to end badly.
But you sit through the credits anyway, hoping that the ending will have been changed.

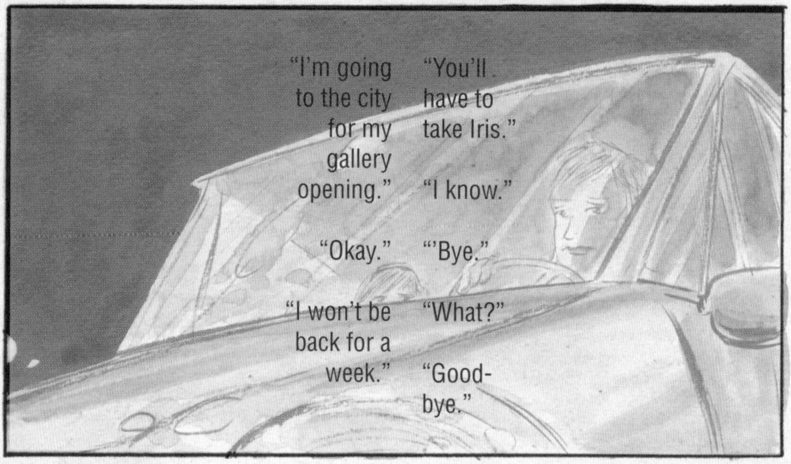
"I'm going to the city for my gallery opening."
"You'll have to take Iris."
"I know."
"Okay."
"'Bye."
"I won't be back for a week."
"What?"
"Good-bye."

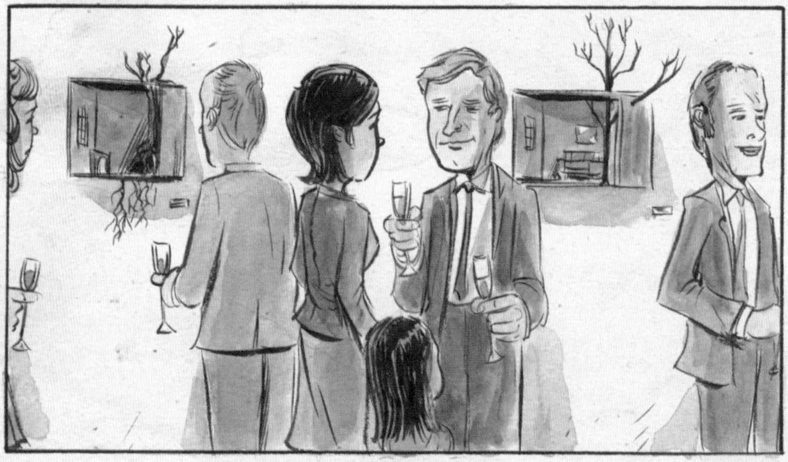

Jo Pressgang

One of Pressgang's earliest pieces recalls her first meeting with her husband in a suburban pizza parlor. The straightforward nature of the construction and strict representational qualities of this piece only echo her later playfulness with form and media.

This large piece details Pressgang's early childhood on the farm. This is a piece from her middle period, and shows her progression to later works. The idealized setting and the exaggerated scale of the tree all represent her early attempts at playing with scale and perspective.

This piece represents the beginning of her modern phase. The structures are starting to show wear and distress. Naturalistic proportions have returned, but organic growth has started to appear in unlikely places. Jo, what's going on with your art?

I was looking at your work the other day. I don't understand it. Maybe, well.... Maybe it's just hard for me to see under my magnifying glasses. But why is everything falling apart? I don't get it.

No. I just... I'm trying something new. I was getting tired of just doing the same stuff over and over again. I'm trying to...I don't know. I'm trying to reflect some of myself. Or put some of myself into it.

I don't like them. If you want to talk to me, talk to me. You don't have to be clever about it. If you're so miserable, then what are you doing here?

Gallery Exhibit
March 6 – May 19

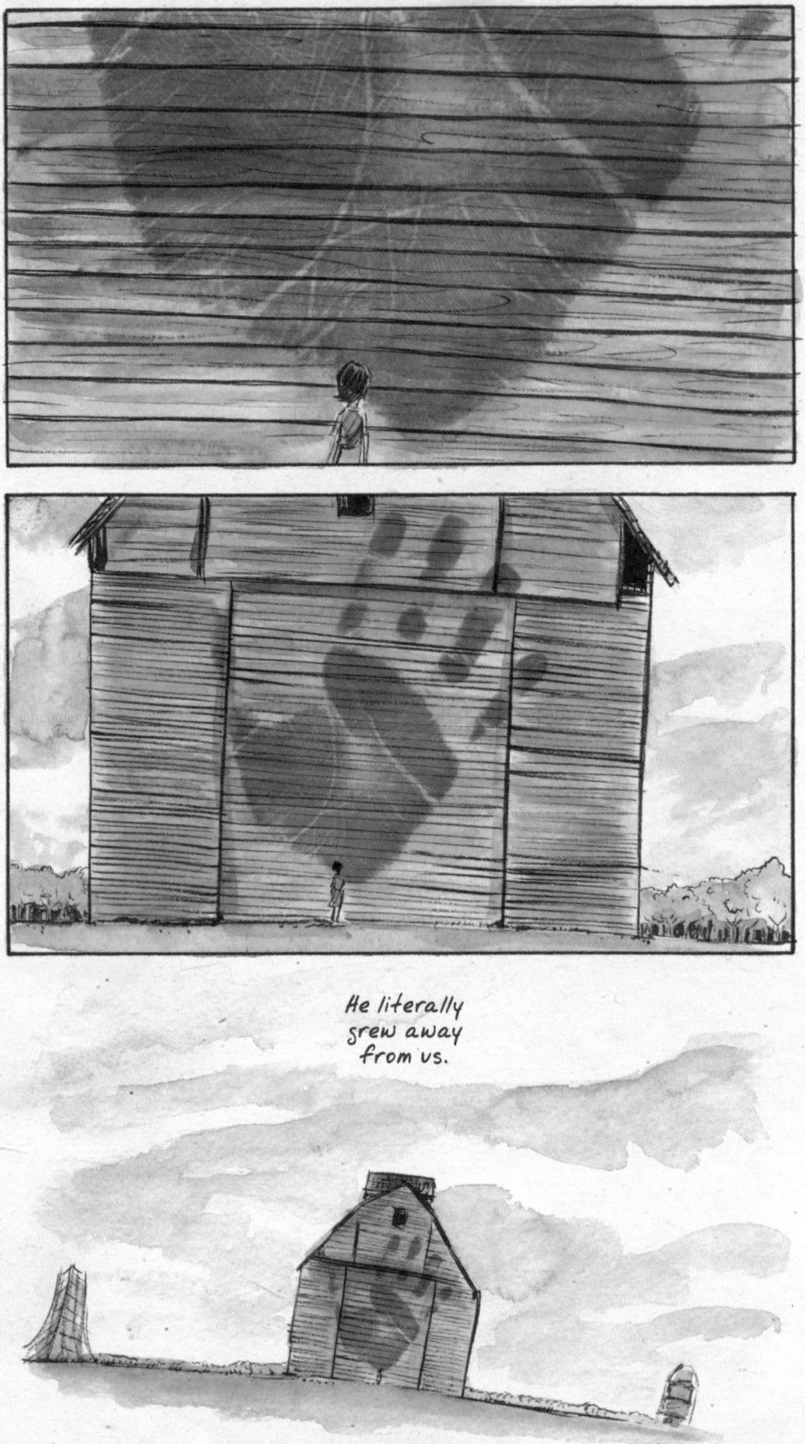
He literally grew away from us.

His vocal chords were so big. His lungs. Everything.

He had to whisper so we could understand him and not burst our eardrums.

I had to shout at him. All he could hear was buzzing.

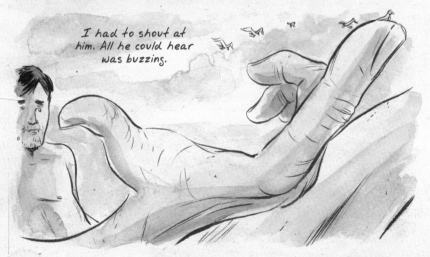

Small Art Makes Big Splash

The prestigious Vowels Gallery in Chicago recently showcased the new, unique talent of Jo Pressgang, the wife of the famous "Giant Man," Craig Pressgang. At first sight, Jo's work is very reminiscent of the renowned Thorne Miniatures, some of which are housed at the nearby Chicago Art Institute.

However, upon closer inspection it is evident that Pressgang's work is aiming even higher. These are not simple historical re-creations on a miniature scale. Each of Pressgang's small constructions houses an enormous depth of emotion and feeling. This is especially evident when viewing her work not only in the context of her later, more famous "destruction pieces," but within the context of her life as the wife of one of the most famous men in the country. How does this inform her work? And how did this demure artist finally step out of the shadow of one of the most famous personalities in the last decade? W

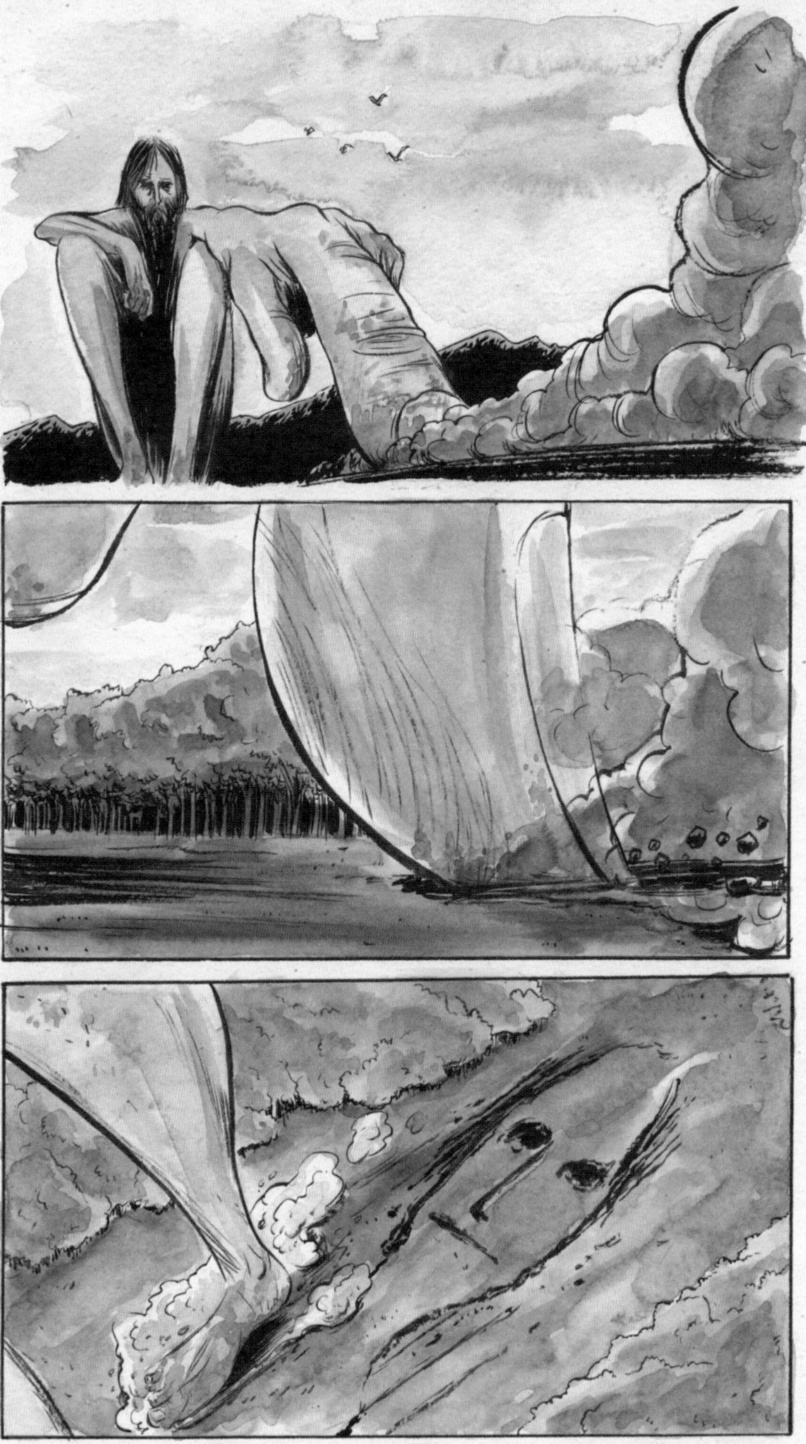

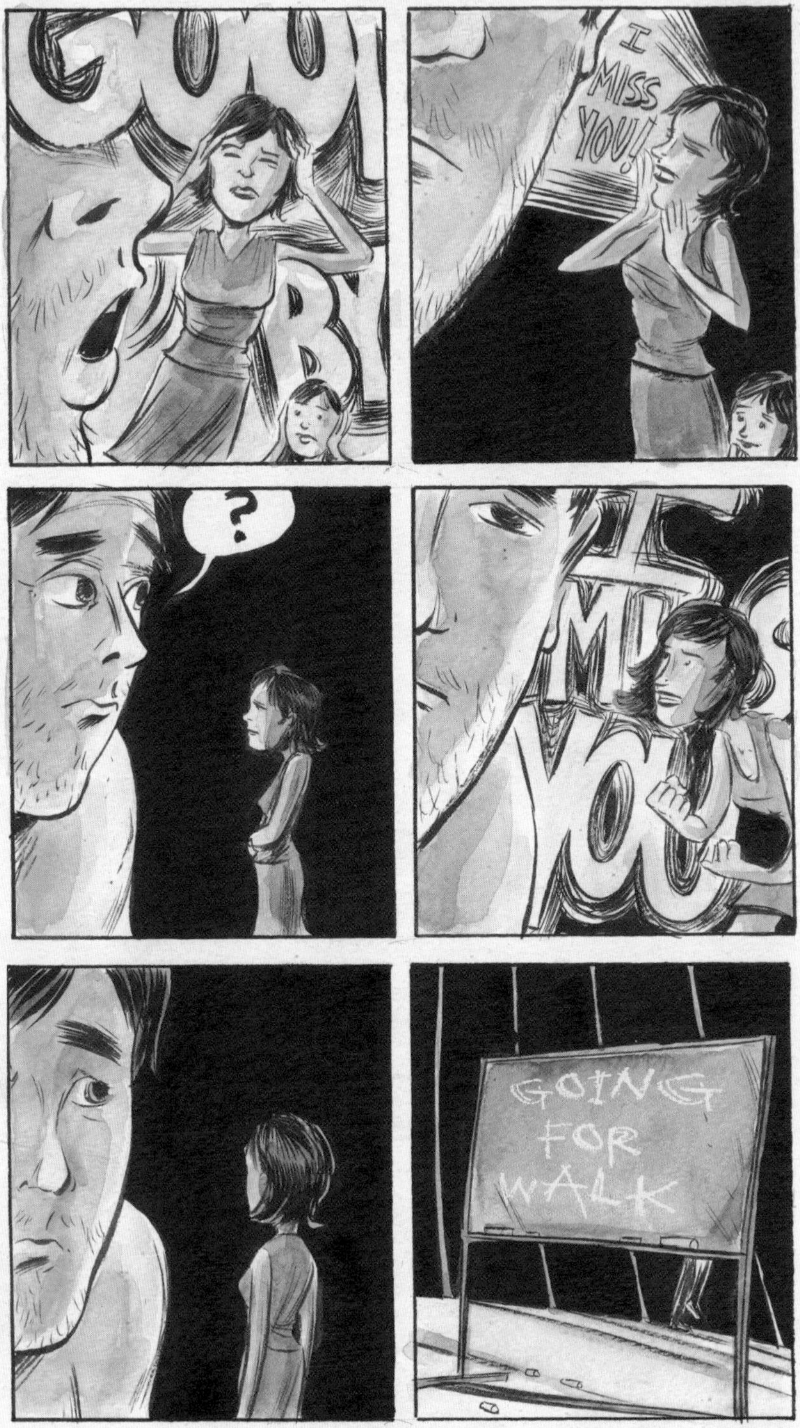
I MISS YOU!
?
GOING FOR WALK

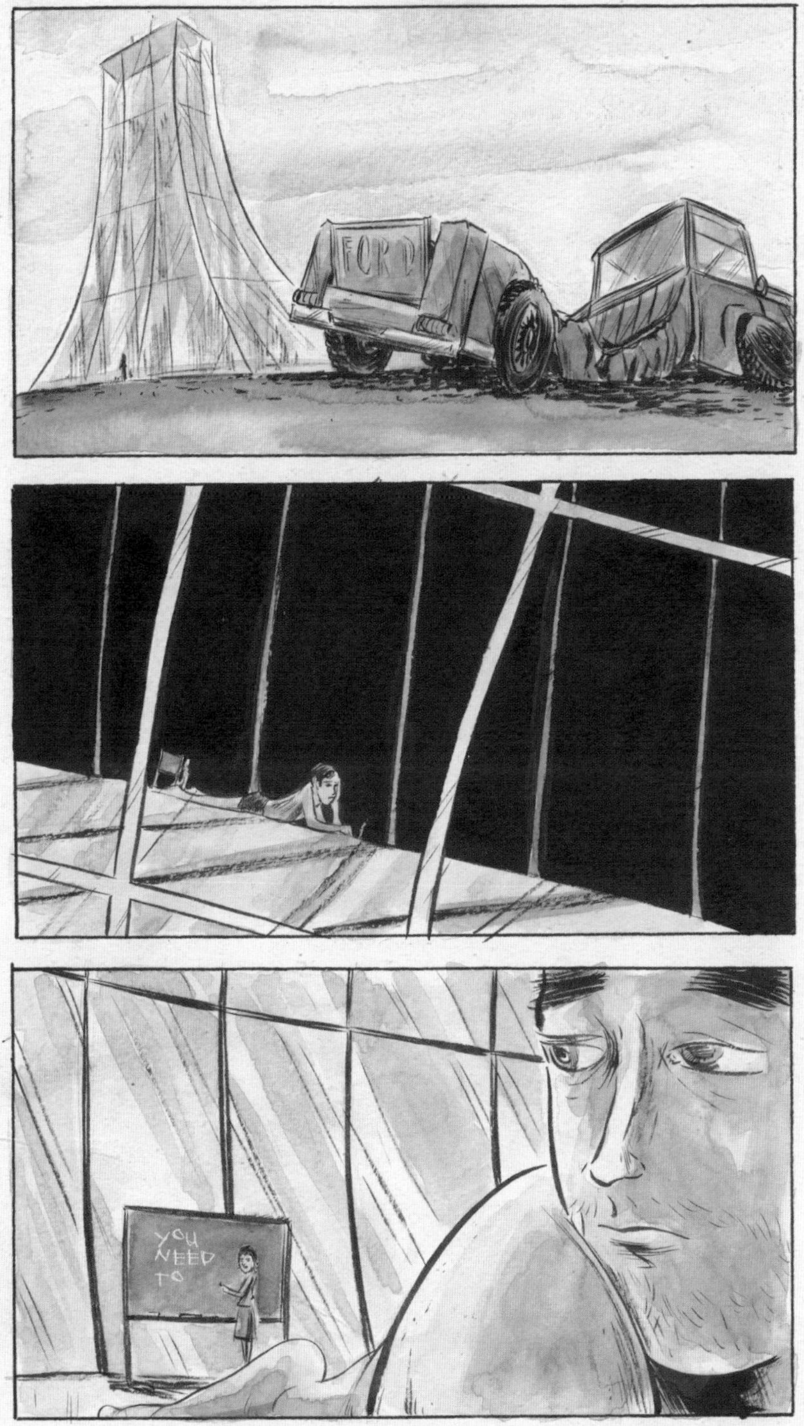
FORD
YOU
NEED
TO

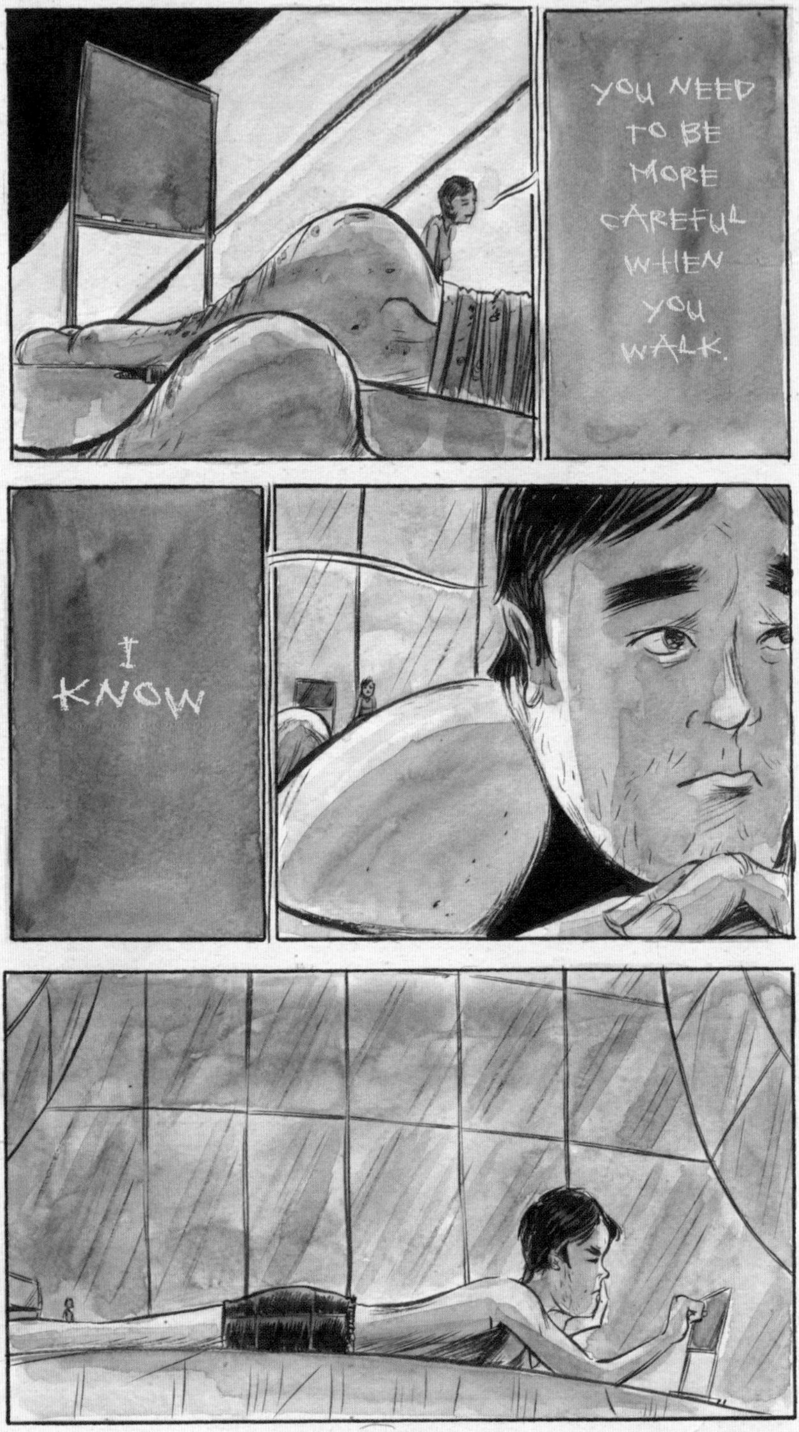
YOU NEED TO BE MORE CAREFUL WHEN YOU WALK.
I KNOW

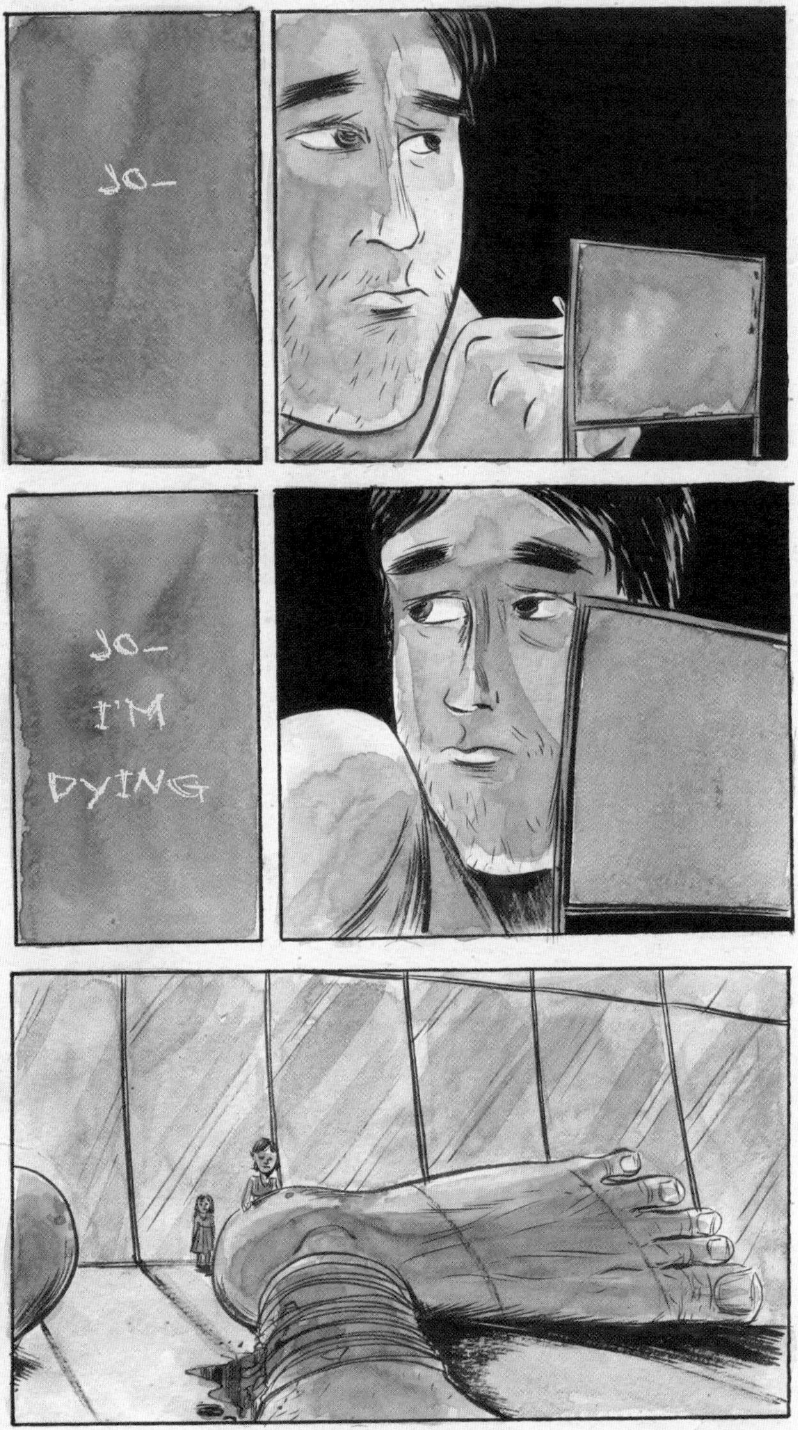
JO–
JO–
I'M
DYING

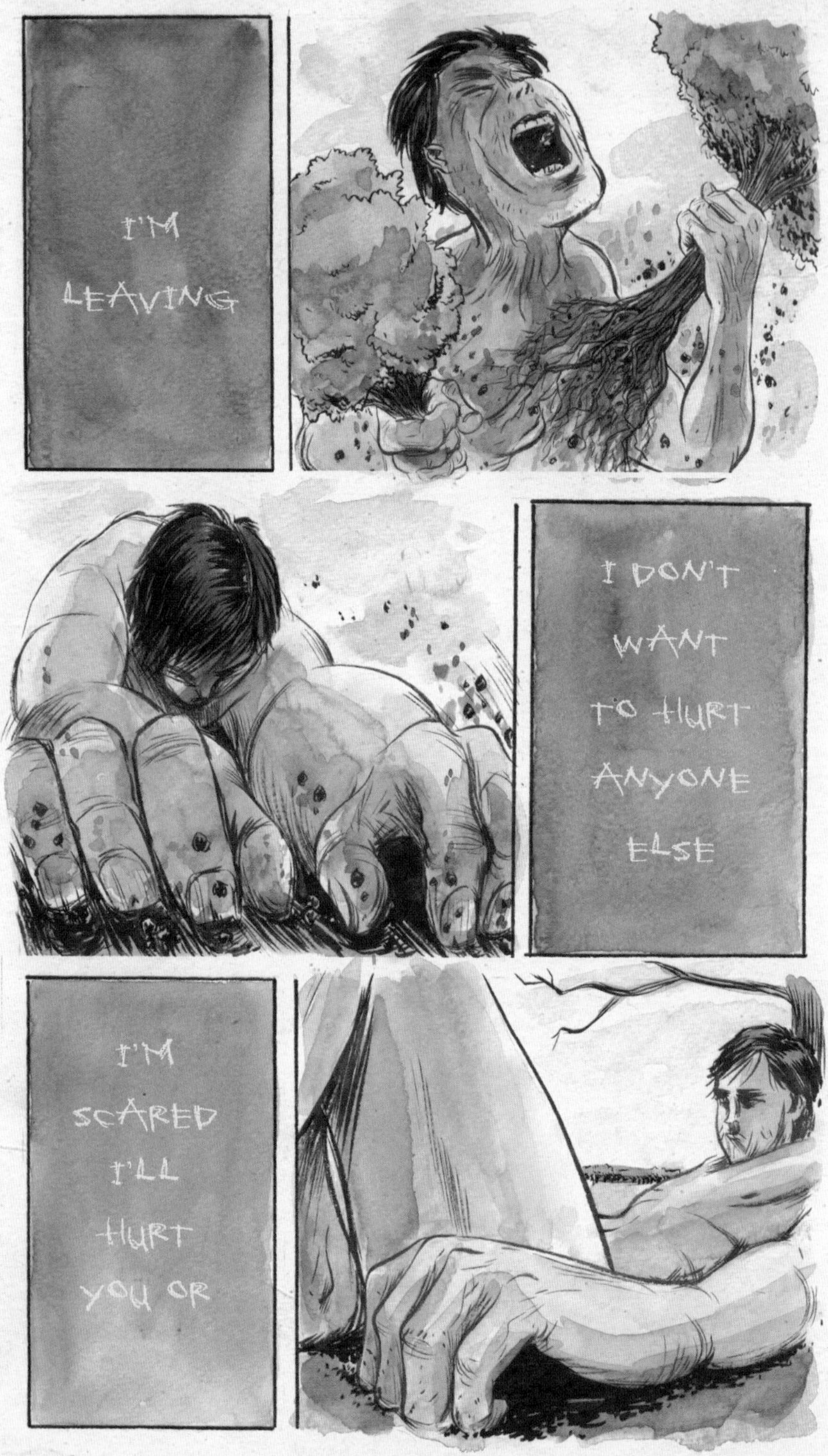
I'M
LEAVING
I DON'T
WANT
TO HURT
ANYONE
ELSE
I'M
SCARED
I'LL
HURT
YOU OR

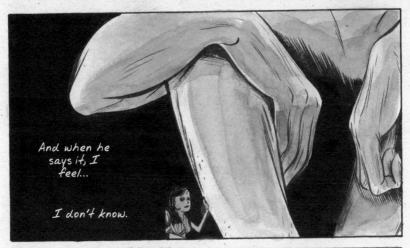

And when he says it, I feel...

I don't know.

A wave of sadness.

And relief.

And total guilt for feeling even a hint of that.

I loved Craig. But he wasn't there anymore.

He was a giant ghost.

I told him
I under-
stood.
Who
knows?

Iris was
old
enough to
under-
stand, I
think.

She related to her
father like you
would to a moun-
tain. Or a familiar
playground.

She'd miss him,
but like you'd
miss the house
you grew up in
as a kid.

I think.

I hope.

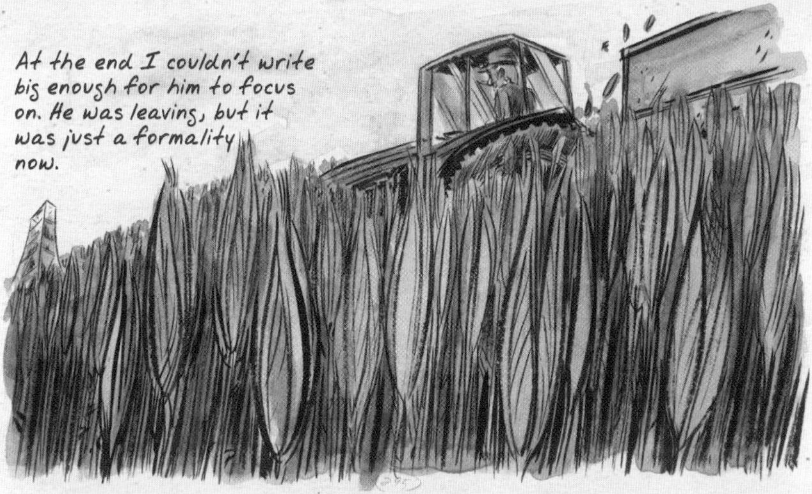
At the end I couldn't write big enough for him to focus on. He was leaving, but it was just a formality now.

WE COULDN'T EVEN TALK AT THE END.

IT WAS STRANGELY SILENT.

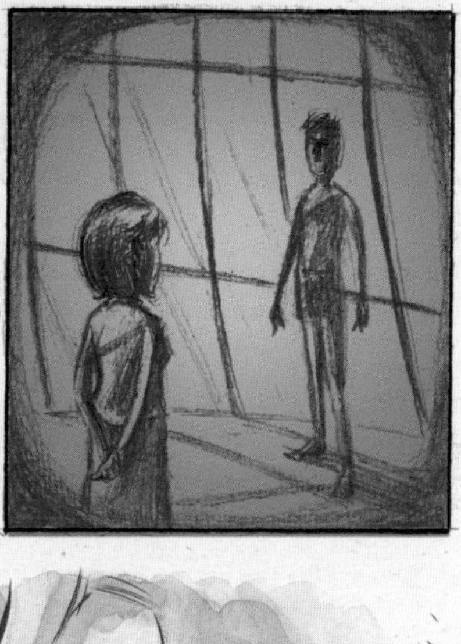

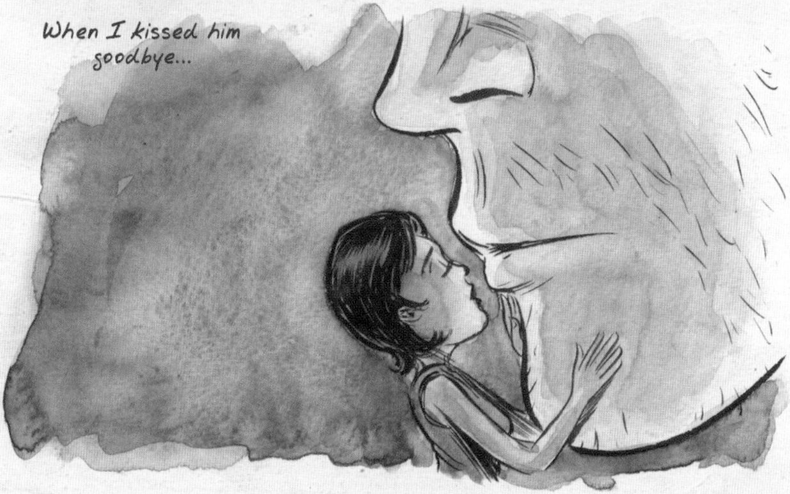
When I kissed him goodbye...

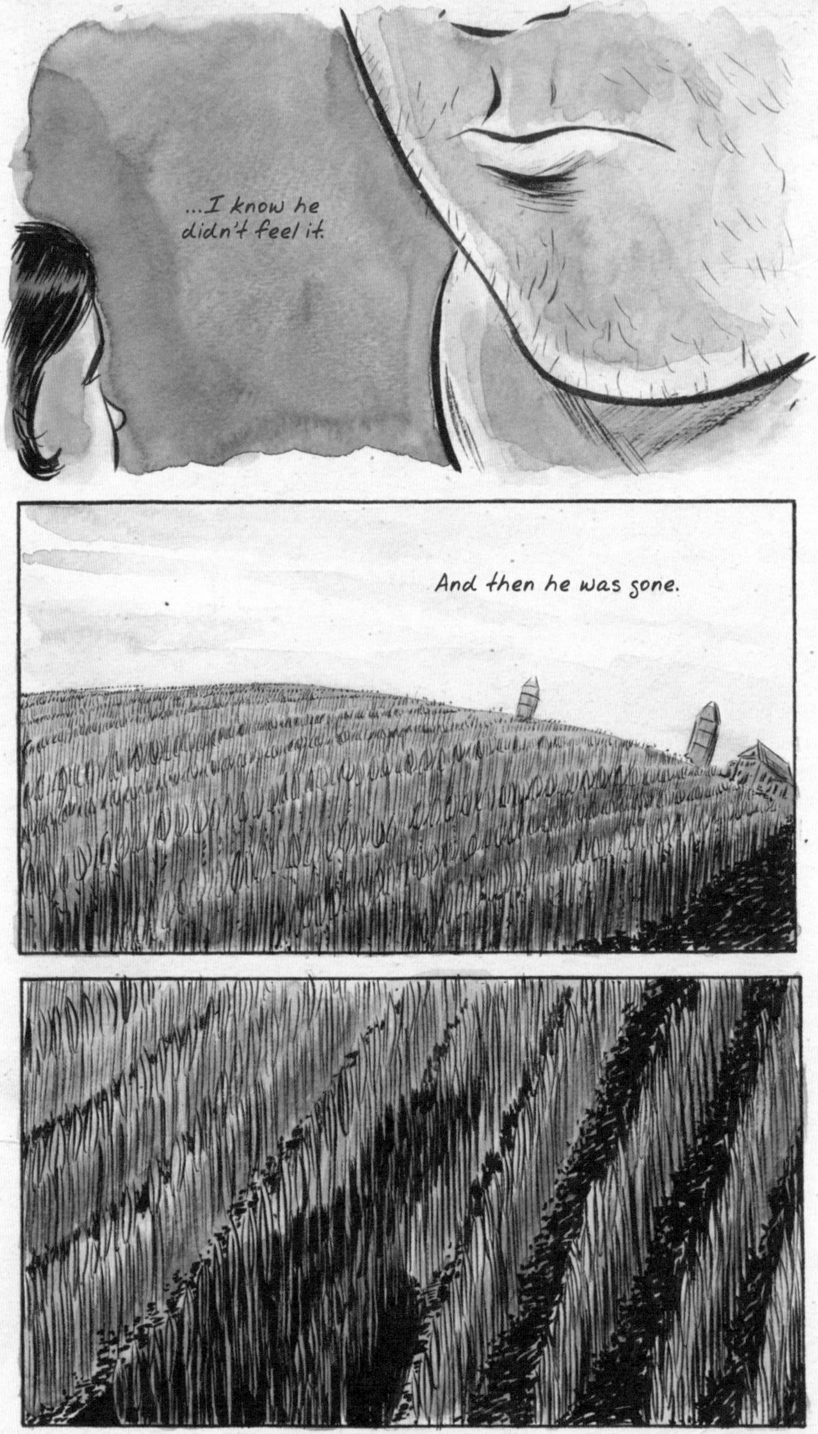
...I know he didn't feel it.
And then he was gone.

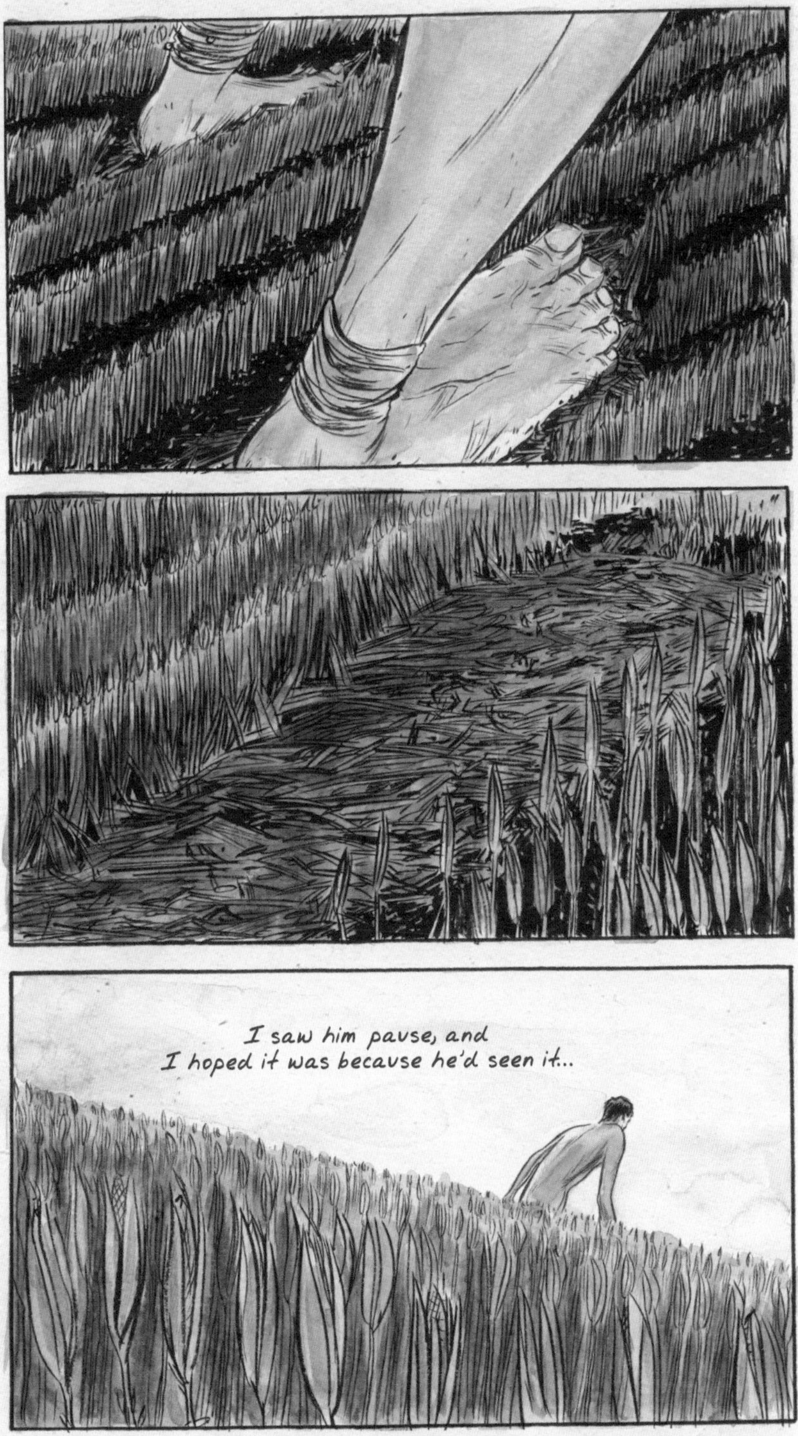
I saw him pause, and
I hoped it was because he'd seen it...

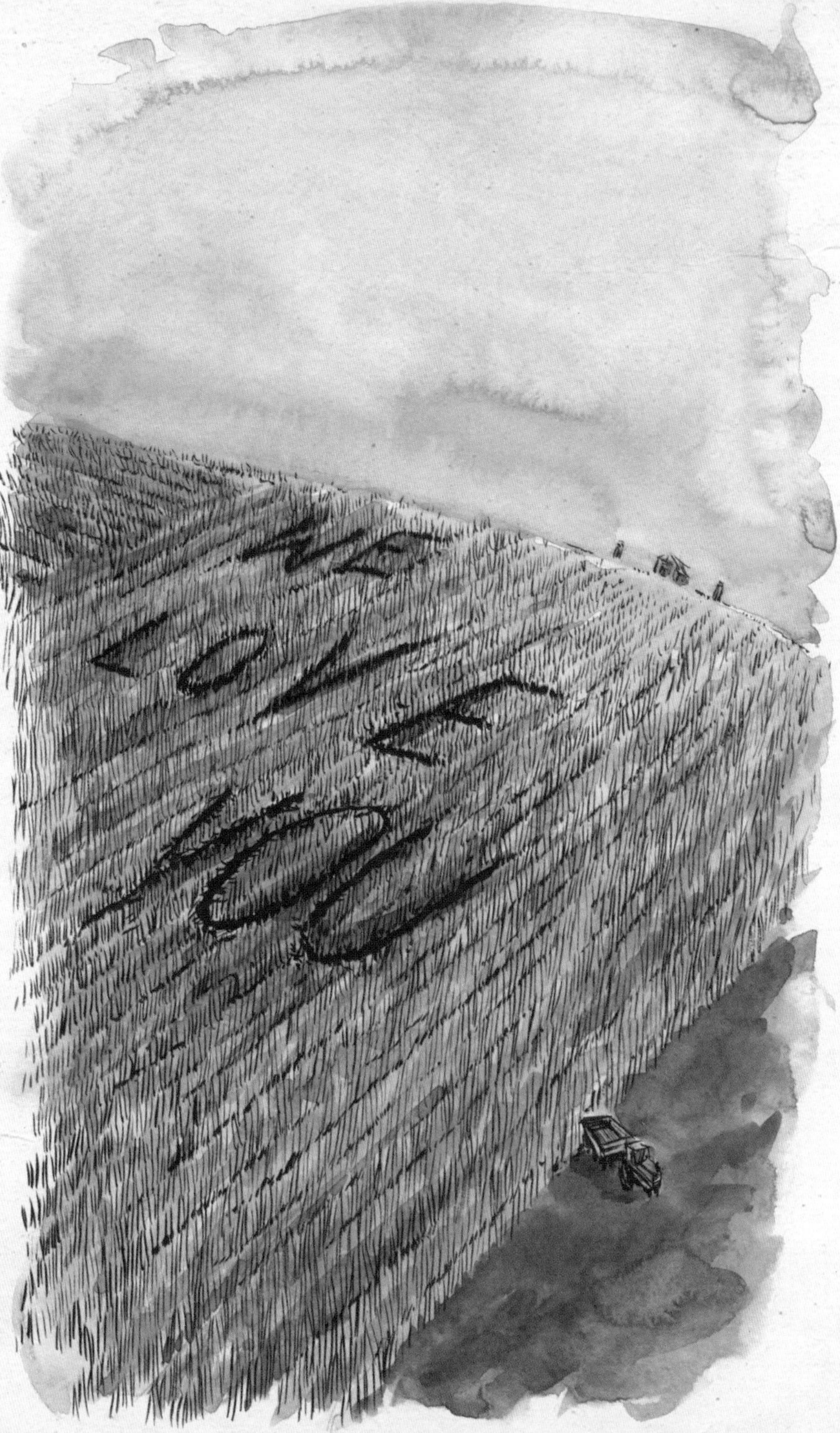

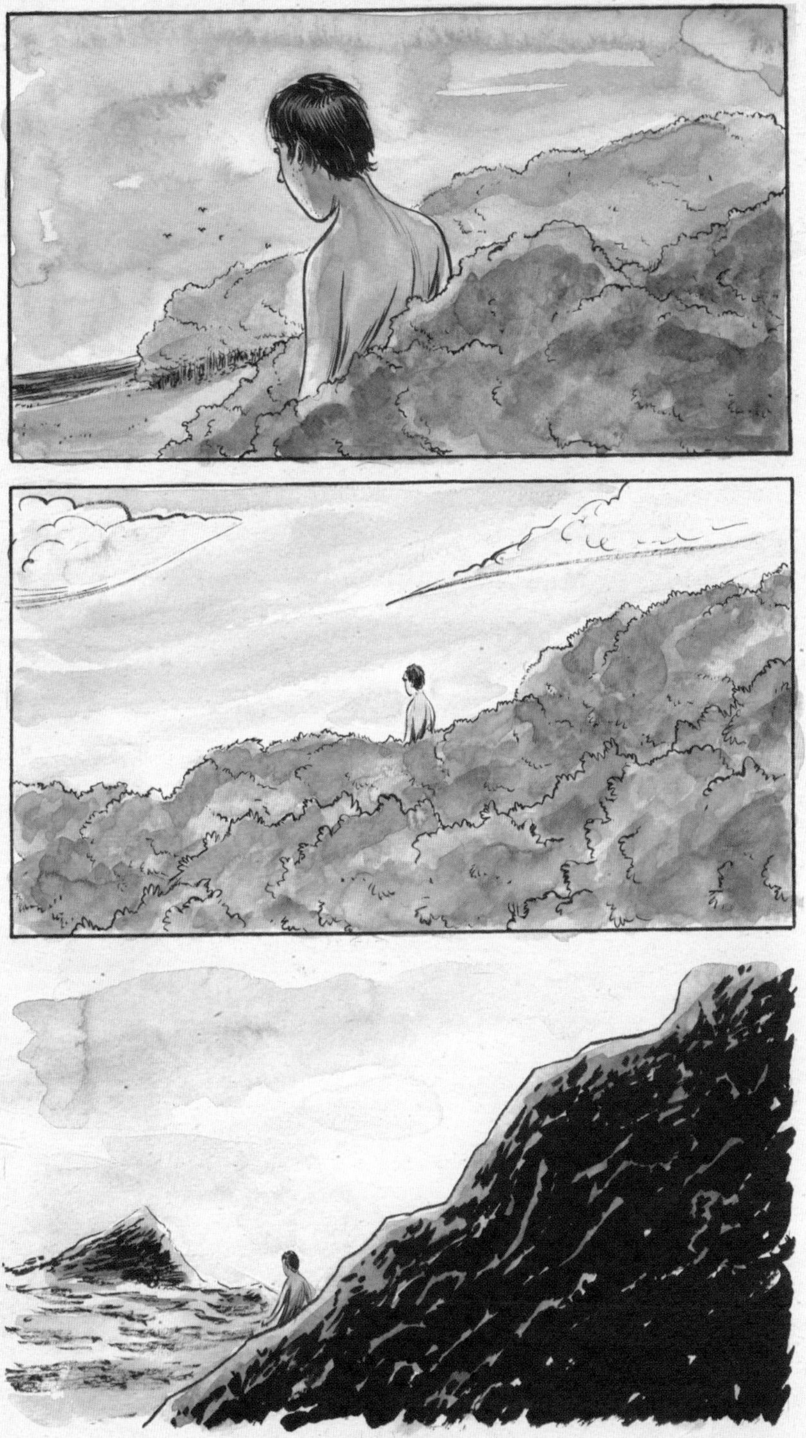

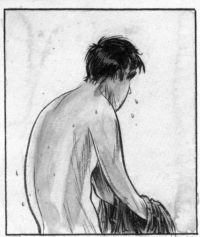

I imagined where he went...

And what he was doing...

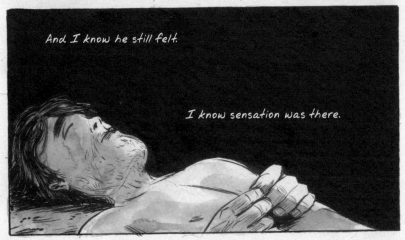

And I know he still felt.

I know sensation was there.

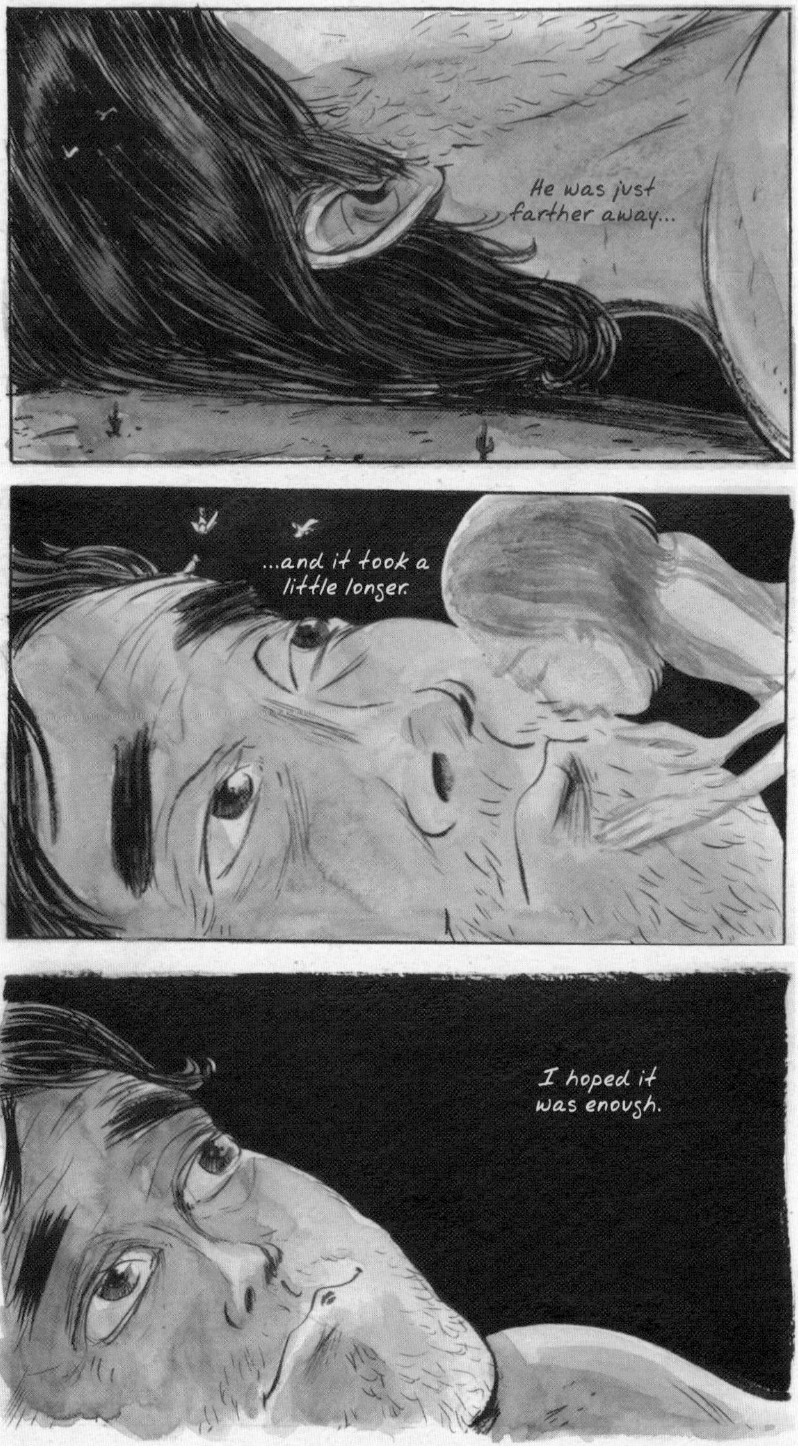
He was just farther away...
...and it took a little longer.
I hoped it was enough.

3RD STORY

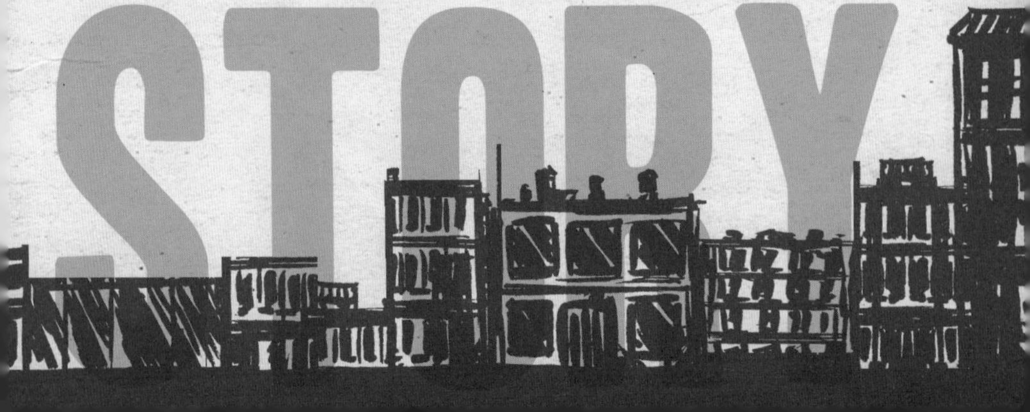

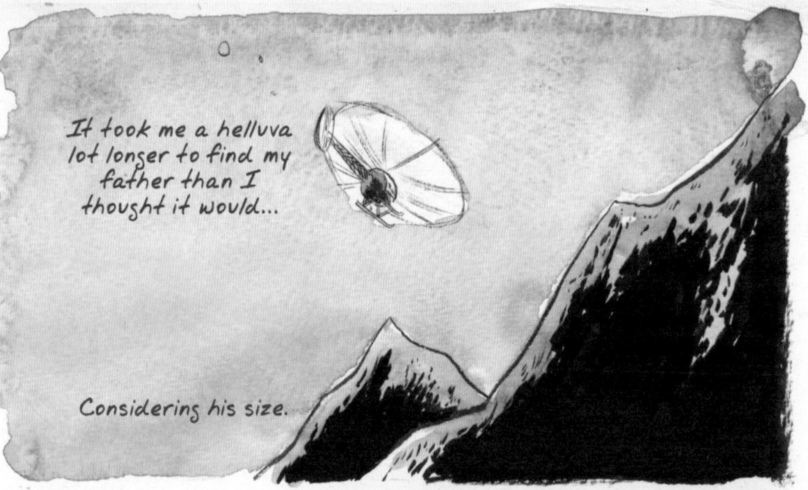
It took me a helluva lot longer to find my father than I thought it would...
Considering his size.

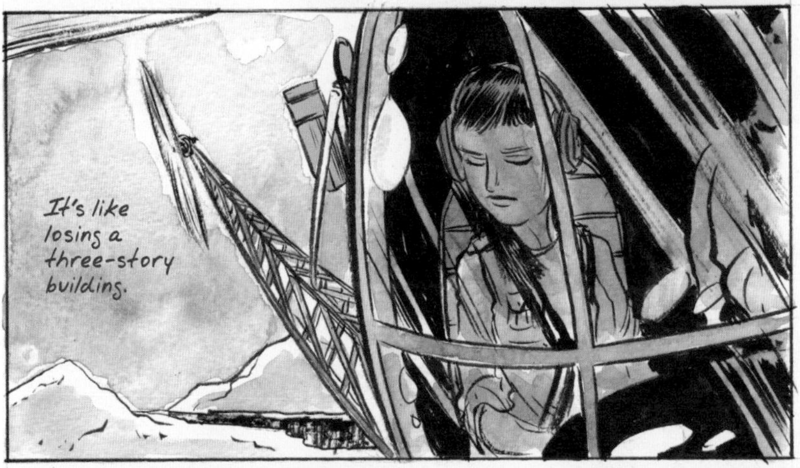
It's like losing a three-story building.

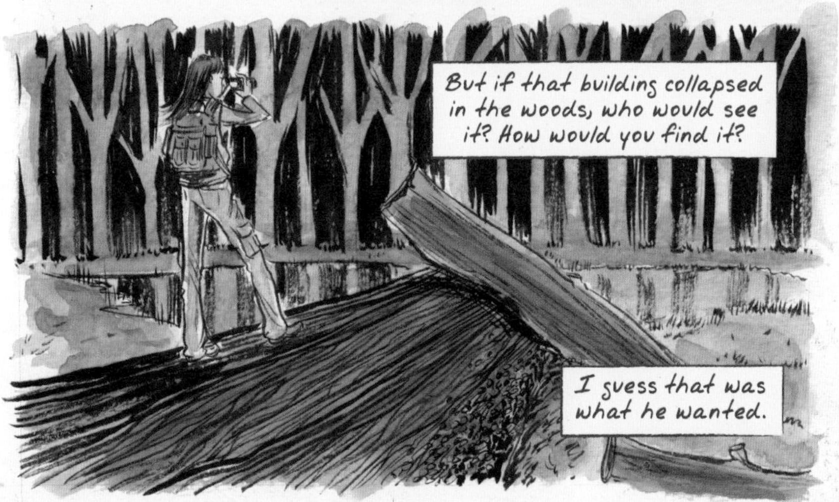
But if that building collapsed in the woods, who would see it? How would you find it?
I guess that was what he wanted.

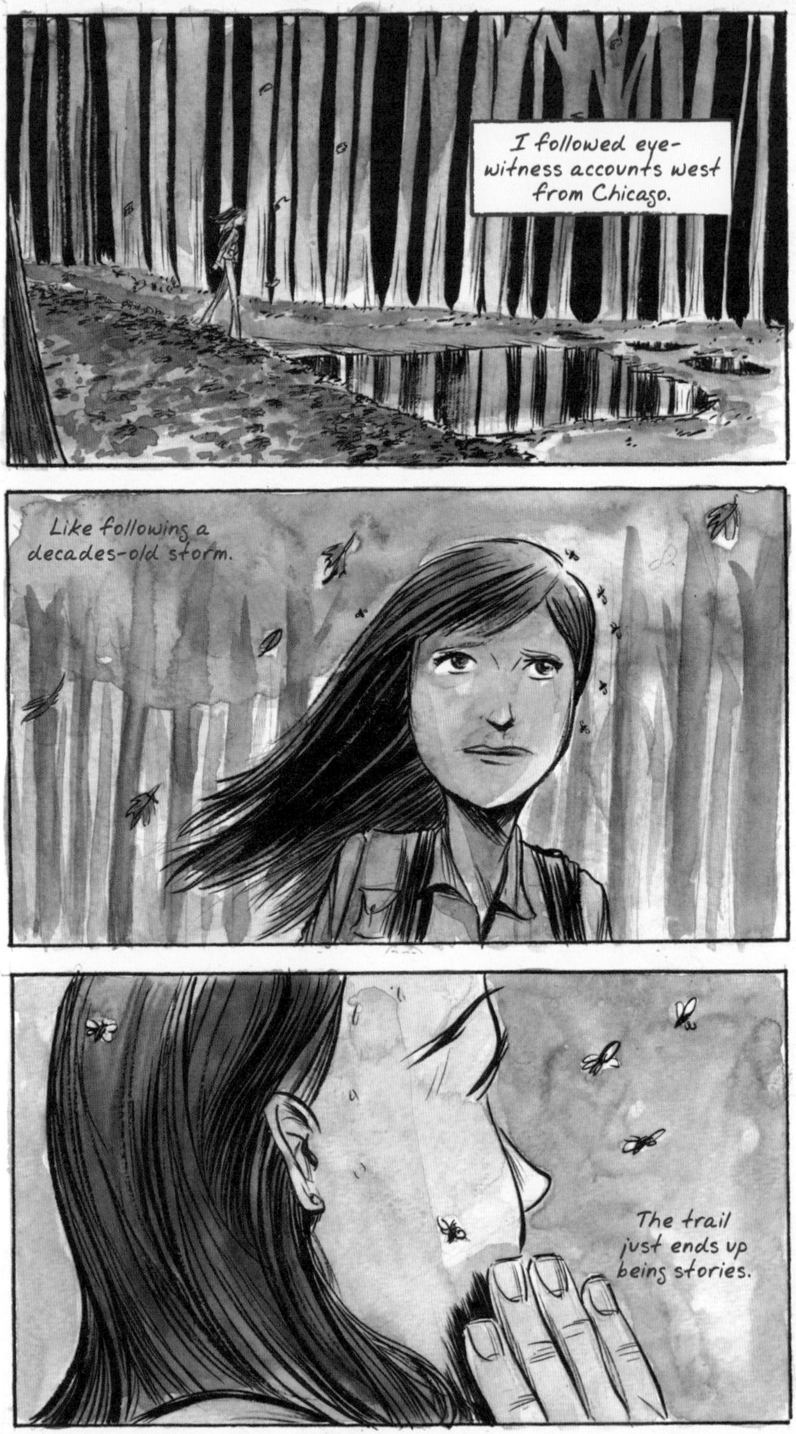
I followed eye-witness accounts west from Chicago.
Like following a decades-old storm.
The trail just ends up being stories.

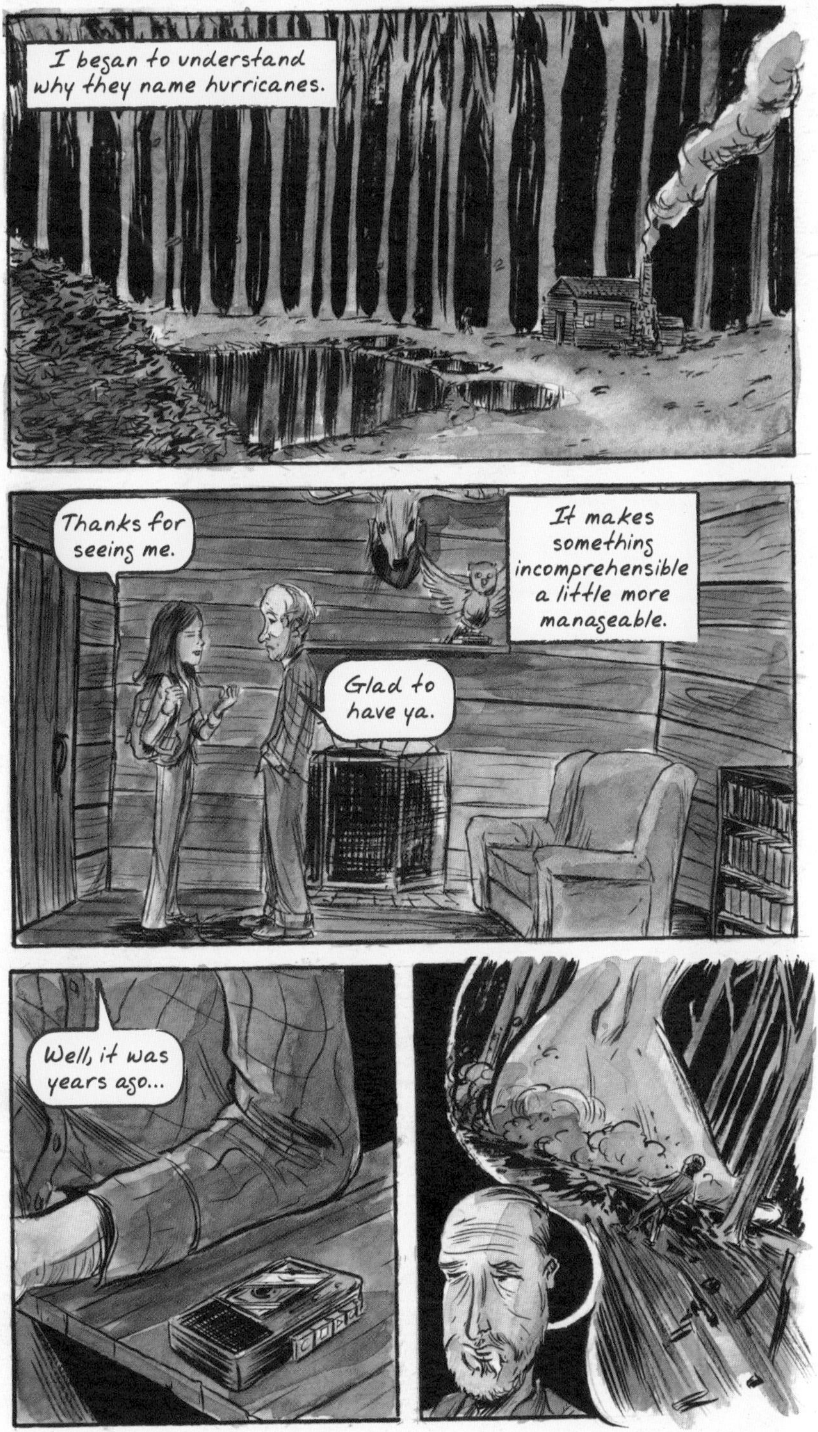
I began to understand why they name hurricanes.
Thanks for seeing me.
It makes something incomprehensible a little more manageable.
Glad to have ya.
Well, it was years ago...

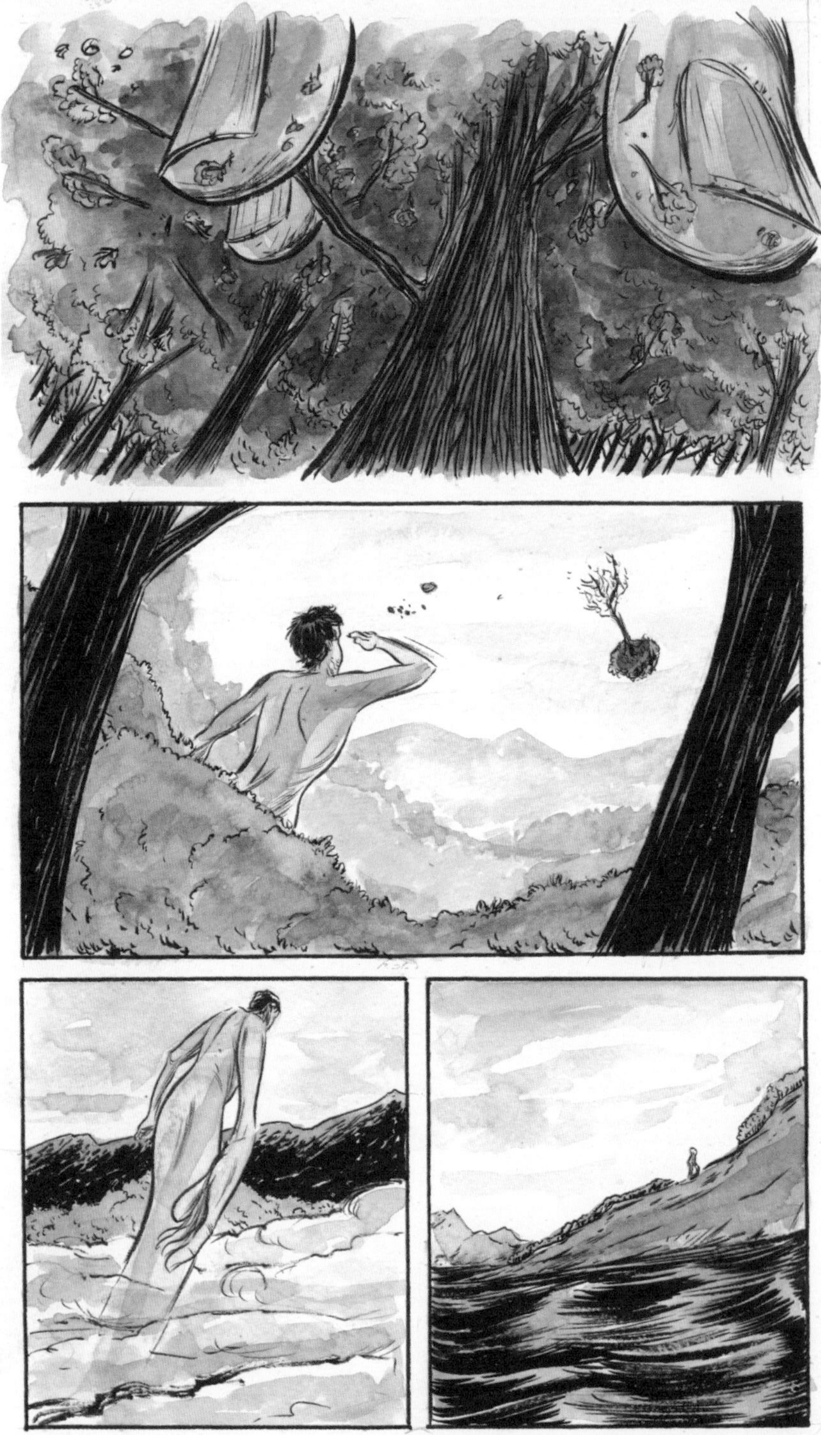

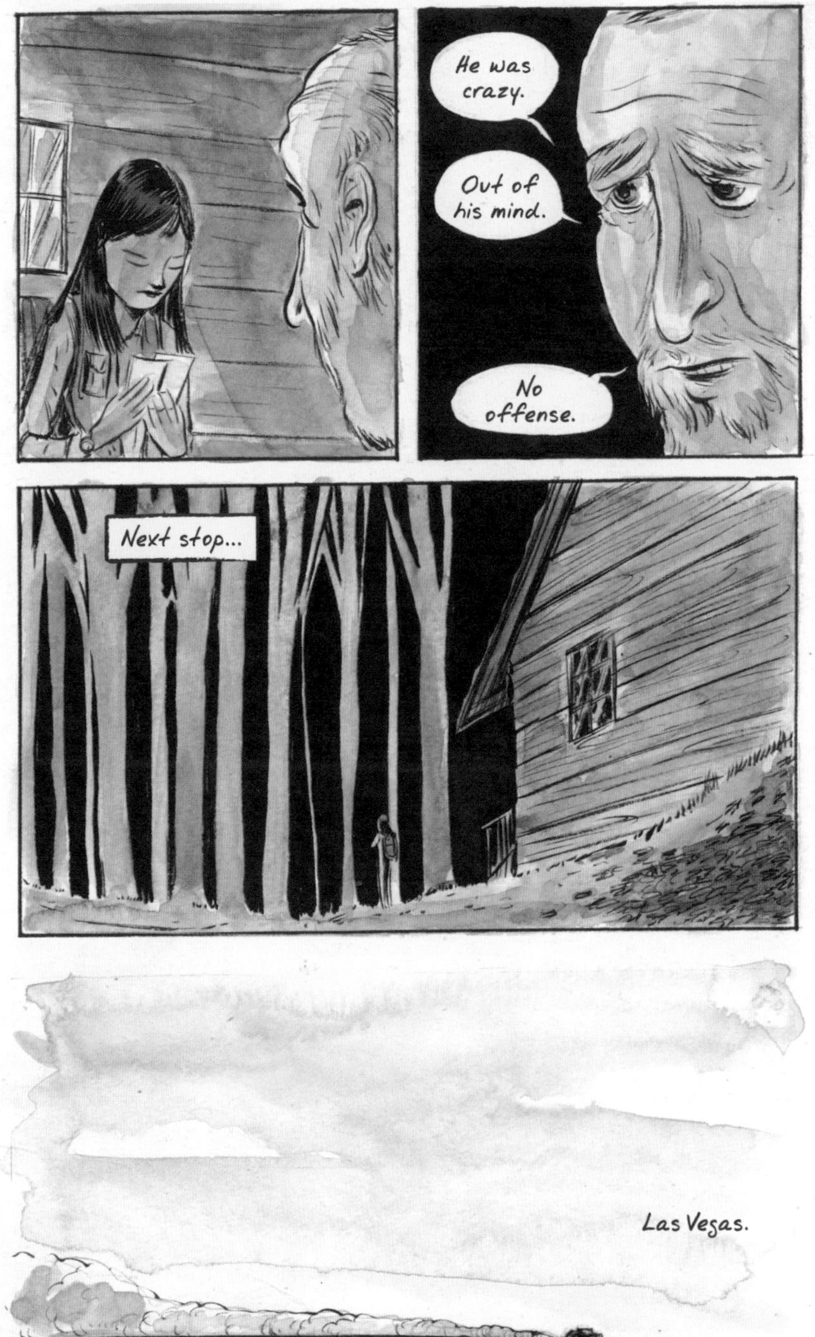
He was crazy.
Out of his mind.
No offense.
Next stop...
Las Vegas.

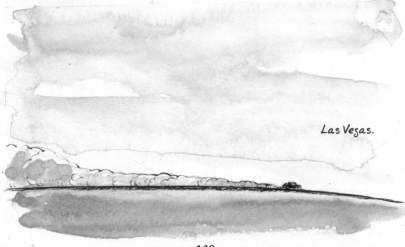

What the hell was I looking for?
Memories clearer than my own, I guess.
LARRY
GATLIN JR.
Riviera
24 HOUR
DANDYFIES
And the site of the famous Vegas photo.
I was ten when this was taken.

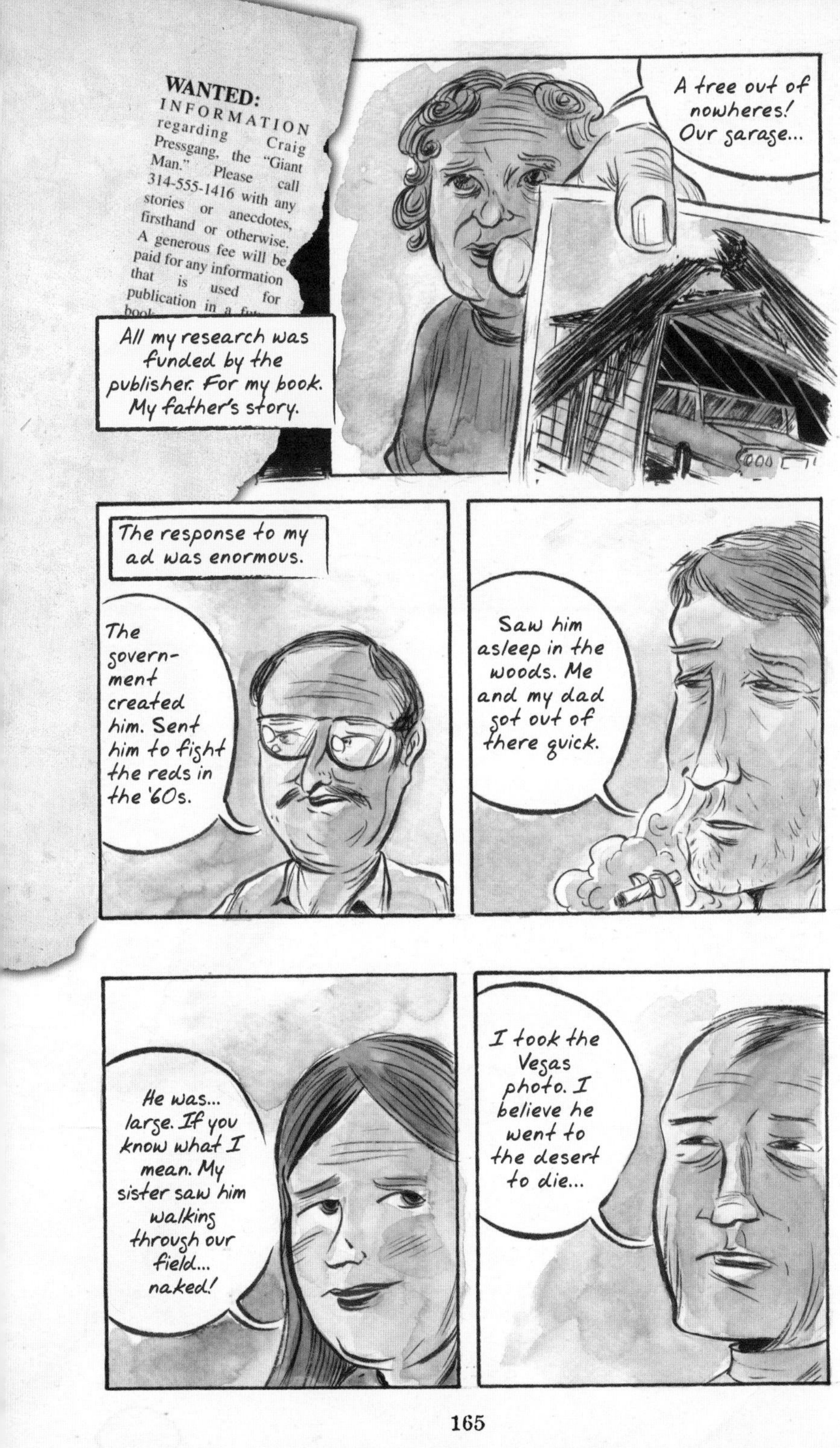
WANTED:
INFORMATION regarding Craig Pressgang, the "Giant Man." Please call 314-555-1416 with any stories or anecdotes, firsthand or otherwise. A generous fee will be paid for any information that is used for publication in a fu-
All my research was funded by the publisher. For my book. My father's story.
A tree out of nowheres! Our garage...
The response to my ad was enormous.
The government created him. Sent him to fight the reds in the '60s.
Saw him asleep in the woods. Me and my dad got out of there quick.
He was... large. If you know what I mean. My sister saw him walking through our field... naked!
I took the Vegas photo. I believe he went to the desert to die...

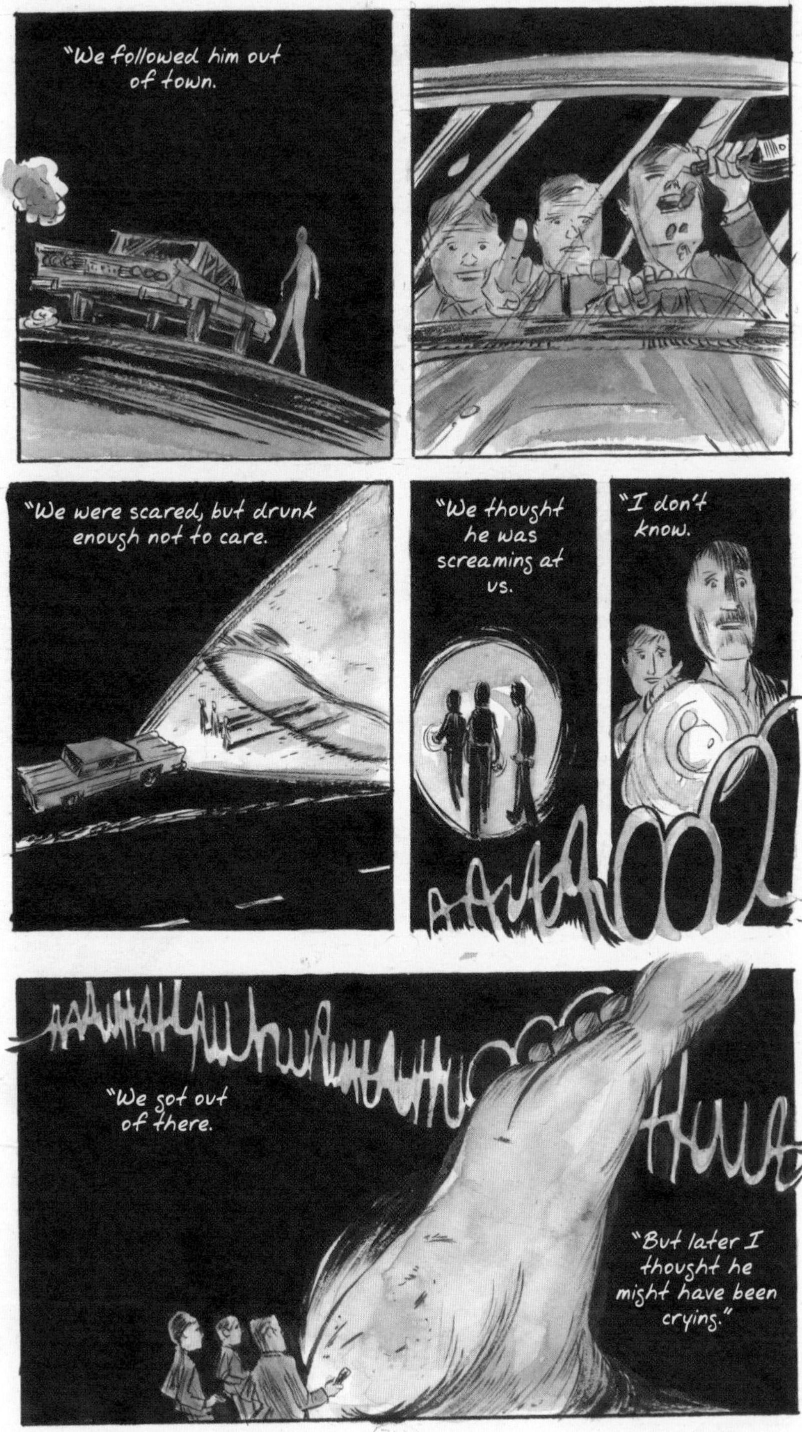
"We followed him out of town.
"We were scared, but drunk enough not to care.
"We thought he was screaming at us.
"I don't know.
"We got out of there.
"But later I thought he might have been crying."

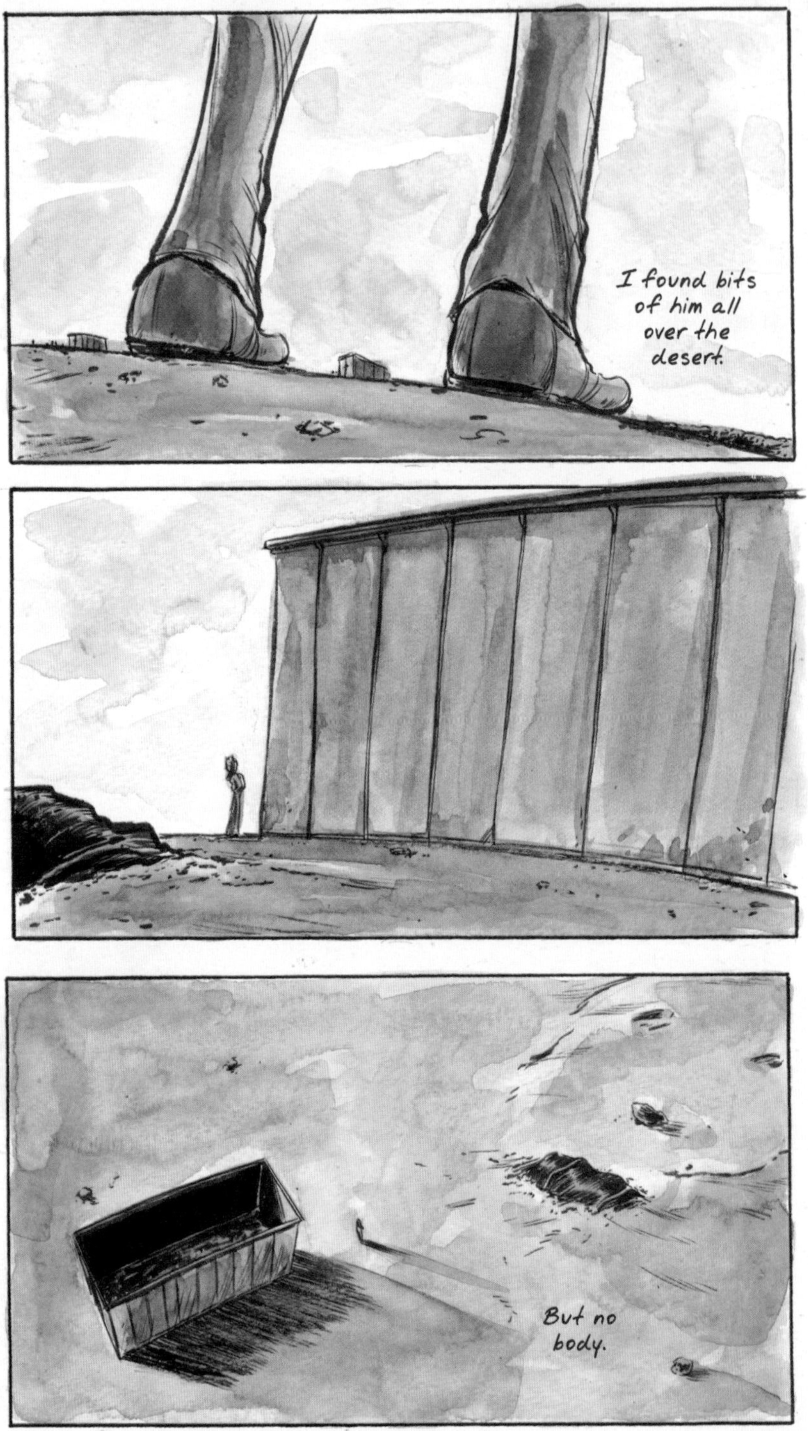
I found bits of him all over the desert.
But no body.

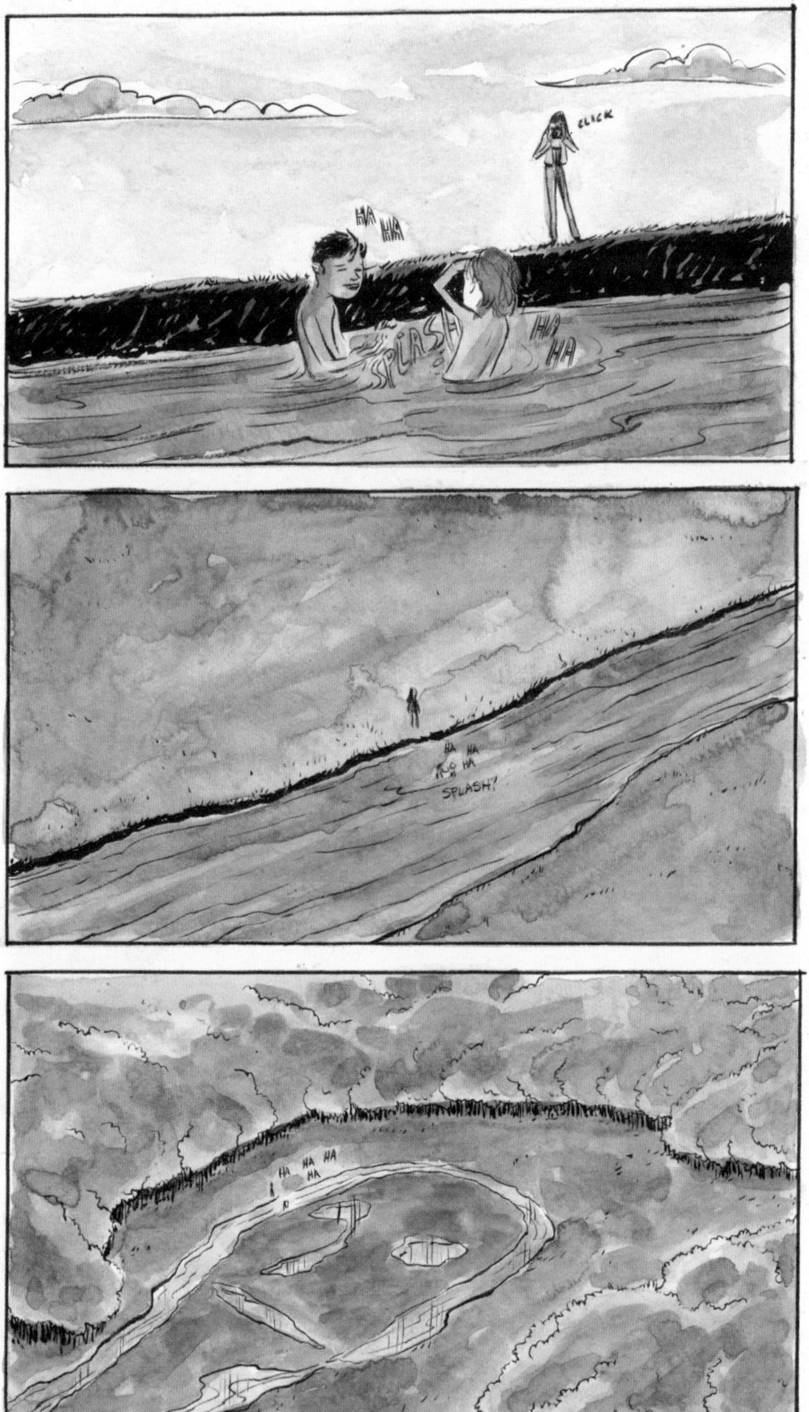
CLICK
HA HA
SPLASH
HA HA
HA HA
HA
SPLASH!
HA HA HA
HA

Then I got a phone call from a guy I'd talked to earlier.

A crackpot.

Iris? I talked to you a few weeks ago?

I worked with your father.

I was C.I.A. I helped him. I know you're writing a book, so I hesitated to tell you.

But you should know. You deserve to know.

I'm assuming you've read this?

iant Man
Pillar of America

The Official Awesome Biography of the World's Tallest Man

Giant Man

Pillar of America

**The Official
Souvenir Biography
of the World's
Tallest Man**

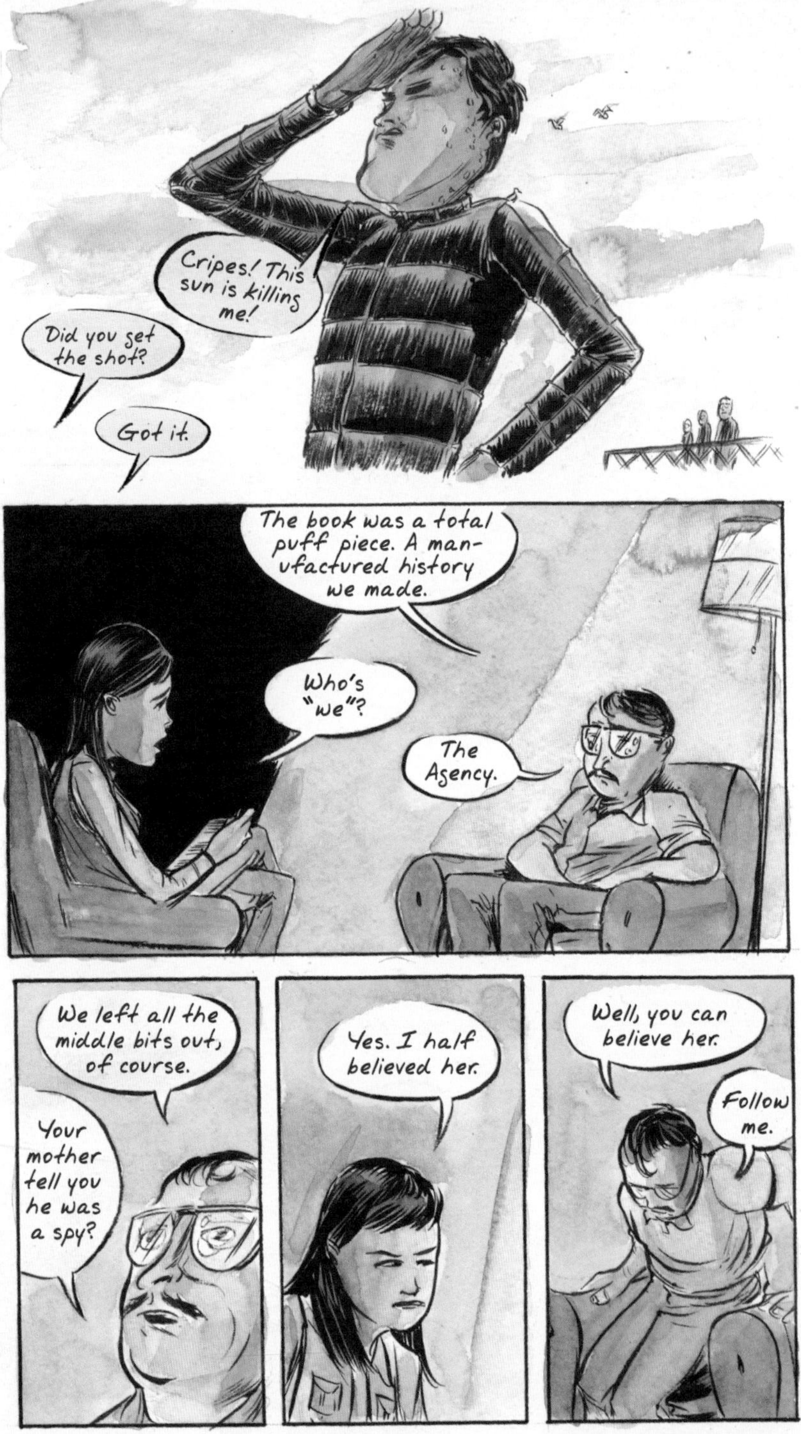
Cripes! This sun is killing me!
Did you get the shot?
Got it.
The book was a total puff piece. A manufactured history we made.
Who's "we"?
The Agency.
We left all the middle bits out, of course.
Your mother tell you he was a spy?
Yes. I half believed her.
Well, you can believe her.
Follow me.

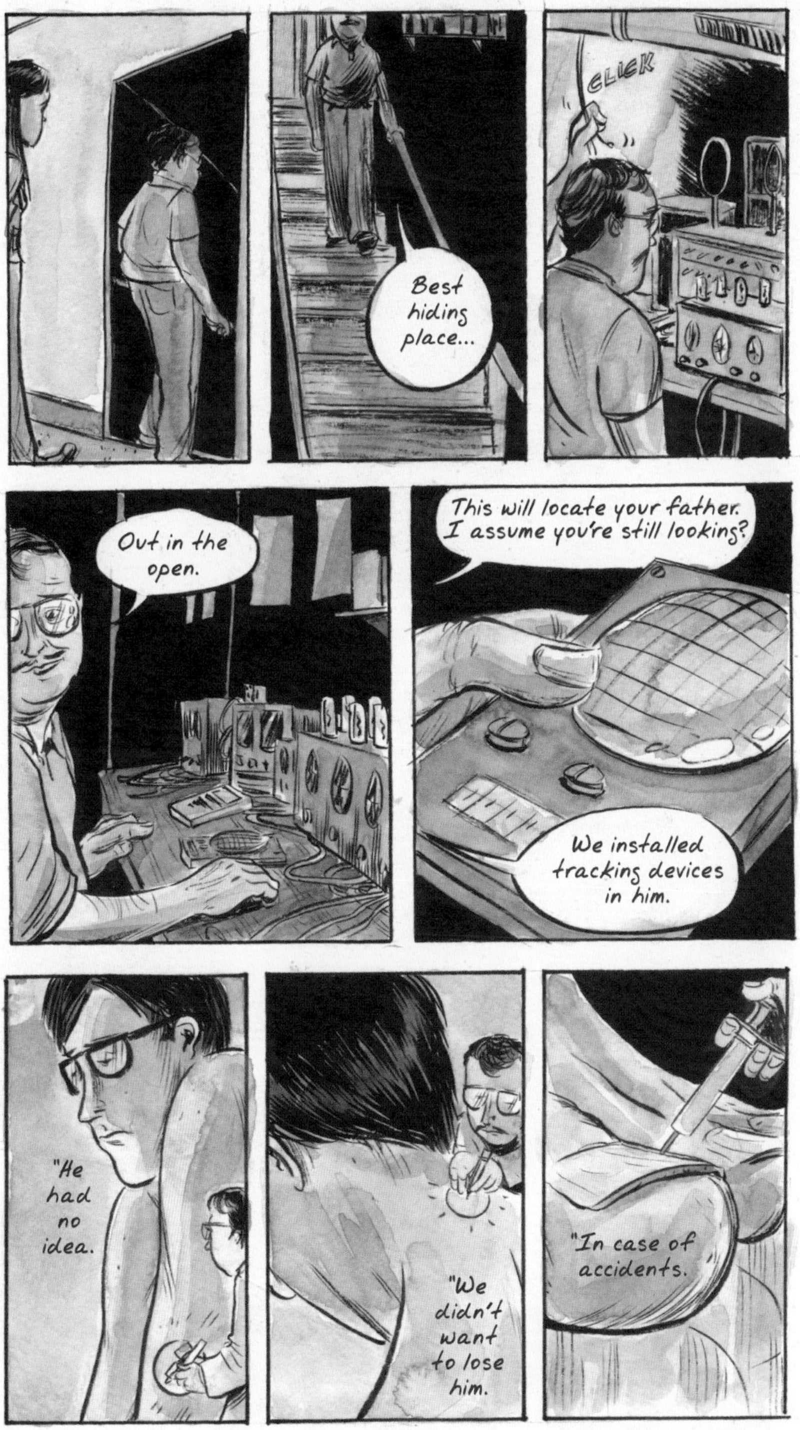
Best hiding place...
CLICK
Out in the open.
This will locate your father. I assume you're still looking?
We installed tracking devices in him.
"He had no idea.
"We didn't want to lose him.
"In case of accidents.

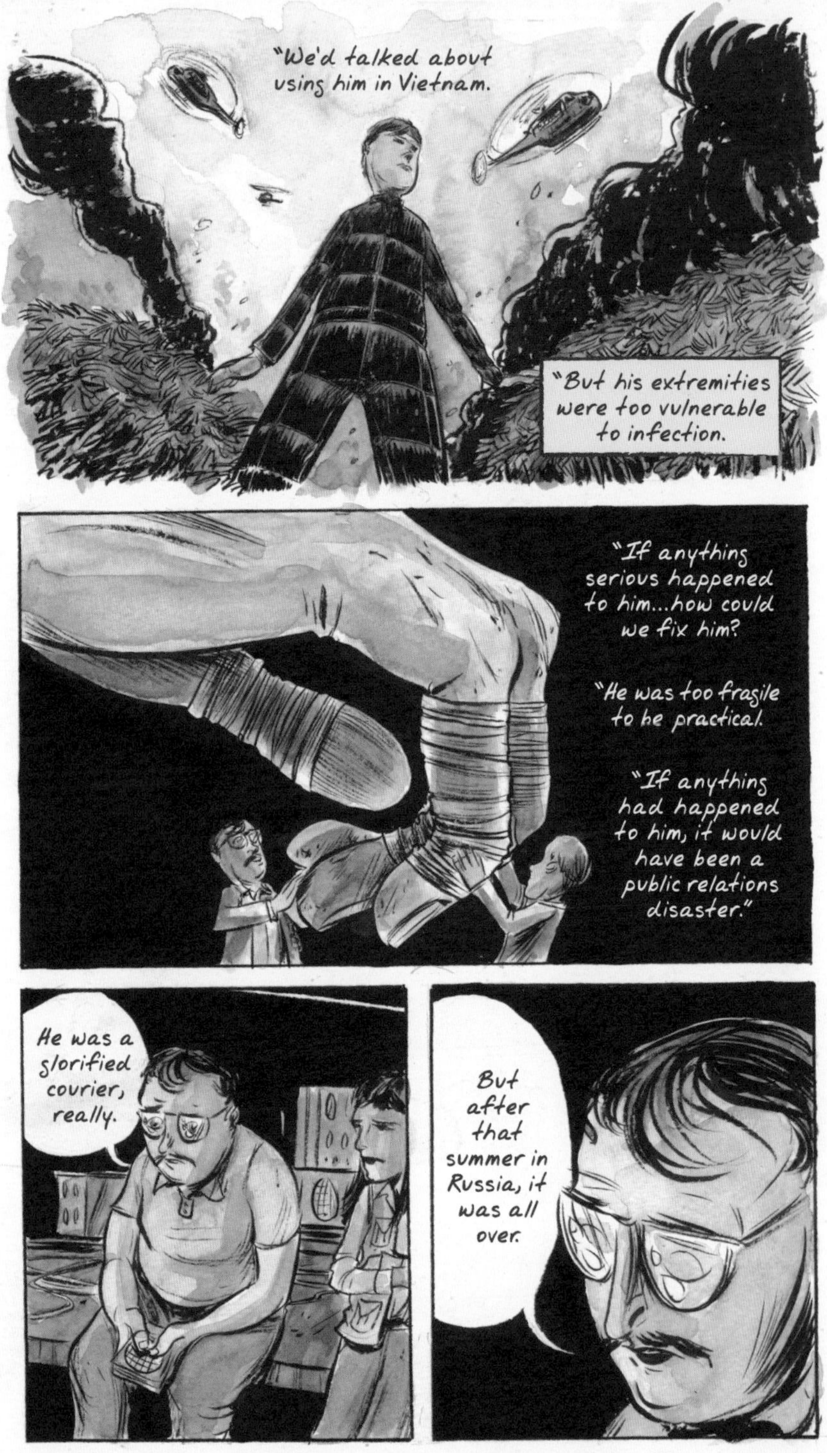
"We'd talked about using him in Vietnam.
"But his extremities were too vulnerable to infection.
"If anything serious happened to him...how could we fix him?
"He was too fragile to be practical.
"If anything had happened to him, it would have been a public relations disaster."
He was a glorified courier, really.
But after that summer in Russia, it was all over.

"But then the Thanksgiving Day Parade happened.

"A time-delay explosive must have been hidden in his ear.

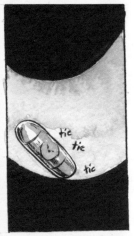

tic
tic

tic

"We were going to decommission him anyway, but the fall made it easy, I guess.

PROOM

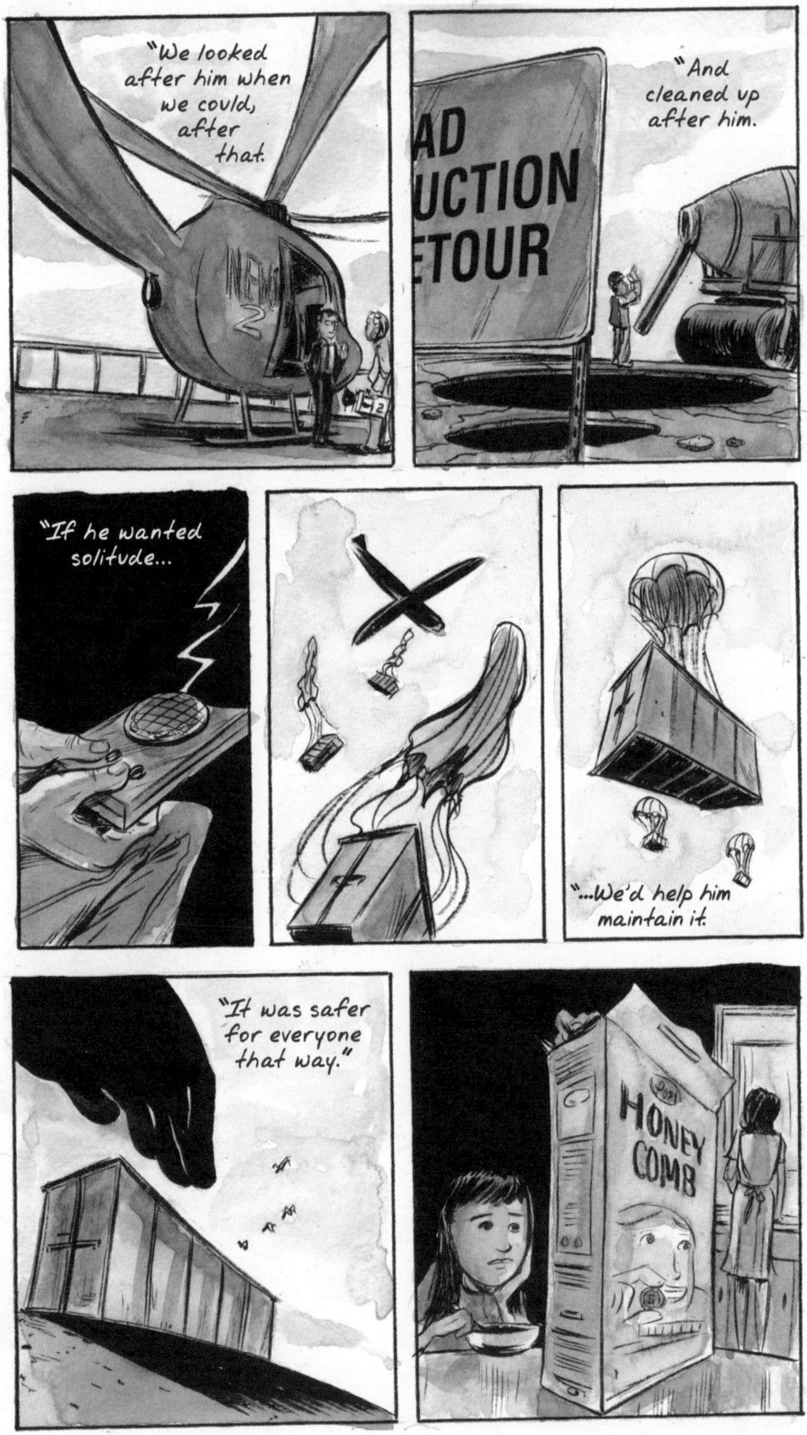
"We looked after him when we could, after that.
NEWS 2
AD
UCTION
ETOUR
"And cleaned up after him.
"If he wanted solitude...
"...We'd help him maintain it.
"It was safer for everyone that way."
HONEY COMB

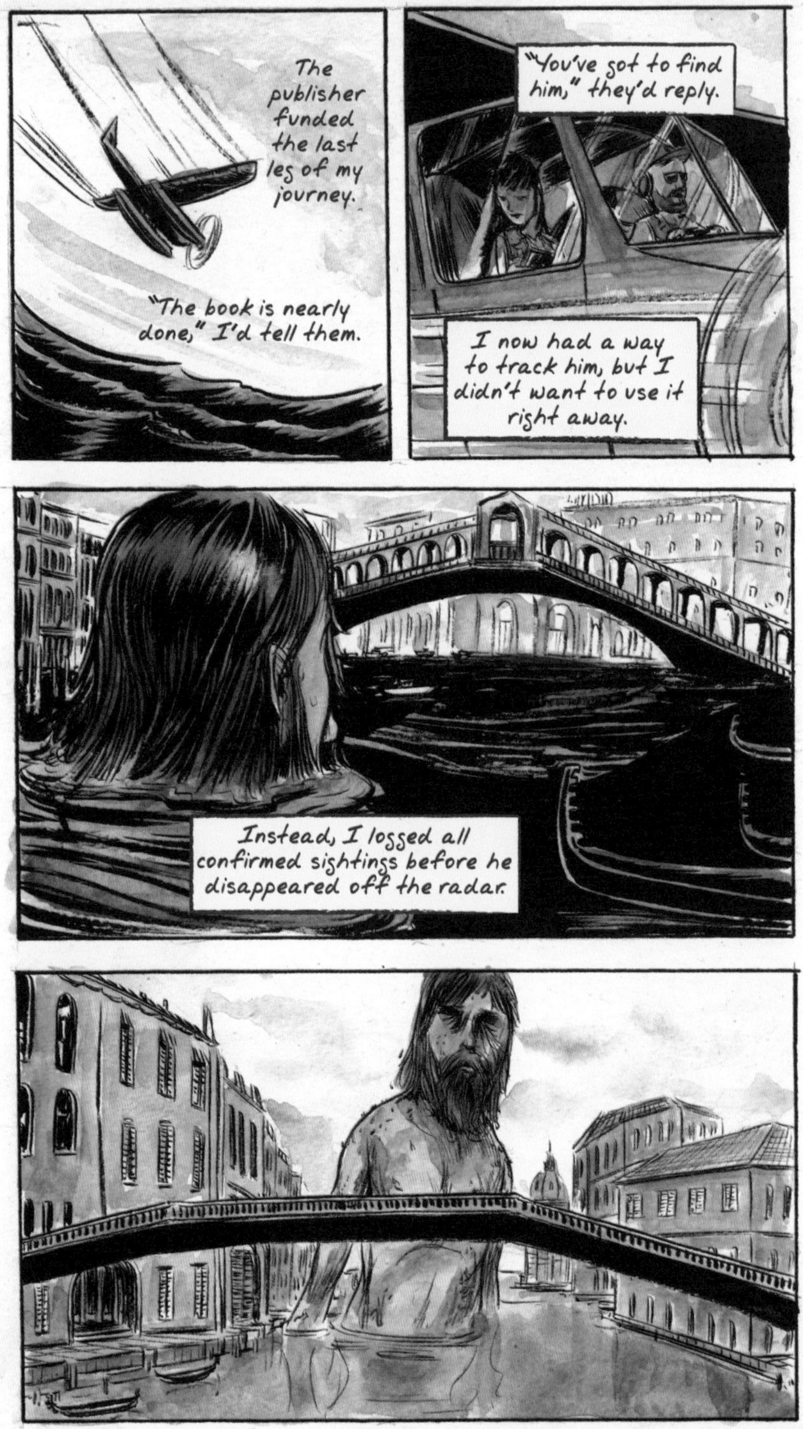
The publisher funded the last leg of my journey.
"The book is nearly done," I'd tell them.
"You've got to find him," they'd reply.
I now had a way to track him, but I didn't want to use it right away.
Instead, I logged all confirmed sightings before he disappeared off the radar.

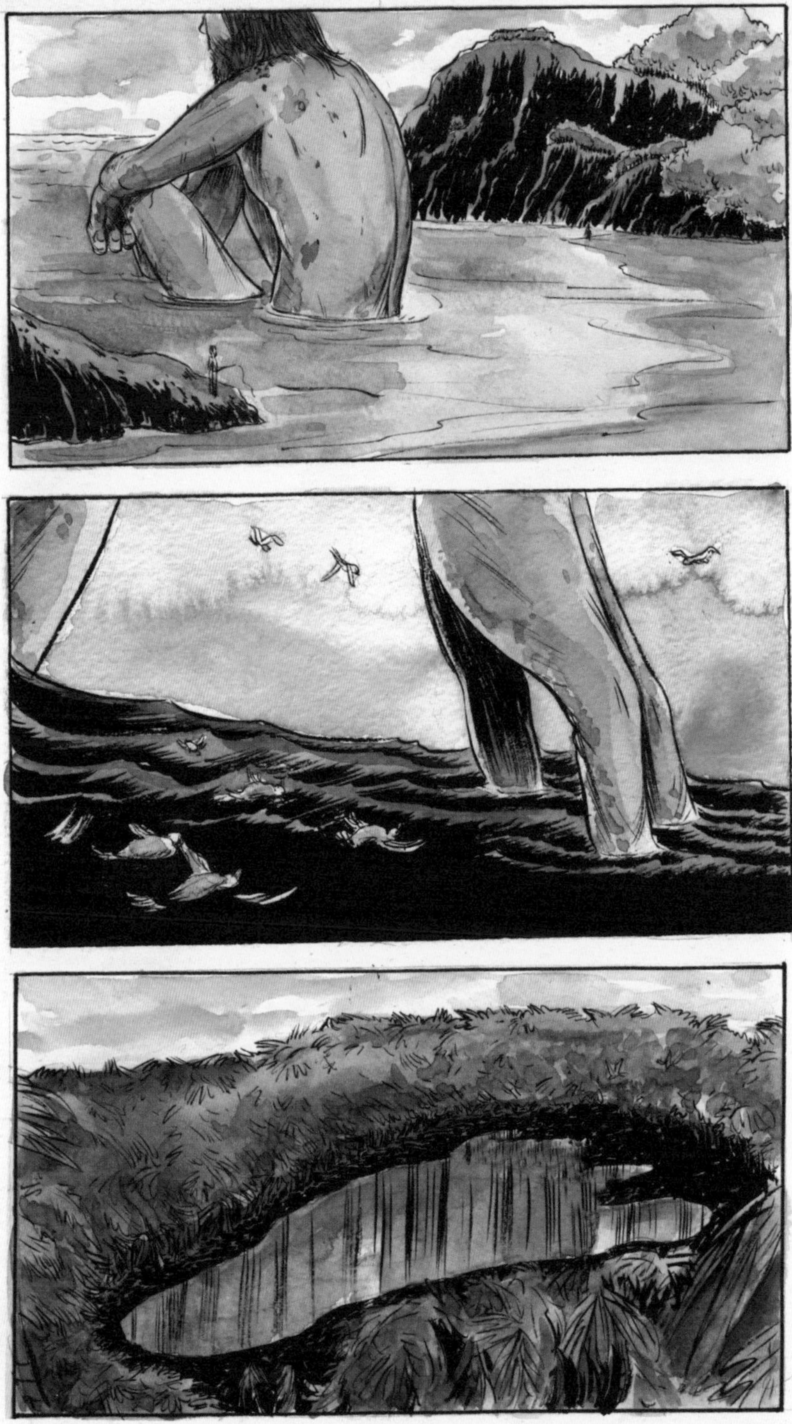

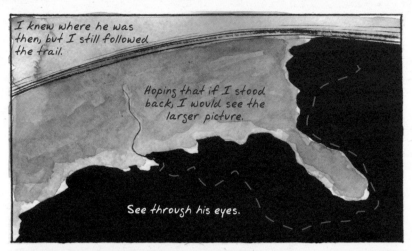

I knew where he was then, but I still followed the trail.

Hoping that if I stood back, I would see the larger picture.

See through his eyes.

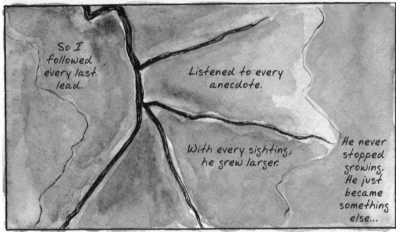

So I followed every last lead.

Listened to every anecdote.

With every sighting, he grew larger.

He never stopped growing. He just became something else...

More unreal.

I felt like I was pursuing fiction.

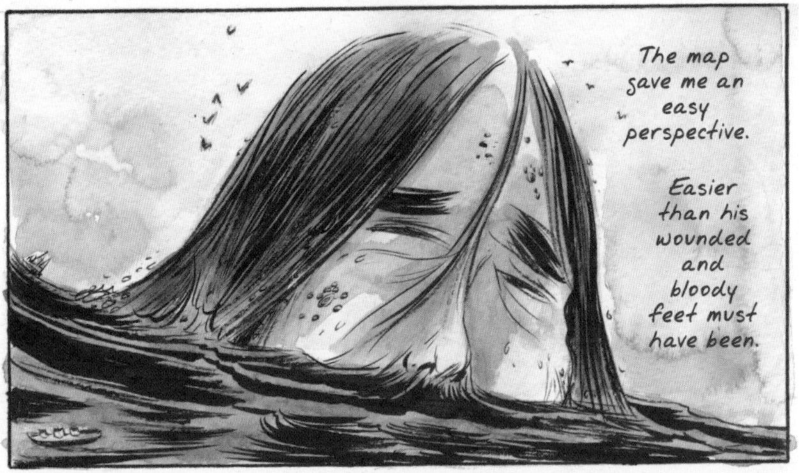
The map gave me an easy perspective.
Easier than his wounded and bloody feet must have been.

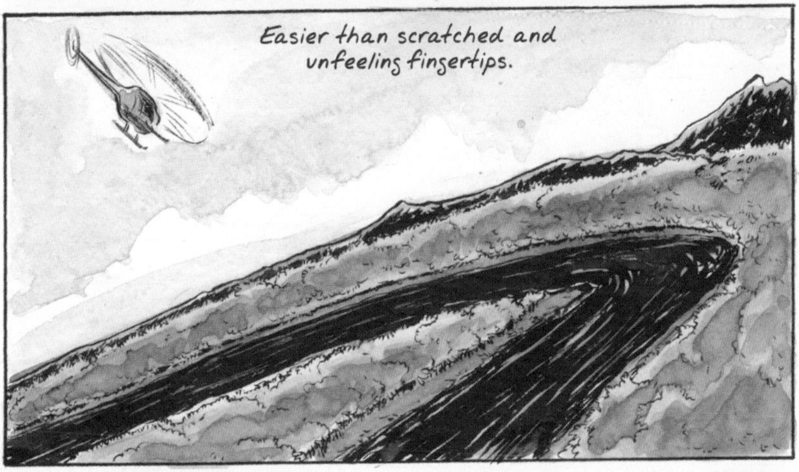
Easier than scratched and unfeeling fingertips.

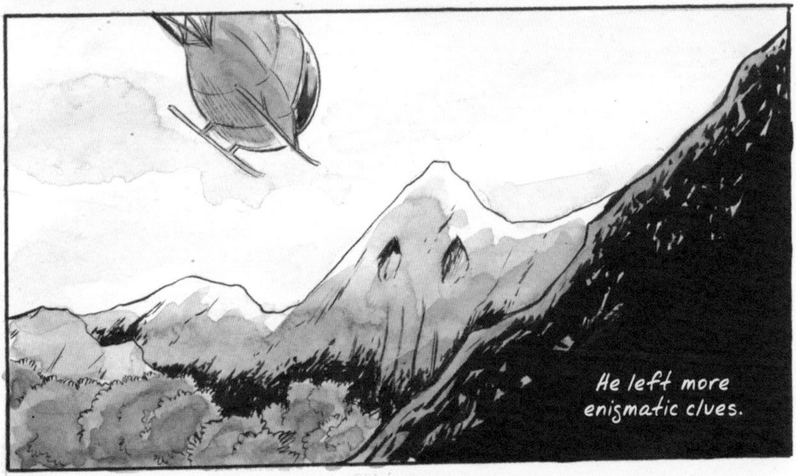
He left more enigmatic clues.

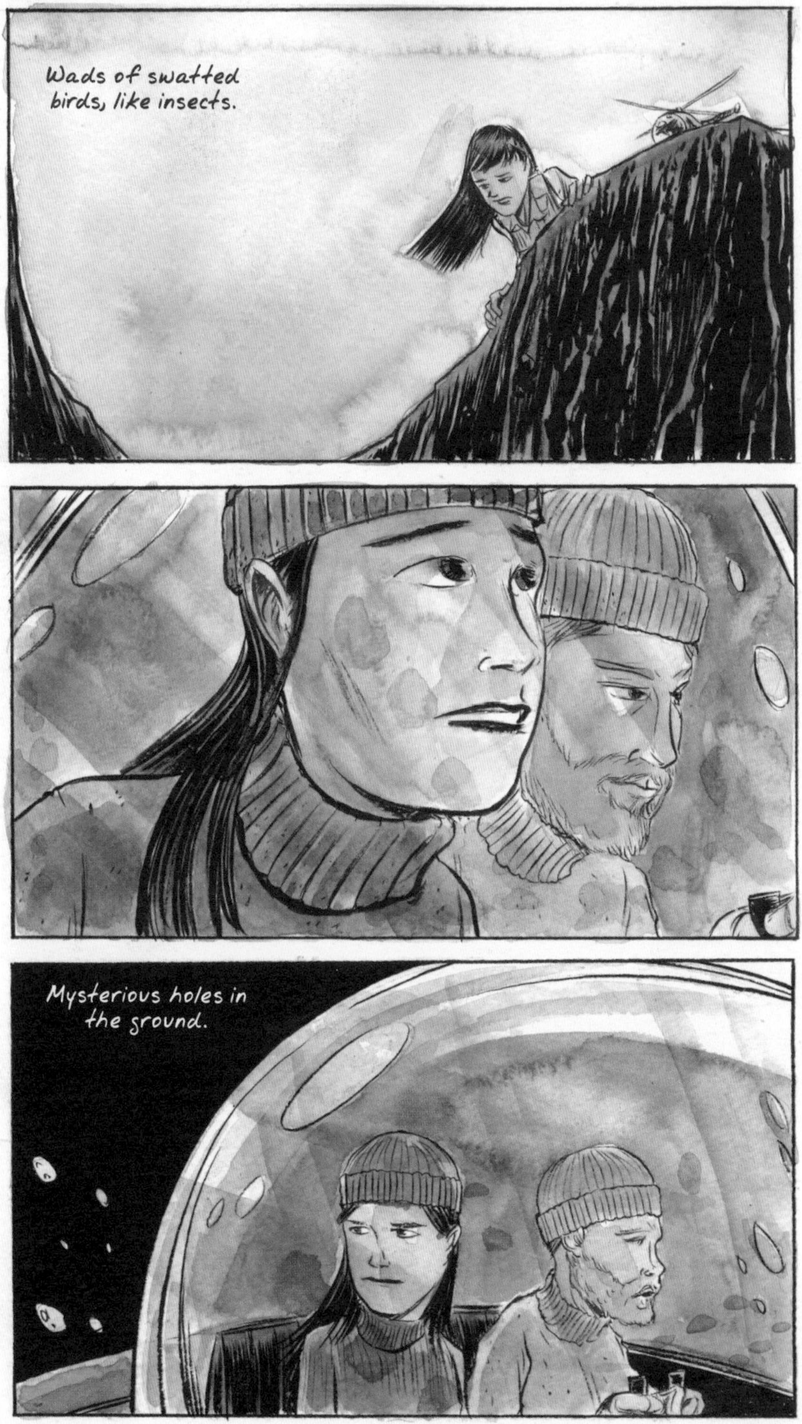
Wads of swatted birds, like insects.
Mysterious holes in the ground.

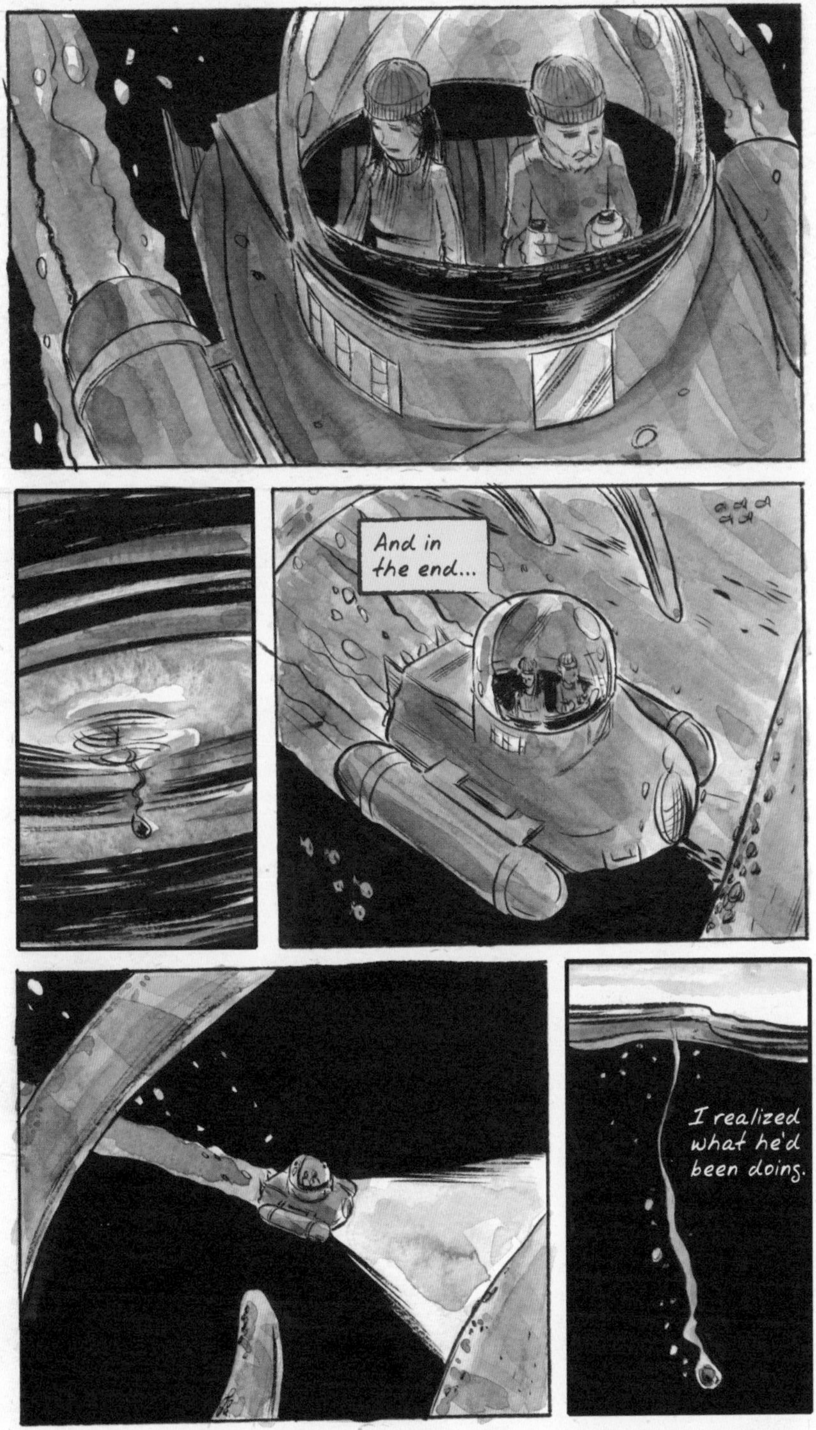
And in the end...
I realized what he'd been doing.

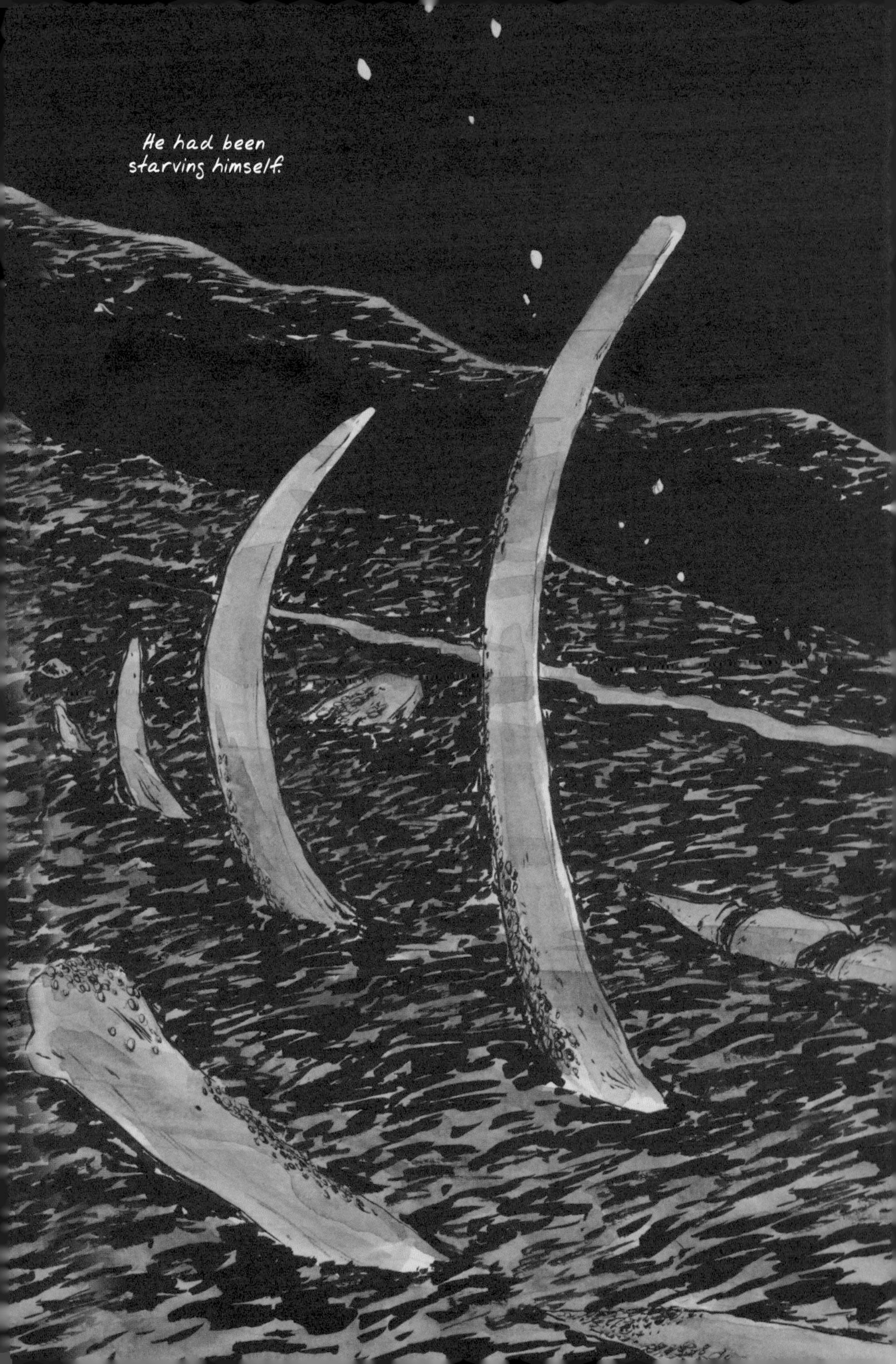
He had been starving himself.

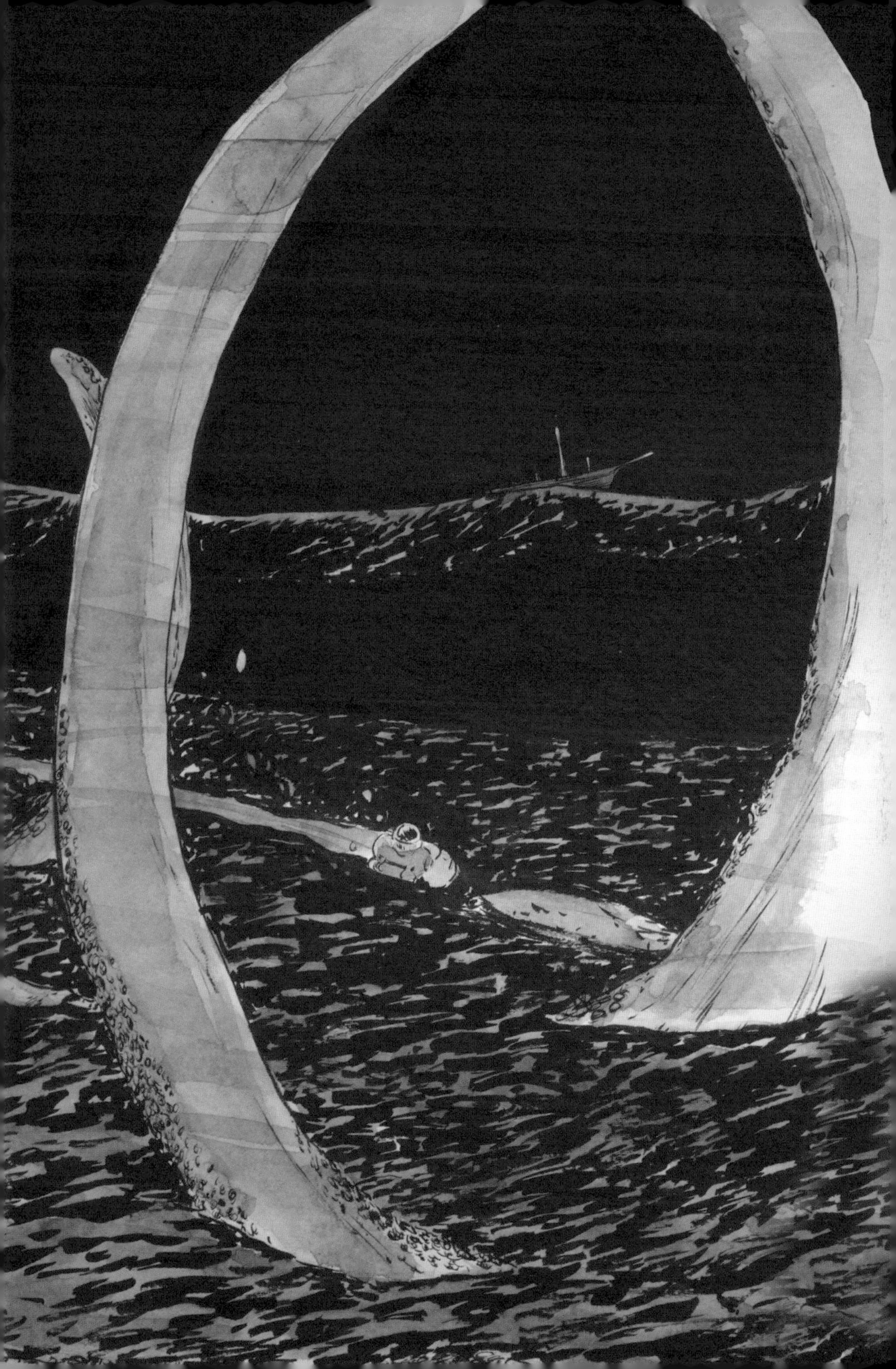

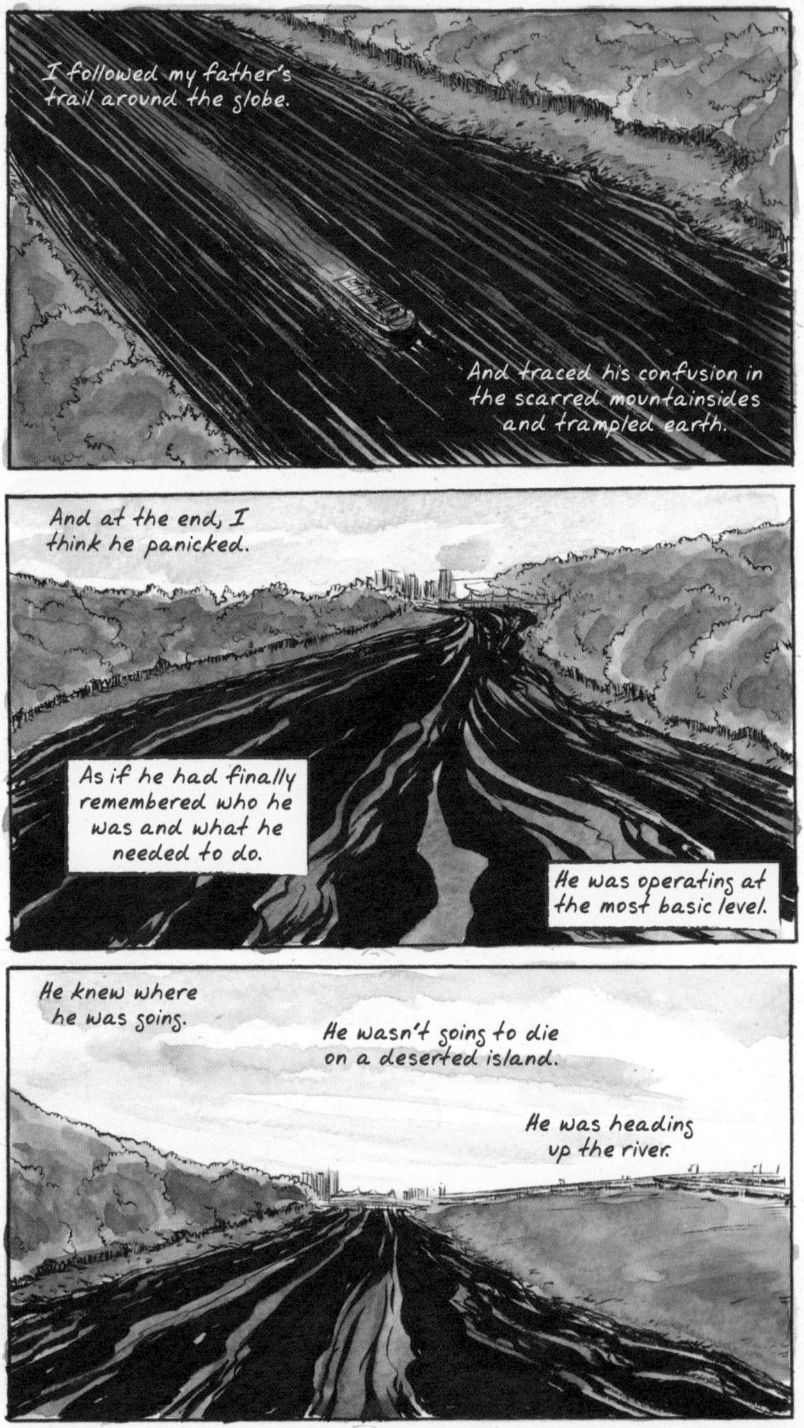
I followed my father's trail around the globe.
And traced his confusion in the scarred mountainsides and trampled earth.
And at the end, I think he panicked.
As if he had finally remembered who he was and what he needed to do.
He was operating at the most basic level.
He knew where he was going.
He wasn't going to die on a deserted island.
He was heading up the river.

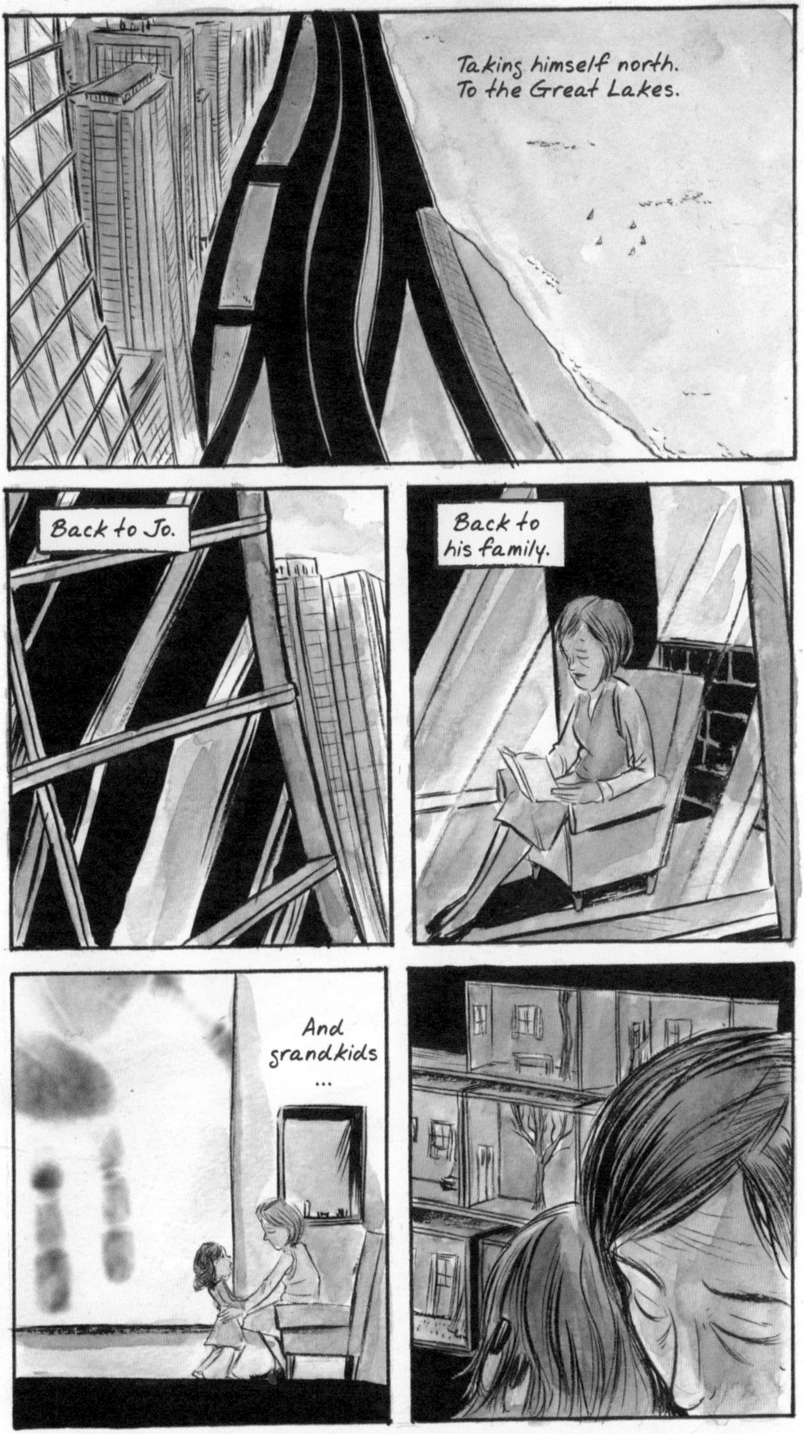

Taking himself north. To the Great Lakes.
Back to Jo.
Back to his family.
And grandkids ...

Taking himself
north. To the Great
Lakes. Back to Jo.
Back to his family.

And grandkids, too
small to see.

The
Secret
History
of the
Giant
Man

The closer I
looked at
everything...

The less I seemed to
understand.

I guess ultimately the only
clue to his identity...

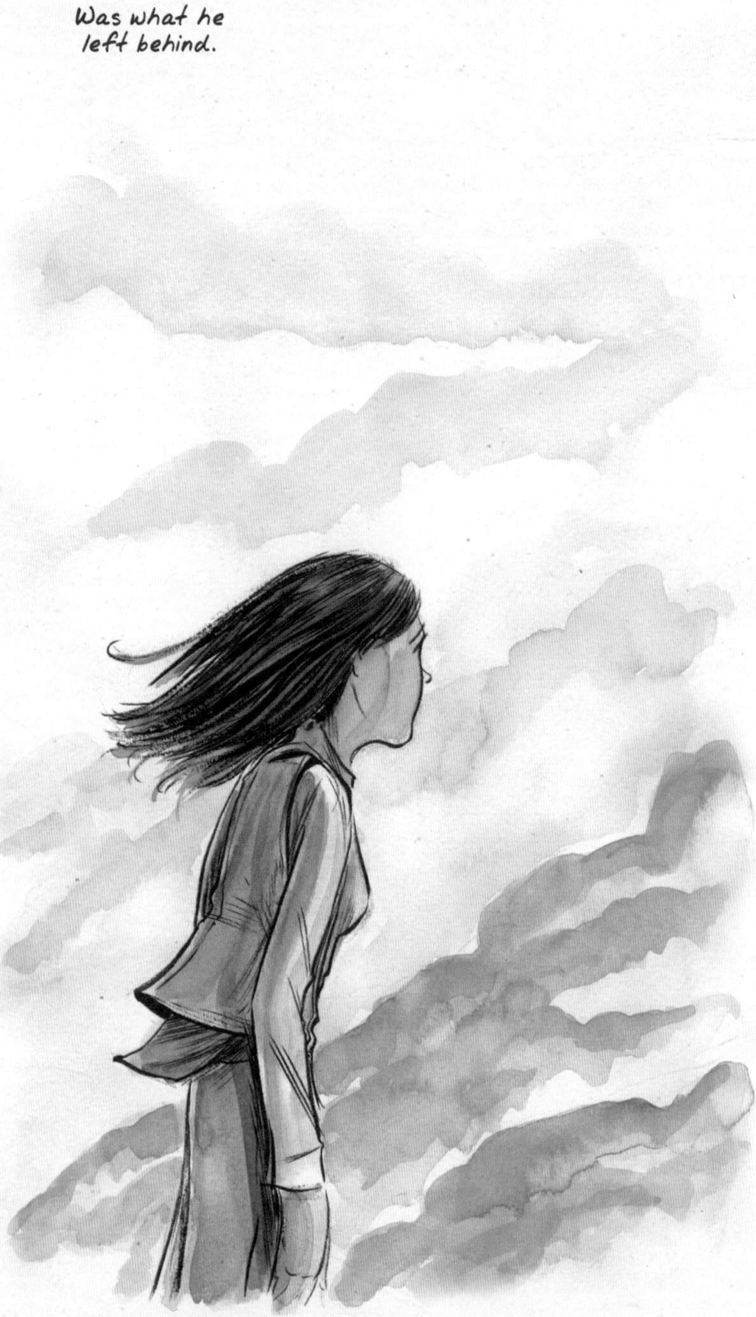
Was what he left behind.

Dedicated to my parents
and grandparents.

Thanks to Brian Hurtt, Luby Kelley,
Jeff Lemire, Emma Kindt for the
sketchbook art on pages 36-37,
and super-thanks to Sharlene and Ella.

About the Author:

Matt Kindt is the Harvey
Award-winning author of
the graphic novels *Super
Spy* and *2 Sisters*, and the
artist and co-creator of
the *Pistolwhip* series of
graphic novels. He has been
nominated for four Eisner
Awards and three Harveys.
Matt lives and works as an
author and illustrator in
St. Louis, Missouri, with
his wife and daughter. For
more information go to
supersecretspy.com

4-09

Photo by Sharlene Kindt

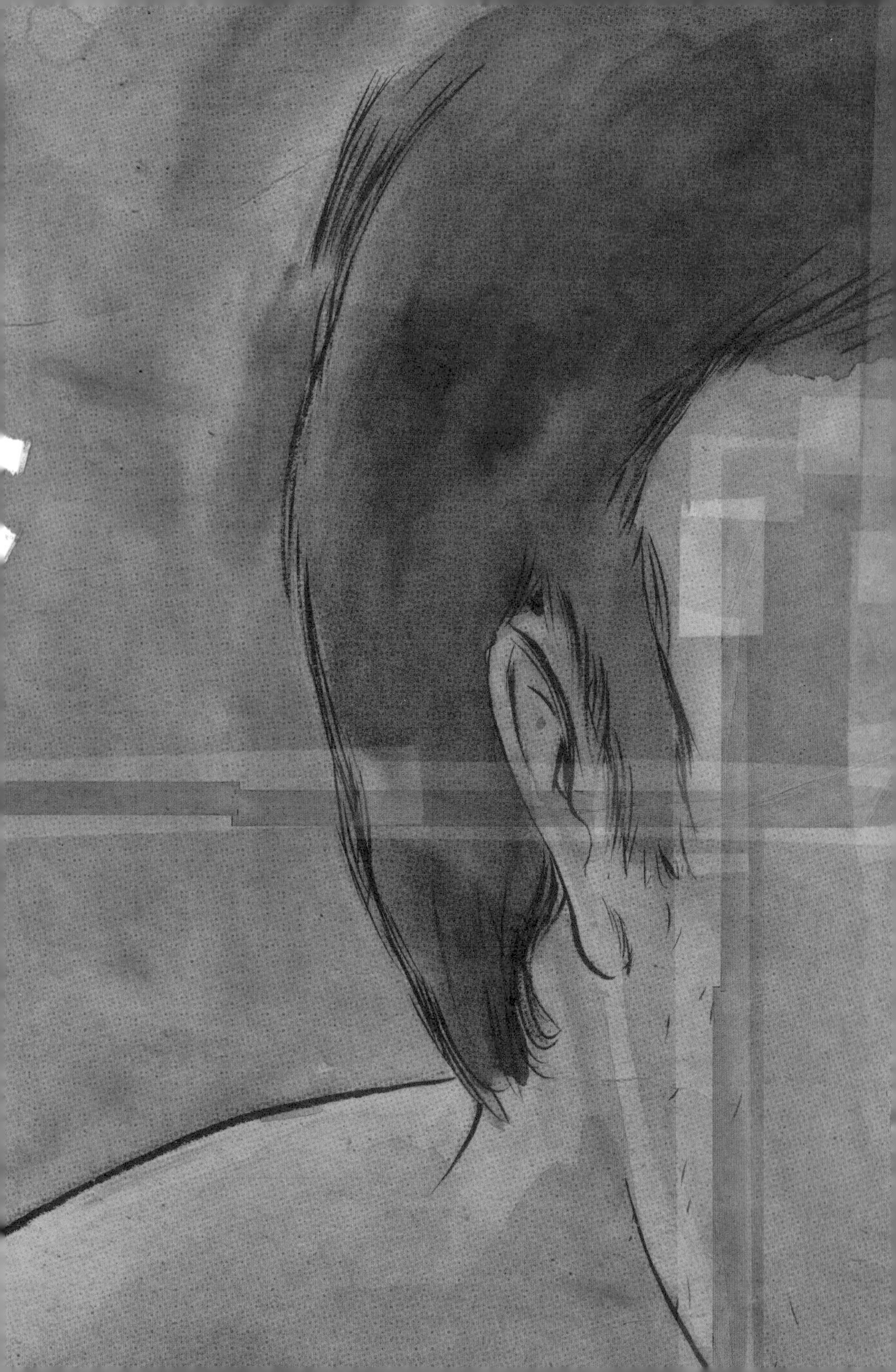